Models of Madness, Models of Medicine

MIRIAM SIEGLER

HUMPHRY OSMOND

HARPER TORCHBOOKS
Harper & Row, Publishers
New York, Hagerstown, San Francisco, London

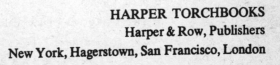

To our families who,
as doctors, patients, nurses, and relatives
have taught us so much

This book was originally published by Macmillan Publishing Company, Inc. It is here reprinted by permission.

MODELS OF MADNESS, MODELS OF MEDICINE. Copyright © 1974 by Miriam Siegler and Humphry Osmond. All rights reserved. Printed in the United States of America. No part of this book may be used or reproduced in any manner without written permission except in the case of brief quotations embodied in critical articles and reviews. For information address Harper & Row, Publishers, Inc., 10 East 53d Street, New York, N.Y. 10022. Published simultaneously in Canada by Fitzhenry & Whiteside Limited, Toronto.

First HARPER COLOPHON edition published 1976

STANDARD BOOK NUMBER: 06–090492–5

80 10 9 8 7 6 5 4 3 2

Acknowledgments are due to the following publishers for permission to quote:
Elaine Cumming and John Cumming, *Closed Ranks*, Harvard University Press, 1957. Celsus, *On Medicine*, translated by W. G. Spencer, The Loeb Classical Library, Harvard University Press, 1935. Patrick Mallam, "Billy O," in Kenneth Dewhurst, editor, *Oxford Medicine*, Sandford Publication, Oxford, England, 1970. Geoffrey Jukes, *Stalingrad: The Turning Point*, Ballantine Books, Inc., a Division of Random House, Inc., 1968. Wilfred Trotter, *The Collected Works of Wilfred Trotter*, Oxford University Press (London), 1941. Clara Claiborne Park, *The Siege*, copyright 1967, by permission of Little, Brown and Co., in association with The Atlantic Monthly Press. René and Jean Dubos, *The White Plague*, copyright 1952, by permission of Little, Brown and Company.

Acknowledgments are due to the *Journal of Orthomolecular Psychiatry*, formerly *Schizophrenia*, for permission to quote extensively from the following articles: Miriam Siegler and Humphry Osmond, "The Impaired Model of Schizophrenia," 1 (1969), 192-202. Humphry Osmond and Miriam Siegler, "Notes on Orthomolecular Psychiatry and Psychotherapy," 2 (1973) 118-126. Miriam Siegler and Humphry Osmond, " 'Closed Ranks' Twenty Years Later," 2 (1973) 150-163. Miriam Siegler and Humphry Osmond, "The Three Medical Models," 3 (1974).

Acknowledgments

AUTHORS WRITE BOOKS, but the time, energy, and effort needed for research costs money: those who give the money, whether they realize it or not, are performing an act of faith. We hope this book will justify that faith. It was supported by funds from the State of New Jersey, General Research Grant of the National Institutes of Health, and the Robert Sterling Foundation. It was initiated by a grant from the American Schizophrenia Foundation made in 1964.

For this, as for most other inquiries, constructive criticism is essential. We have been fortunate to be helped by a number of gifted and distinguished people who include the late Dr. Paul Haun, M.D., V. Terrell Davis, M.D., Professor Desmond Curran, FRCP, CBE, Zigmund Lebensohn, M.D., J. D. W. Pierce, FRCP, Francis Braceland, M.D., Michael Mendelson, M.D., Walter Barton, M.D., Professor Paul Huston, M.D., who was kind enough to introduce this book, and his colleagues of the Psychopathology Committee of the Group for the Advancement of Psychiatry. We are much indebted to them for focusing our attention on our failure to be explicit regarding the nature of models. This has allowed us, we hope, to remedy a shortcoming with the help of Dr. David Park, a physicist with special knowledge of these matters.

We are also indebted to valued colleagues of current or previous researchers: Professor Abram Hoffer, M.D., FRCP (Canada), Professor Robert Sommer, Ph.D., and to Dr. Frances Cheek, Ph.D., who housed the models in their early stages in the Section of Experimental Sociology at the Bureau of Research in Neurology and Psychiatry in Princeton, New Jersey.

Then there are three men who are in a slightly different category. Professor T. T. Paterson developed the concept of Aesculapian authority and what we owe to him is self-evident. Mr. Stevens Newell played a vital part in researching our models of alcoholism. We had the incomparable advice of the late Bill W. (Mr. William B. Wilson), co-founder of Alcoholics Anonymous, who told us, oddly enough, that we were among the first to ask him how he believed A.A. worked rather than telling him why it had succeeded.

To transmute our many research papers into a book, we have been lucky enough to have the tactful guidance of our editor, Mr. Michael Denneny, whose interest and concern for the content of our studies led him to insist upon their being presented in an appropriate form.

For want of critics, colleagues, and editors, this would have been a much worse book. Without the help of our secretaries and research assistants, there would have been no book at all. For their efforts spread over many years we wish to thank Mrs. Irma Pressey, Mrs. Charlotte Hardy, Mrs. Phyllis Loften, Mrs. Barbara Pinney, and Miss Ingrid Lane, who have typed and retyped evolving manuscripts with great forbearance and pursued current and sometimes nonexistent references with patient zeal.

Contents

Foreword

AN INCIDENT WHICH occurred in 1964 set the stage for this book. One of the authors was astonished by "the frequent and often acerbic differences of opinion" among the staff members in a mental health center. She related her perplexity to the other author, who replied, "Why, that's because they are using different models." Since that occurrence Siegler and Osmond have collaborated in the study of models of madness. Their book appears at a time of enormous turmoil in psychiatry, which some writers refer to as an identity crisis. An editorial in a prestigious medical journal,* "Quo Vadis, Psychiatry?" calls attention to the salient points: mental illness is thought by some to be a myth, the scope of psychiatry is nebulous, some psychiatric schools stray too far from medicine and their adherents do not use medical procedures in diagnosis or treatment.

Conflicts are not new in medicine, certainly not in psychiatry. Recall, for example, the acrimonious disputes between the medical and theological views of madness prominent in the Middle Ages or the loud clashes among the opposing doctrines of psychotherapy in our own century.

Competing theories of disease, conflicting methods of treatment, or inappropriate professional activities may confuse professional goals. Only with reasonable guidelines for the solution of its dif-

* *Journal of the American Medical Association* 226 (Oct. 22, 1973), p. 464.

ficulties can a profession stabilize itself. The authors assert that the most basic guideline for psychiatry is to remain *within the realm of medicine*. They defend the medical model of madness because they believe it has the most to offer the patient, his family, and society, and defend it by comparing their conception of the medical model with seven nonmedical models of madness: the moral, the impaired, the psychoanalytic, the family interaction, the psychedelic, the social, and the conspiratorial. All of these models present a concept of madness, indicate what should be done about it and how those involved ought to behave.

What is the medical model? Medicine is a craft or practical art. The best way to characterize a practical art is to observe its typical activity. When a patient is brought to the emergency room of a hospital, a compressed drama of the clinical model unfolds. Doctors quickly examine the patient. Three questions immediately arise: What was found in the examination? What does he have? What can be done about it? The fear of imminent death adds urgency to the scene. In this transaction there is no blame, the illness is something that *happens* to the person, not something he is or does—a very important consideration for the sick role.

Here we have the medical model in essence. By exercising a special kind of authority, physicians confer the sick role on people, thus placing them within the medical model.

Paterson has called this "Aesculapian authority." It is an unusually powerful authority. Because of it, people will make their bodies and minds accessible for examinations—often embarrassing and painful ones—accept prolonged or dangerous treatments, and meekly follow the doctor's orders. Indeed, the power of Aesculapian authority is so great that in certain circumstances it can override any other authority in society.

The sick role is also a powerful role, found in some form, in virtually all cultures. According to the sociologist Parsons it has four elements, which Siegler and Osmond summarize. A sick person "is exempted from some or all of his normal social role responsibilities . . . cannot help being ill and cannot get well by an act of decision or will . . . is expected to want to get well as soon as possible," and ". . . is expected to seek appropriate help, usually

that of a physician, and to cooperate with that help toward the
end of getting well."

The authors' presentation of the clinical medical model with
its dual foci of Aesculapian authority and the sick role, along with
the twelve further dimensions they explicate, is the most important
contribution of the book. It clarifies for physicians many things
rarely put into words, particularly the meaning of Aesculapian
authority and the sick role. Nor have many of us thought so clearly
about some of the other dimensions of the model, such as rights
and duties of patient, of family and of society. The medical model
appears much more complex than we have ordinarily thought.

The second major contribution of the book is the comparison
of the medical model with the seven nonmedical models of madness. In the hands of Siegler and Osmond all of these nonmedical
models are inadequate in one or more of their dimensions when
compared to the medical model. The message for psychiatrists who
have deserted the medical model, or only use a part of it and "bits
and pieces" of other models, is a clear and urgent demand to re-
examine their practices. *Psychiatry is a branch of medicine*.

The twelve dimensions of the models need a comment, for in
the writers' view another dimension possibly should be added to
the list, namely that of differential diagnosis. Differential diagnosis
is usually thought of as distinguishing between two allied conditions by contrasting their symptoms. This differential can also
extend to the histories, the courses and the signs of the two conditions. Diagnosticians face a persistent question: What other
condition might this illness be? This question is asked frequently
at the first examination of the patient, but an answer must await
the results of additional special examinations or laboratory tests,
or more history of the illness. First studies of a patient often produce an impression only, not a definitive diagnosis. Sometimes one
must patiently observe the course of an illness, or the response of
the patient to a therapeutic trial. (Sometimes only an autopsy de-
termines the diagnosis.) After one makes a diagnosis, treatment
begins. But the illness may take an unexpected turn with atypical
symptoms or signs. Does this mean that the diagnostician erred?
Has another disease compounded the clinical picture? Are the new

symptoms the result of the treatment? The ability to make a differential diagnosis initially and throughout the course of an illness is an important talent required of physicians.

The practitioners of the nonmedical models do not have the broad training or experience in general medicine nor in somatopsychic or psychosomatic signs and symptoms to make the differential diagnosis that the psychiatrist's training and experience enable him to make. This can obviously lead to disaster for the patient.

A few words about models. Models, like diseases, are abstractions. They are inventions of the human mind to place facts, events, and theories in an orderly manner. They are not necessarily true or false. Models which are the closest to reality and the most comprehensive seem more satisfying intellectually.

The status of a model, like a theory, changes with new discoveries and the influence of the times. For example, in the Middle Ages when the moral model was more widely accepted than it is today, a diagnostic trick was used to separate epileptic convulsions believed due to demoniac possession from those due to natural causes. If a seizure stopped when words of scripture were uttered in the victim's ear, the case was one for a clergyman, since the devil cannot bear to hear scripture and would desert the person's body. If the seizure did not stop, a physician was called.

Even adherence to a specific model does not free one from error. Early in this century bacterial infection as a cause of disease exerted a powerful influence in medicine. An etiologic hypothesis for schizophrenia was that the patient harbored a hidden focus of infection. Operations were done successively in hope of removing the focus; each operation in the chain was performed in the following order after the previous one had failed: removal of tonsils, teeth, appendix, gallbladder and half the colon. The "schizococcus" has never been found. This procedure had a short life since it failed to prove its worth.

Model confusion appears most easily when there are many unknowns and a variety of social attitudes. Alcoholism is one such case. Social drinking is often considered normal, but if it turns into weekend binges, *moral* condemnation may enter the picture.

If the drinker drives erratically and is arrested he finds himself in the *legal* system which confines him to its corrective institution, the jail. Continued uncontrolled drinking, which places him in the *impaired* model, may lead finally to delirium tremens and hepatic cirrhosis; then he lands in a hospital where temporarily at least he easily fits the *medical* model. After discharge, what then? Prolonged intensive psychotherapy, an antabuse regimen, attendance at Alcoholics Anonymous, adversive conditioning, family therapy, or what? The alcoholic can easily move from one model to another.

"Model muddlement" (a phrase of the authors) occurs in psychiatry, too, for reasons inherent in psychiatry itself. Psychiatry concentrates on subjective phenomena which are susceptible only to the crudest of measurements. The patient must tell us his experiences. He may be a poor reporter, he may falsify, he may deny, he may distort, he may forget. Considerable interviewing skill is often required to determine the validity of the patient's account of his illness. His behavior may prompt a variety of interpretations including a decision as to whether his experiences go beyond the uncertain boundaries of normal.

Because the brain is effectively encased in a bony skull, techniques for studying it have developed slowly. This is particularly true of the correlation of mental states with brain pathology or malfunction. Electrotherapy, introduced late in the 1930s, which certainly affects the brain, is a highly successful treatment for depression. We do not know why it works. Nor do we know why the antipsychotic drugs are effective for schizophrenia, the antidepressants for depression, and lithium for the control of cyclic manic depressive disease. But these new drugs have vigorously stimulated neuropsychopharmacology to develop new research tools. They have reduced the population of state hospitals markedly and made possible the growth of psychiatric units in general hospitals where the majority of the seriously mentally ill now receive treatment.

In 1945, an historian of neurology, Walter Riese, made an interesting comment about diseases of the brain. He said,

Indeed, in no other field does a physician seem to be so discouraged and helpless as in the diseases of the central nervous system, and with some exceptions, neurology is still the science of the uncurable, and psychiatry the science which teaches us to care for the sick rather than to treat or cure him.*

Fortunately the situation has improved for both neurology and psychiatry since 1945.

Psychiatrists have developed over many years a number of psychotherapeutic techniques to help their patients, and some techniques have grown up outside of psychiatry. In general, some of these methods are helpful as supportive measures in some major mental disorders, but do not materially affect the basic disease. They are useful in some neuroses and some personality disorders. An adequate discussion of the value of psychotherapy is not the purpose here. We only wish to note that nonmedical therapists are found widely in the health field, sometimes in competition with physicians. Obstetrics has the midwife, orthopedics the physical therapist, and ophthalmology the optometrist.

We should mention, too, that physicians sometimes move into areas occupied by other craftsmen. The plastic surgeon who lifts faces might be called a beautician or perhaps even a mental health worker. Dentists are in an analogous situation. My dentist once remarked that after years of practice he had decided he was mostly a beautician since 80 percent of his work was cleaning teeth for persons who hoped his services would help them have prettier smiles. Jurisdictional strife exists within medicine itself: Who treats extruded spinal discs, the neurosurgeon or the orthopedic surgeon?

All these observations indicate that there is often conflict among the practitioners in the health field, both in defining areas of practice and in concepts of disease. Psychiatry does not have a corner on "model muddlement." But it does have an obligation to straighten out its own muddle.

Despite the conflicts and cries throughout many centuries, the conquest of madness has progressed markedly within the field of medicine. Turn back to the vast pandemonium of madness which confronted Pinel, when in 1793, he assumed a post in the Bicêtre, a hospital for the mad in Paris. By careful clinical description he

* Riese, W. "History and Principles of Classification of Nervous Diseases." *Bulletin of the History of Medicine* 38 (1945), p. 509.

developed broad categories for the patients: the feebleminded, functional psychoses and brain diseases. Since his time many of the inborn errors of metabolism leading to mental deficiency have been identified and are diagnosed by pediatricians. Special educators instruct the majority of mental defectives now called slow learners. Brain tumors, often diagnosed by neurologists, are treated by neurosurgeons. Toxic reactions are diagnosed and treated by physicians without regard to specialty. Vitamin-deficiency psychoses are largely prevented by dietary measures. General paresis, once accounting for 10 percent of the resident population of state hospitals, has become a rarity due to early treatment of syphilis.

This leaves the functional psychoses, the neuroses and personality disorders more strictly within the realm of psychiatry. Medical genetics have opened new research areas in the functional psychoses. The antipsychotic, antidepressant and antianxiety drugs have improved the treatment of the functional psychoses and of the neuroses. A large number of the depression and anxiety cases are treated by physicians generally. These are dramatic and significant advances. *None* of the seven nonmedical models made, or could make, this progress; it was all achieved *within the medical model*.

I wrote earlier in this preface that the important contributions of this book are the clarification of the concept of the medical model, with its attributes of the Aesculapian authority and the sick role, and the comparison of this model with seven nonmedical models by means of the twelve dimensions. This bare-bones statement does not convey the penetrating analysis of the comparisons, nor the richness of observations drawn from the history of medicine, from literature, from clinical practice and from activities of psychiatrists who work outside the medical model. One will find examples of the physician's role from Moliere and Osler, the sick role from Thomas Mann, and the illuminating failure of a community psychiatry project in Canada. Such examples together with an engaging style of writing make for delightful, interesting and easy reading. But be not deceived. *Models of Madness, Models of Medicine* is a book to be reread and pondered.

PAUL E. HUSTON, M.D., PH.D.

With them it is as though an artist were to gather the hands, feet, head and other members for his images from diverse models, each part excellently drawn, but not related to a single body, and since they in no way match each other, the result would be monster rather than man.

Copernicus, *De revolutionibus orbium caelestium*

1

Introduction

SCIENCE, UNLIKE ART, is a system of derivative ideas filtered through centuries. Consequently, originality in science is not only infrequent but unwelcome,[1] and even the most original ideas have a history, often a much longer one than their authors suppose. We know the immediate background against which these models developed. During the study that resulted in the paper "Attitudes Toward Naming the Illness,"[2] which began in 1964, one of us (Siegler) was making a series of observations in a mental health center. She had great difficulty in understanding the frequent and often acerbic differences of opinion which arose between staff members. She mentioned this to Osmond and emphasized that these squabbles made no sense to her. He replied, "Why, that's because they are using different models." That question and its answer are the genesis of this book.

Any intelligent and critical person allowed to overhear conferences in most psychiatric centers, in this or other countries today, would be profoundly puzzled, not merely by the differences of opinion but by the lack of common ground among the discussants. Conversations can be heard which strongly resemble the Mad Hatter's tea party, and even when clearcut differences of opinion occur which might result in rational confrontation and serious debate, the contestants are likely, after a few rhetorical statements, to ride off in all directions. The question, What are they arguing about? was one which any critical observer might have raised, but perhaps the real question is: Why was that particular answer made?

That answer derived from some fifteen years of study of the model psychoses, combined with knowledge derived from them, and concern with the experiential worlds of the mentally ill [3] and the social consequences of altered perceptions.[4] From 1950 onward, in collaboration with Drs. John Smythies, Abram Hoffer, and many others, Osmond had undertaken extensive studies of what came to be known as *model psychoses,* in Roland Fischer's [5] useful term. We had produced these models using a variety of chemical substances, such as the well-known mescaline, LSD, etc.,[6] and the less well-known, but probably more significant, adrenaline derivatives, such as adrenochrome and adrenolutin.[7] As a result of these studies, we had developed the first of our experiential instruments for exploring the *Umwelt,* or self-world, of the mentally ill, the H.O.D. test.[8] This test supported our clinical findings that perceptual anomalies play a crucial part in schizophrenia and in particular determine many, if not most, of the social consequences of that illness. Though now unfamiliar, this view was probably held by most psychiatrists until the beginning of this century. In the last thirty or forty years it has been displaced, but never disproved. Very shortly after we had developed the H.O.D. test, Abram Hoffer and Sidney Fogel [9] began to construct an experimental model of schizophrenia based not upon drugs but upon posthypnotically induced perceptual anomalies. This has been greatly refined and elaborated by Bernard Aaronson.[10]

In 1961 the first paper on "Models of Madness," published in the *New Scientist,*[11] stated: "Although the idea of using models of madness in psychiatry is at least a century old, it has not been greatly used until the last decade or so." The idea of using models of a biological or psychological kind within psychiatry was therefore familiar to us in 1964, and there was a substantial literature available on this subject. The idea that there might be different models of medicine in general, and psychiatry in particular, was also in the air at that time. The division of medicine into *clinical* medicine, *public health* medicine, and what we have called *science* medicine is extremely old, going back at least to the Greeks,[12] but it is not unfair to suggest that its very antiquity and familiarity had, as so often happens, encouraged neglect rather than concern. Very few people, so far as we have been able to discover, were much interested in the relationship between these three kinds of medicine or in changes which might occur in consequence of that relationship, with advances in all three.

Although hardly anyone doubted that the three sorts of medicine existed, they were taken for granted and were supposed to jog along together without interfering with each other. In practice it was recognized that they sometimes did conflict. Books such as *Arrowsmith*[13] and *The Citadel*[14] would hardly have become best sellers if the medical and lay public had not suspected that sometimes the gearing between the three hardly meshed at all. The comforting fiction that in getting one's medical degree one was invested with the triune authority of clinical, public health, and science medicine was a further burden for the conscientious and a greater source of exhilaration for the lackadaisical. Wisely, perhaps, must young physicians, like their teachers, seldom gave the matter a moment's thought and thus were already preparing to join the ranks of their moral and ethical elders.

Nevertheless, at least one notable medical philosopher and thinker, Dr. Wilfred Trotter, gave a considerable amount of his powerful and well-coordinated thinking to this matter. As one might expect from the author of *The Instincts of the Herd in War and Peace*,[15] who was not only a great surgeon but was recognized as a scientist as well by his election to the Royal Society,* his discussions of the relationship between clinical and science, or technical, medicine are not only extraordinarily shrewd but as apt today as they were nearly forty years ago.

* According to Ernest Jones, *Life and Work of Sigmund Freud*. Vol. 2 (New York: Basic Books, 1955), pp. 28, 41. Trotter also played some part in drawing Jones's attention to Freud's writings in 1903. He and Jones were the only English doctors present when the first International Psychoanalytic Congress was held in the Hotel Bristol at Salzburg on Sunday, April 26, 1908. Freud and Trotter did not meet again until thirty years later in London, toward the close of both their lives.

Trotter, following Plato, describes clinical medicine as a practical art, like that of the farmer, the builder, the blacksmith, the joiner, or the sailor. He goes on to say:

A practical art has no complete and sure foundation of ascertained principles. Its possessions are made up of separate and fragmentary conquests from the unknown. The items of its knowledge are therefore incompletely definable and are preserved as the traditionary rules of the art. These are not *applied* like scientific principles to the particular case, but are *interpreted* for its treatment in accordance with the judgment, intuition and personal skill of the artist. It thus comes about that in a practical art satisfactory action is judged not wholly by its object being attained, but by whether the artist followed the established rules, whether, as we say, he proceeded "secundem artum." In a true applied science, failure can be due only to ignorance; in a practical art where so much is indefinable, success as a sole test for correct action is obviously impracticable. To adopt for a practical art the standard of attainment applicable to an applied science is not to improve its status, it is only to convert it to quackery.[16]

Trotter here lays the foundation for distinguishing science medicine from clinical medicine, and in the process alerts us to an idea of central importance: clinical medicine is best seen as a puzzling and poorly understood activity and should be approached anthropologically, as one would approach a religious ritual of some primitive people. Instead of assuming that it is a conscious and rational activity, the rules of which are known to its practitioners, we should assume the opposite: that its rules are so deeply imbedded in human culture and lie so much outside awareness that its practitioners know as little about it as most of us do about the grammar and origin of our language. We cannot ask doctors and patients directly why they do what they do because they usually do not know why; we must observe them first and then try to make the rules of the enterprise explicit.

Because the art of medicine has sometimes been mistakenly seen as an applied science, it has been difficult to understand why doctors are so conservative; indeed, they are often berated for this. But Trotter helps us to understand the origin of this conservatism:

The method of the practical art was the first instrument forged by man for the subjugation of chaos. At the dawn of civilization the preservation of knowledge was far more important than its discovery. The accidental fruits of experience and the creations of genius could be saved from an infallible oblivion only by being preserved in the precepts and tradition of a practical art. The superlative need for preservation made the arts inherently conservative, for there was, and is, no unequivocal difference between the change that was progress and the change that was decay. New knowledge was therefore accepted as reluctantly as old custom was given up.[17]

When we take our bodies to a doctor for repair, what we want, in part, is what the owner of an irreplaceable Stradivarius wants when he takes it to a violin-maker—a craftsman who has forgotten nothing.

Lest one imagine that this conservatism is no longer needed, we should recall that within the last 130 years there was an admirable and very successful system of treatment and care for psychotic patients called "moral treatment," whose rules and traditions have been so completely lost that we cannot say of a single mental hospital today: this is a moral treatment hospital. A more recent example is that of studies on the efficacy of psychotherapy in schizophrenia: although the consensus is that these studies have failed to show that psychotherapy benefits sufferers from this illness, it is still a very widely used form of treatment, for it has become a tradition to give it, and so long as there is no agreed alternative it will continue to be employed.

The conservatism necessary to medicine as a practical art does not prevent doctors from taking action long before all the facts are known. Trotter [18] illustrates this by citing the case of scurvy. In 1745 James Lind described the cure of scurvy by lemon juice, but it was 162 years later that the scientific experiments of Holst and Fröhlich established its cause. Trotter says: "The practical art of medicine alone knew the urgency of the problems [of rickets and scurvy]. . . ." The scientist, then, may be prevented from acting by his exacting standards, and may be disinclined to act because of his detachment from the urgency of the problem; in these instances the clinical doctor may have a practical if unproved solution to a problem long before the scientist.

Trotter was well aware of the troubles which were beginning to afflict clinical medicine in his day as science medicine was burgeoning:

The ancient and honourable art of medicine is being increasingly and inevitably pressed on by applied science, and suffers as well from misunderstanding and loss of prestige. It remains, however, the backbone of medical practice and indispensable to mankind. There is therefore an especial need today that its characteristic mode of activity should be understood, and should not be confused with those of the other elements that make up the complex of medicine.[19]

In following Trotter's lead, we shall concern ourselves with the "characteristic mode of activity" of clinical medicine, and thereby hope to unravel some of the confusion which plagues psychiatry and medicine today.

Once one has differentiated clinical medicine from the other elements, the question arises whether a single man can combine the three very different roles in his person. That great, exemplary doctor, Sir William Osler, demonstrated clearly throughout his life that it was possible for one man to combine the roles of clinical, public health, and science doctor. Osler wielded with an extraordinary and deceptive ease the "threefold brand" of medicine. One might call them faith, hope, and charity: the public health, the science, and the clinical models. Because of his enormous skill he made it look something that any fool could do and he made perhaps thousands of younger people wish to emulate him. What he realized well enough, and what apparently got lost by the time the Flexner Commission report came out, was that the greatest of his gifts was the last, the clinical model—no amount of effort given to the other two would make up for lack of it. When urging students to join the noble band of general practitioners who formed "the very sinews of the profession, generous hearted men with well balanced cool heads, not scientific always, but learned in the wisdom not of the laboratories but of the sick room," he added: ". . . and finally, gentlemen, remember, you are here not to be made chemists or physiologists or anatomists, but to learn how to recognize and treat disease, how to become practical physicians." [20]

During the period since the publication of our first joint paper on models in 1966, "Models of Madness," [21] the notion of using models to solve some of the problems besetting psychiatry has been very much "in the air," but has shown little sign of coming down to earth. We find it remarkable that while there has been a great deal of discussion by psychiatrists, psychologists, sociologists, and others regarding models, there has been a paucity of actual model-making other than our own. In psychiatry and its environs there has been a much greater tendency to talk about models than to study, use, develop, and understand them. We have been surprised at the lack of criticism of our method of model-making, the general acceptance of the dimensions which we employed, the failure—with one notable exception, the impaired model [22]—of social scientists to provide us with other usable models.

One psychiatrist, T. Kraft,[23] has employed our dimensions to construct a new model of alcoholism, the social anxiety model. We are, of course, pleased to see him organize his view of alcoholism in a way which makes it possible to compare it with that of others. However, at this writing he has not yet done the critical part of the work to which one commits oneself as a model-maker: comparing his model, dimension by dimension, with the alternative models. A single model makes a noise like the sound of one hand clapping.

We have also come upon what one might consider a rival set of models,[24] but these came long after our own and seem to derive from them in a truncated and distorted way. We expressed our opinion rather tartly [25] regarding this particular effort at model-making, but that was due to its incompetence, not because we want to discourage other model-makers. Indeed, we welcome efforts by others to produce better and more effective models than those which we will display and discuss here. So far, however, we can say without conceit that no serious rivals exist. This does not mean that they never will.

A number of colleagues have suggested, rather strangely, that all models are out of date, while others claim that they themselves use "all the models." However, they have been reluctant to show us either how one would conduct oneself using the first proposition or, regarding the second, demonstrate how they have combined in one grand super model the eight models we have discussed here without producing not a super model but a super muddle. This cannot be due to a lack of interest in these matters. For instance, in the *Roche Report* of January 15, 1971, there is an article entitled "Exploring Psychiatry's Own Identity Crisis," by Dr. Arnold J. Mandell,[26] Professor and Chairman of the Department of Psychiatry at the University of California School of Medicine at San Diego. Dr. Mandell sees contemporary psychiatry going through an identity crisis in an attempt to decide whether it is a mental health delivery system, a field of training, an area for research, or all or none of these things. One wonders what Silas Weir Mitchell,[27] who reproved the psychiatrists of the 1890s, reminding them that they were among the "first of specialists," would think about this second adolescence. Dr. Mandell adds: "There is no unity, understanding or acceptance of a role expected by society." Instead, he believes that psychiatry is thrashing around in several directions at once, sometimes successfully and often ineffectively. He suggests that "the psychiatric hospital with its medical model may be an institution of the past." He contrasts the problem of the psychiatrist as a brain biologist with his activity as a member of a behavioral science group. He ends: "Whether the psychiatrist's identity can expand to incorporate new knowledge and a new social role remains to be seen."

However, in spite of Dr. Mandell's view that the medical model may be part of an "institution of the past," we learn nothing from him as to what exactly the medical model is. It is hard to see how anything can be described as obsolete until we know exactly what it is and why it can no longer survive. It is frequently supposed that simply because the medical model is, as we shall show, very old indeed, it must therefore be obsolete. While this may be a culturally favored view in North America, it has little social or biological validity; supposedly obsolete and indeed extinct biological systems like the coelacanth have sustained themselves quite satisfactorily for millions of years after their supposed obsolescence occurred.

Not long after this, a dissident group of the American Psychiatric Association (A.P.A.), in a statement of principles appearing in

Psychiatric News, February 3, 1971, stated that the A.P.A. must concern itself with:

. . . racism, poverty, institutional violence and discrimination on the basis of sex, creed or ethnic background, the fact that these social injustices do not per se "cause" mental illness should not prevent us from taking a strong stand against them and their effect on human dignity, well-being and optimal psychological development which are, of course, central to mental health.[28]

This suggests a psychiatry unlimited on the grandest scale. However, in the correspondence column of *Psychiatric News* (December 1, 1971), Dr. Edward W. Hughes, Jr., M.D., criticizes the decision of the A.P.A. to drop the internship requirements, which he considers reflects psychiatry's growing ambivalence and anxiety about its identity and the social pressure to produce more therapists as fast as possible.

With psychologists and other non-psychiatrists rapidly moving into the vacuum of mental health care, the A.P.A. is hastily beginning to delude itself that more psychiatrists can be manufactured by diluting a most important year of clinical experience, under the guise that this will allow medical schools the opportunity to innovate in this manufacturing process.

He ends:

Hopefully, our senior members will be able to make up their minds so that we younger ones will know what we are supposed to be and what we should become. Sitting in the office, grinding out a vague process of psychotherapy seems to be too abstract for definition. But isn't this enough, if it ever can be measured, if done well, to help us find ourselves as physician psychiatrists? [29]

These, then, are only a few of the concerns expressed by psychiatrists. Other professions express theirs, too. Many surgeons and internists criticize psychiatrists for not being doctors, a theme reminding one of Silas Weir Mitchell's remarks in 1894 as to what became the American Psychiatric Association:

You were the first specialists and you never got back into line. It is easy to see how this came about. You soon began to live apart and you still do so. Your hospitals are not our hospitals; your ways are not our ways. You live out of range of critical shot; you are not preceded and followed in your ward work by clever rivals, or watched by able residents fresh with the learning of the school.[30]

Mitchell went on to say that he had seen mental hospitals that "smelt and looked like second-class lodging-houses" and that the psychiatrists had taught their colleagues little from their experience of having seen ninety-one thousand patients. Mitchell's observations still echo uneasily down the years.

In the *Medical Post* of February 9, 1971,[31] Dr. Dennis Kussin, President of the Association of Residents in Psychiatry at McGill University wrote: "One of the difficulties in teaching psychiatry is deciding what should be taught. . . . There are so many different theories, each school has its own approach." One resident said: "If you knew the pet theories of the examiner, you could direct your answer accordingly, but of course, you hardly ever know the examiner's particular leanings." Dr. Frederick A. Freyhan, Director of Psychiatric Research at St. Vincent's Hospital and Medical Center in New York, wrote: "The achievements of modern pharmacology have yet to be matched with corresponding revisions of psychiatric theory, practice and education." In the same article, Dr. Thomas Ban said: "Psychiatry must either become a branch of medicine or move out of the medical schools and become a social science."

In such circumstances, it is understandable that other specialties in medicine tend to be less perplexed and perhaps just a little smug when viewing psychiatry's misfortunes. Yet we shall show that they too have their troubles, and it is possible that the development of conceptual models such as those which we shall discuss here may be no less useful to medicine generally than they are likely to be for psychiatry.

We do not expect to resolve the problem of language which assails the psychiatric establishment at this moment. However, we do believe that we have made a modest step forward, which suggests that at least some of the troubles besetting psychiatry today derive from a failure to understand that different models are being used. If these different models are to be harnessed together, this will be difficult, if not impossible, until some account is taken of the very different roles and goals imposed by the use of these many models. Before undertaking any study of the models themselves, however, it is essential to know how they came to be constructed and how we use them today.

Constructing the Models

We have evolved a method for constructing models in an attempt to explain and perhaps alleviate the confusion in psychiatry, which nowadays resembles the Tower of Babel. Our psychiatric situation is perhaps even more chaotic than that of the legendary tower, for in that famous example of failed communication, each person was presumably speaking one language consistently, although not the same language as his fellow tower-builders. What we have in psychiatry is worse: each person uses a hodgepodge of bits and pieces of ideas, theories, notions, and ideologies in order to engage in a supposedly common enterprise with others similarly confused.

A common enterprise: that is the key. For if concerted action was never required, what difference would it make whether one were consistent or not? Very few of us always hold a clear and consistent view of this complex, puzzling, and ever-changing universe. Each of us collects scraps and shreds of theories about politics, economics, art, religion, philosophy, science, child psychology, etc., and so long as we are not asked to take any responsible action, we are content to live in a state of chronic, undifferentiated model-muddle. We know dimly that somewhere there is someone who has gone to the trouble of discovering the connection (or lack of connection) between the gold standard, low tariffs and the single tax, between free will and evolution, between thumb-sucking and school performance, and we are grateful for these grand efforts on our behalf, but we also know that we will probably never understand them and that it probably doesn't matter very much.

However, when we are confronted with suffering people and their families, who demand that we exert ourselves on their behalf because we have declared ourselves to be expert in the field of their suffering, then it does matter what we say and do, and what we do depends upon the theories or models which we hold regarding those misfortunes we are supposed to alleviate. That is why we look to those few who have worked out some consistent position to guide our stumbling efforts. To write a book or set up a program which consistently uses a particular theory of madness that can be differentiated from all other theories is an intellectual achievement, a step beyond our usual state of eclectic muddlement. Unluckily, those giants of thought and system, to whom we turn for guidance, frequently hold points of view which are irreconcilable with each other. If we chose clearly articulated theories, one might be proved "true" and all others "false," thus giving us generally acceptable grounds for action. Alas, that most desirable of solutions, an orthodoxy such as Freud commended to Jung in the earlier part of this century, is not at present open to us, for there is no psychiatric theory at the moment which is so good and so universally accepted that exemplary members of this profession are prepared to use it, to insist that it be used by their co-professionals and thus end the controversy. Indeed, we have come to suspect that this failure to reach agreement lies not in the theories themselves so much as in the philosophical implications of those theories.

What then are we to do? There are too many theories, no one theory has universal acceptance, those who hold consistent theories disagree with each other violently, while at our door those afflicted with madness wait in desperate hope to learn what we plan for them. To make sense of this chaos, we must first gather together the disparate points of view and sort them into some kind of preliminary groups or types. In short, we must make a classification system.

There are immediate advantages to any classification system, however crude. The most obvious is that it makes it much easier to remember and recognize large amounts of data if they have been classified in some way or other. If one had to learn to recognize large numbers of animals, then one would probably begin by sorting them into categories, using the Linnaean or some other system. In setting up a library there must be some basis for arranging the books, otherwise they would never be found when wanted. They could be arranged by color or by weight, but somehow we recognize instinctively that we require criteria for this kind of sorting which feel fundamental rather than accidental.

A classification system makes it easier for the user or consumer to chose intelligently. In a library one wants to know how to find the novels of one author rather than another, or to find books on hog-raising rather than on hair-styling. If the book jackets were all blank, then the only way would be to look through the pages of each book, an appalling and unnecessary chore. In psychiatry, too, the user or consumer has choices: is he or she looking for a doctor who specializes in psychiatric diseases, or is one really asking for a guru or guide to point one toward enlightenment? But in this library the covers are all blank and one has to leaf through many pages to see if one has obtained the right expert. This not only wastes time and money, but prolongs the suffering of the person seeking help.

In that mental health center where we did our original work and where this problem forced itself unexpectedly upon our attention, our inquiry into the attitudes of patients, families, and staff enabled us to make a preliminary sorting into four different points of view, which we called medical, psychoanalytic, social, and moral. Because this center had doctors, nurses, social workers, and psychologists on its staff, in a hospital which had wards, charts, examination tables, blood pressure apparatuses, etc., and there were discussions about etiology, diagnosis, treatment and prognosis, we knew that we had the makings of a medical model. The psychoanalytic model was there, too, for we heard talk of ego strength, of unresolved conflicts, of adolescent turmoil, and of parents who unconsciously undermined the therapy of their children. It also became clear, from our inquiries and from the center's programs, that the patients, residents, or whatever they were to be called, were often seen as a sort of disadvantaged minority requiring social rehabilitation. The language of morality was also used; good behavior was encouraged and led to privileges and early discharge, while bad behavior was frowned upon and led to gloomy predictions about the inmate's future. We had, now, the making of four models.

By surveying the psychiatric literature of that day (1964), we found two other points of view which were not at that time in evidence in our particular mental health center, and from them we constructed two additional models. One was the family interaction model, whose representative journal, *Family Process,* was then just two years old. The other was what we came to call the conspiratorial model, best represented at the time by the writings of Thomas Szasz, whose book *Law, Liberty and Psychiatry* [32] was published in 1963. We now had a classification system of six models, which we described in our initial paper, "Models of Madness," [33] in 1966.

Sometime later two other points of view came to our attention which we felt should be included among our models. An empirical study by Gerald Gordon [34] suggested the possibility of making an impaired model. Gordon set out to validate Parsons's sick role and discovered, in the process, the impaired role. Once we constructed a model from Gordon's study, we found that it described the custodial features of many state hospitals much more exactly than the medical model. Large parts of these institutions are not really hospitals at all, but homes for the impaired, as the title "asylum" often given them implied honestly and accurately enough. Had we not already constructed our original six models, we would have probably missed the significance of Gordon's important discovery.

Our eighth model, which we have called the psychedelic, was constructed to explain the writings of R. D. Laing, [35] in which madness is seen as a mind-expanding trip. Although this view, that the mad really see things more clearly than the rest of us, seemed a startling innovation, we discovered that it is just as old and persistent as the other views.

If one is making a classification system, how does one know when there are enough categories? How many models ought there to be? We felt that there must be enough to reflect major current differences of opinion, while not so many as to create an awkward or cumbersome system. A system of one hundred models might well be worse than no system at all, while one of only two or three models would be insufficiently complex to shed much light on our problem. We believe that we will know when additional models must be constructed as soon as we find views expressed in the literature, in programs, or in those suffering from madness which cannot reasonably be fitted into any of our existing models.

It is sometimes said that you cannot compare apples and oranges, but this is not so; you can if you are willing to call them both "fruit." Because our models lie in different disciplines (medicine, law, philosophy, psychology, religion, etc.), we have the apples-and-oranges problem, and so we must compare our models in terms of common qualities. All of our models presuppose that there is a "mad" person who believes himself, or whom others believe, to have difficulty in occupying a normal social role; that there is a practitioner of some sort with special knowledge of this kind of event; and that there is a family and a community which have some interest in defining the situation. All the models deal with the question of what sort of thing madness is, what should be done about it, and how those involved ought to behave. These common elements provide the dimensions of our models. In this book we shall concern ourselves with twelve dimensions: definition or diagnosis; etiology; behavior (how it is to be interpreted); treatment; prognosis or outcome; suicide; the function of the hospital or other institution; personnel (who the practitioners shall be); the rights and duties of the patient, client, etc.; the rights and duties of the family; the rights and duties of community or society; and the goal of the model.

A model, as we shall use the term in this book, is an arrangement of an ideology, theory, point of view, etc., in such a manner that it can be compared with other ideologies, theories, points of view, etc. Comparability is the essence of model-making. To be in the model-making business, you require at least two models of at least two dimensions each. For example, if you want to buy a boat or a refrigerator, you want to know many things about it in order to make an intelligent choice: its size, its cost, its reliability, its capacity, etc.; in other words, you want a model with a sufficient number of relevant dimensions. What you also want is two or more

TABLE I: MODELS OF MADNESS

	Medical Model	Moral Model	Impaired Model	Psychoanalytic Model	Social Model	Psychedelic Model	Conspiratorial Model	Family Interaction Model
1. Definition/ diagnosis	Doctor determines disease; informs patient clearly; rules out other diseases. Diagnosis determines treatment and prognosis.	Moral practitioner determines extent of unacceptable, dysfunctional or immoral behavior.	Person is permanently handicapped or disabled; e.g., incurably insane.	A continuum of emotional difficulties from mild neurosis to severe psychosis. Diagnosis unimportant; each case unique.	Mental Illness is a symptom of a "sick" society, another aspect of poverty and discrimination.	Madness is really a mind-expanding "trip"; things appear more clear than ordinarily possible.	Madness exists only in the eye of the beholder; the so-called madman is simply the victim of labeling.	The whole family is "sick"; the one brought for help is only the "index patient," who may be the healthiest member of the family.
2. Etiology	Etiology important but not always known. Natural causes are assumed.	Unimportant. Bad behavior was learned somewhere.	Unimportant how person became impaired; often from birth.	Very important. Must reconstruct analysand's life from dreams, free associations, history-taking.	Socially disadvantaged families produce psychological problems in their members. Rate of social change is too fast or not fast enough.	Schizophrenics have been driven mad by their families, who try to get them to conform.	People are identified as mentally ill because others conspire to label them; the conspirators cannot tolerate deviance.	Patient is "sick" because acts out family pathology; family is "sick" because parents came from "sick" families, etc.
3. Subject's behavior	Indicates patient's illness. May help diagnosis.	Taken at face value; measured, not interpreted.	Behavior interpreted as normal with allowances made for handicap.	Interpreted symbolically. Therapist must de-code it, find out what it really means.	Behavior symptomatic of social pathology.	An attempt to break the bind their families have put them in.	Stems directly from the way he is treated by those conspiring against him.	All behavior in the family consists of moves and maneuvers in the family game.
4. Treatment	Medical, surgical treatments, nursing care; specific to diagnosis if possible. Contraindications possible.	Important. Modify "bad" behavior with positive and negative sanctions.	No treatment for an impairment. Rehabilitative measures important.	A special one-to-one relation with therapist involving transference.	Improve social, economic, political status of mentally ill and their families.	A guided "trip" into madness and back again.	"Treatment" is really a kind of brain-washing to induce conformity.	Family therapy.
5. Prognosis	Important. Follows from diagnosis. Doctor cannot promise cure but usually offers some hope.	Good, if client cooperates and practitioner can construct workable sanctioning system or reinforcement schedule.	No change expected for better or worse.	Depends on analysand's place on continuum, e.g., prognosis poor for psychotics. Depends on whether analysand really wants to get well.	Recovery depends on social change.	A guided "trip" may lead to enlightenment.	A vicious circle: the more someone is treated as mentally ill, the more he will behave that way.	If family therapy is successful, family will give up games and index patient will give up symptoms.

TABLE I: MODELS OF MADNESS (Continued)

	Medical Model	Moral Model	Impaired Model	Psychoanalytic Model	Social Model	Psychedelic Model	Conspiratorial Model	Family Interaction Model
6. *Suicide*	A serious risk in many psychiatric disorders. Doctor must watch for signs that patient is at risk.	A choice or option which ends all further possibility of behavioral change.	Not expected if person accepts his handicap.	Aggression turned against the self, or unwillingness to face real problems.	A symptom of anomie, despair.	"Trips" are risky; there is no guarantee that a person won't commit suicide.	A way out of the vicious circle.	A final move in the family game by a member who sees no other moves open.
7. *Function of institution*	Hospital is a place where patients are treated and cared for; patients never *live* there or work *for* the hospital.	Correctional institution where person stays until his behavior improves; voluntarily or involuntarily.	Home for impaired provides protection, care, work, rehabilitation.	Any place where analysand can be analyzed, away from family that made him "sick."	Asylum for the severely damaged; or storefront clinic; or headquarters for the social revolution.	To provide a good atmosphere for guided "trips."	All institutions for schizophrenics degrade and invalidate human beings.	Hospital anti-therapeutic, unless whole family is treated there.
8. *Personnel*	Doctors treat the ill, nurses care for them, other staff rehabilitate them.	Moral practitioners possessing knowledge on how to alter behavior, e.g., behavior therapists, clergymen, ward attendants.	Personnel must be skilled at rehabilitation; must be kind to the impaired.	Psychoanalysts or psychotherapists. Must have undergone analysis themselves.	Social psychiatrists, social workers, storefront clinic workers, social revolutionaries.	Guides who have been there and back.	Conspirators: all who conspire to label a person as mentally ill. Anti-conspirators: all who combat this, e.g., civil liberties lawyers, writers of exposé articles, etc.	Family therapists, game analysts.
9. *Rights and duties of subject*	Right to the sick role: exemption from normal responsibilities; no blame; right to special care. Duty to try to get well; to seek help and cooperate with that help.	Right to expect a serious effort to restore him to society. Duty to cooperate in effort to change his behavior.	Right to be protected from abuse, exploitation, persecution. Duty to behave as much as possible like normal person, within limits of impairment.	Right to have his behavior seen as symbolic, not judged morally. Right to sympathy for his long-standing emotional problems. Duty to cooperate with the therapy.	Right to expect social reforms to remove any special disadvantages. Right to care as social victims. Duty to cooperate with social change.	Right to well-guided "trip" in setting conducive to inner exploration. Duty to accept restraint if he is too much for others.	In a total institution the inmate has no rights and no duties.	Right to expect other members of family to agree to be defined as "sick" and to co-operate with family therapy. Duty to cooperate with family therapy.

TABLE I: MODELS OF MADNESS (Continued)

	Medical Model	Moral Model	Impaired Model	Psychoanalytic Model	Social Model	Psychedelic Model	Conspiratorial Model	Family Interaction Model
10. Rights and duties of families	Right to sympathy; right to be informed about illness and progress. Duty to cooperate with treatment.	Right to expect that experts have better sanctioning system than they have. Duty to encourage their immoral members to seek behavior therapy.	Right to know degree of impairment; right to be spared unreasonable hope. Duty to encourage impaired person to live as normally as possible.	No rights, not even being informed of progress. Duty not to interfere with therapy.	Right to expect social reforms to prevent social pathology. Duty to cooperate with social change.	No rights. Duty to allow their mad member to go on voyage of self-healing. No right to label him and send him to hospital.	Forfeited its usual rights by labeling one member as mentally ill and acting against him. Duty not to do this.	Right to be treated as "sick." Duty to cooperate with family therapy.
11. Rights and duties of society	Right to be protected from ill people who are a danger to others. Duty to provide medical care in one form or another.	Right to defend itself from members who endanger others by violating social norms or laws. Duty to provide possibility of rehabilitation.	Right to be protected from dangers due to impairment (e.g., insane drivers). Duty to protect impaired from abuse, exploitation, persecution.	No rights. Duty to see immoral behavior of analysands as symptoms of emotional disturbance.	No rights. Duty to change, or stop changing, so social pathology is not transmitted to individuals via their families.	No rights in relation to mad people. Duty to allow more "breakthrough."	Right to lock up those who have broken laws, but not those who are merely socially deviant.	No rights. Possibly, duty to provide family therapy.
12. Goal of model	Treat patients for illnesses; restore them to health if possible; otherwise prevent illness from getting worse. Reduce blame by conferring sick role. Accumulate medical knowledge.	Alter behavior to bring person into line with acceptable social norms.	To protect and care for permanently impaired persons; to provide rehabilitation for those able to function at a reduced level.	To resolve the analysand's long-standing unconscious emotional conflicts.	To reform society and create a healthy environment in which families can raise children without mental illness.	To allow certain people, now seen as mad, to develop their potential for inner exploration and to change the world through their insights.	Conspirators: to maintain the status quo by punishing deviance. Anticonspirators: to champion the persecuted.	To restore pathological families to mental health. To understand family dynamics.

models, for no amount of information about one model will tell you whether or not some other model might not be better. A boat which is the right size might be too expensive, while one that is inexpensive might be too small. The same is true of the various models used in psychiatry. The psychoanalytic model can give a more complete account of etiology than any of the other models, but it is exceptionally poor at discussing the rights and duties of the family. The medical model, which has fairly clear and well-known directions for the family, is often hazy about etiology.

If all those who participate in psychiatric enterprises had used only one model, and had used it consistently, we would never have been put to the trouble of constructing these models, but since very few people are highly consistent and most are not at all, we have made the models to show what it would look like if they were used purely and consistently. Table 1 (p. 16) presents the models in this idealized form.

Our classification system, as it appears in Table 1, implies that all the models are equal, but in fact there is one model which is more equal than the others; this is the medical model. What are the reasons for its special status? First, psychiatry *is* a branch of medicine, and even those psychiatrists espousing radical antimedical models, such as Drs. Laing and Szasz, are physicians who have not formally dissociated themselves from their medical profession and who seem unlikely to do so. Even in the most radical programs, the familiar scenes of medical practice still occur: the doctor prescribes the pill; the suffering person wants to know when he will be able to work; the family is presented with a bill.

A further reason for the privileged status of the medical model in our system is that we were already biased in its favor when we began our inquiries, although we did not then know why this was so. It might have been better if these models were constructed by someone of Olympian detachment, equally familiar with them all, and not especially involved in any one. But this does not seem to be the way research of any kind is undertaken, and it is certainly not what happened with us. This book shows why we believe the medical model to be the best choice for those suffering from schizophrenia.

In addition to these two situational advantages in our schema, now that we are able to compare the medical model with the other models, it seems to have a significant advantage in relation to conditions such as schizophrenia, in that it alone offers a dignified status for the person who cannot occupy his usual social role for reasons completely beyond his control. This unexpected aspect of the medical model emerged gradually during our explorations and has become central to our understanding of the conflicts and confusions which reverberate among the models.

We now propose to show how each of the seven nonmedical models compares with the medical model in contemporary psychiatry, and to show why the medical model, for all its shortcomings, is much stronger than it first appears.

2

The Discontinuous Models of Madness

OUR MODELS CAN be divided into two classes, which reflect two fundamentally different ways of viewing human misfortune: the discontinuous and the continuous. Three of our models, the medical, the moral, and the impaired, can be described as discontinuous in the sense that they put forth a partial or restricted rather than a global view of the problem of madness. In these three models, some aspect of madness is dealt with in an immediate but limited way: symptoms are treated, misbehavior is corrected, or impairment is assessed. There is no attempt at a total explanation or solution for the whole of madness.

In medicine it is assumed that our knowledge of nature is fragmentary and that whatever the ultimate cause of illnesses may be, we are obliged to work out immediate and practical solutions to particular crises without allowing ourselves to be distracted from this humble pursuit by cosmic considerations. It is further assumed that illnesses are distinguishable from each other, and that treatments which are helpful in one illness are not necessarily helpful and may even be harmful in another. Measurement is essential to sustain this discontinuous view of medicine. Physical examinations of the patient and samples of blood or urine are used to determine the particular illness and its particular treatment. Some measurements which are no longer acceptable, such as the qualitative pulse or uroscopy, no doubt served a useful function in maintaining this discontinuous view of disease. Judgments are also made about the severity of illnesses, for people are said to have a serious case of this illness, or a mild case of that. As Trotter has emphasized, clinical medicine is not expected to exhibit logical consistency.

The moral model, too, is discontinuous. Just as treatment ought to fit the illness, so should punishment fit the crime. Crimes are categorized as to type and as to heinousness, while punishments are calibrated according to severity. The system of privileges which still prevails in the wards of some mental hospitals and is now being revived as behavior therapy in others reflects this model: good and bad behavior has been measured in cigarettes or tokens disbursed and in hours spent in seclusion.

The third discontinuous model is the impaired. There are clearly many different kinds of impairment and no one expects that arrangements which are suitable for the blind will be equally helpful for the deaf or the crippled. Here, as in medicine, measurement is almost essential, for a person who has only 5 percent vision has a much worse degree of impairment than one with, say, 50 percent, and while an I.Q. of 90 may be seen as a variation on normality, an I.Q. of 30 is a permanent limitation requiring the impaired role. In relation to madness, the impaired model has been poorly developed and tends to focus on crude obvious distinctions, such as whether a person is continent or incontinent, or whether he can work productively without supervision. Since those people who have been ill with schizophrenia for many years often have social, educational, vocational, and other impairments, much more refined measurements are needed than are presently available.

The affect of those who use these discontinuous models tends to be cheerful and optimistic, an unexpected but wholly beneficial effect of their limited and realistic goals. The neurosurgeons, orthomolecular psychiatrists, ward attendants, behavior modification experts, and others who use discontinuous models in psychiatry are content to deal with each separate event as it comes along and do not concern themselves too much about how everything fits together. Because of this high morale in those who use discontinuous models, a similar expectation is generated in those who are afflicted in these various ways and is required of them even in the face of crushing difficulties. Once again this seems to stem from limited expectations, for there is always something that can be done to decrease a symptom, correct a behavior pattern, or gain a little ground with an impairment. Even when ground cannot be gained, loss may be prevented and this, too, becomes an occasion for raising morale. The use of measurement makes it possible to be encouraged by the smallest increments of success.

Discontinuous models suffer from a lack of comprehensiveness; what they offer are partial and sometimes only trivial solutions to vast problems, such as madness, which are clearly enormous in scope. However, what they lose in comprehensiveness is gained in the willingness to take simple, practical, and sometimes verifiable steps to alleviate suffering. Perhaps one cannot have it both ways: a theory which is stretched so thin that it covers everything does not ever offer much comfort and protection at any particular spot.

The Medical Model

Suppose that a Martian spy were assigned to learn the meaning of our phrase "the medical model." How would he go about it? He might decide that the first logical step was to read the medical literature, including current books and articles, the history of medicine, and the socio-anthropology of medicine. But here, oddly enough, he would find no reference to the medical model. He would find such references only in the literature of psychiatry and psychology, and almost always in the context of how or why the medical model ought to be abandoned.[1] Before plunging further into this vast and confusing literature, our spy might pause and reason to himself: if it is called the "medical model," it must be used (even if not written about) in that activity called "medicine." In order to find out what the medical model looks like, then, one must examine medicine in action, or read accounts of that action.

Fortunately, there is a recent book, *Five Patients*,[2] which gives an account of the daily activities of a general hospital said to be the best in the land. Surely here one could learn what the medical model is. The author says that in order to understand the job this hospital does, one must view it on the basis of a twenty-four-hour day, 365 days a year.

On that basis, the hospital sees a new patient in the emergency ward every eight minutes, X-rays are taken on a patient every five minutes, a new patient is admitted every twenty minutes. And a new operation is begun every thirty minutes.

The medical model, then, deals with urgent matters at a fast pace. The author describes the emergency ward, a microcosm of the hospital as a whole:

After a student has examined the patient, the resident conducts a second examination, and then comes out to talk to the student about the case. The resident generally has only three questions: "What did you find? What do you think he has? What do you want to do for him?"

Interestingly, these are the only really important questions in all clinical medicine.

Our spy now has a highly condensed account of the medical model at work, from which he can reconstitute its various components. First, a person voluntarily comes to a building called a "hospital" where he agrees to be called a "patient" and where he is referred to as a "case." If he is unable to come on his own two feet, he may be brought by others who stand for him and for whom he would do the same. He then agrees to be handled with extraordinary physical intimacy by strangers called "doctors" in a way allowed to no one else, not even a sexual partner. The function of this examination is to find out what the patient "has"— not what he "is" or "does." This means: into what category of previously described illnesses or injuries does this patient best fit? If the doctor shows an exclusive concern with the uniqueness of the patient's self and does not inquire into the diagnosis—the question of what he "has"—the patient is likely to feel profoundly uneasy and may conclude that he has come to the wrong place. For many people are willing to interact with one's unique self, in a variety of relationships, but only doctors are interested in what one "has."

On the basis of the diagnosis, the doctor may decide upon a treatment, which is what the doctor wants to do for the patient. Most medical treatments are either unpleasant, disgusting, painful, expensive, life-threatening, or sometimes all of these, and no one would agree to them unless he believed that his health or life was at stake. We must assume that our spy understands what death is, for without the possibility of death—or grave disability—the medical model makes very little sense. The urgency of medicine, the fast pace, the intensity of the doctor-patient relationship, however brief, the willingness to agree to drastic procedures—all must be understood in the context of possible and sometimes imminent death.

This brings us to prognosis, another essential medical function. The doctor must maintain the patient's hope and his will to live, while giving him a realistic idea of the likely course and outcome of the illness.

At this point it is important to notice what components are *not* implied in the medical model. It is not necessary to have a known etiology, a successful treatment, or a favorable prognosis in order to sustain the medical model; in fact, the absence of all three is typical of major diseases. As the etiology of a disease becomes known, both prevention and treatments for it become more successful and the prognosis improves, the disease tends to disappear from the center of the medical scene, to be replaced by other diseases with unknown etiology, unsuccessful treatments, and unfavorable prognoses.

Returning to the psychiatric literature on the medical model, our spy finds that psychiatrists and psychologists are in favor of abandoning the medical model for a variety of reasons. Some wish to abandon it because they believe there is insufficient evidence of a biogenic basis for psychiatric disorders. Others believe that if a person is hospitalized as a psychiatric patient, this can only mean that the prognosis is regarded as hopeless, and that if he should ever leave the hospital, he will be stigmatized forever after. Another view is that the person who says that he is mentally ill is a malingerer, trying to get the privileges of the sick role without any legitimate basis for doing so. Still others hold that the real issue is who shall treat the mentally ill: if a medical model is used, it will mean that only doctors can treat them, whereas if a nonmedical model is used, other kinds of professionals will be needed. And last but not least, some psychiatrists and psychologists contend that mental illness is a metaphor and was not intended to be taken literally, but arose out of a humane desire to gain better treatment for certain kinds of deviants.

Now that our spy knows what the medical model looks like, it is clear what the problem is. Those who wish to abandon the medical model are not using it and do not know what it would look like if used in psychiatry. Our spy now looks for an account of the medical model in psychiatry which looks as much as possible like the medical model described in *Five Patients*. He finds a paper called "The Treatment of Schizophrenia Based on the Medical Model" [3] which meets this requirement. In his summary, David Hawkins says:

Clinical experience with a new approach to schizophrenia based upon the medical model has been described in a series of 315 patients. This involves: informing the patient of the diagnosis, educating the patient and family about the illness, use of the H.O.D. test, daily exercise, and a medical regimen consisting of phenothiazines, pyridoxine, niacin or niacinamide, and ascorbic acid. This proved to be inexpensive, financially possible for all, and patient acceptance and cooperation were high.

On the subject of outcome and probable etiology, he says:

The clinical manifestations of schizophrenia abated in our patients in response to a biochemically oriented treatment approach, which considers this illness to be the result of perceptual distortions based on a genetically transmitted disorder.

Elsewhere in the article, our spy learns that patients are seen infrequently, on an average of once a month; that they are urged to join self-help groups; and that they are advised about a special diet. Whether or not one agrees with this doctor's findings, there is no doubt that he is, as he claims, using a medical model, which he is able to describe with the same brevity and clarity as the author of *Five Patients*. Hawkins evidently does believe that there is sufficient evidence of a biogenic basis for psychiatric disorders; he does not believe that the prognosis is hopeless, nor that a medical diagnosis stigmatizes a person forever, and he does not hold that a person claiming to be mentally ill is a malingerer. Although he does believe that medical doctors should diagnose and prescribe for medical illnesses, he also works closely with psychologists, social workers, rehabilitation workers, and self-help groups in order to help his patients with the nonmedical aspects of their lives. In this he resembles those treating tuberculosis, diabetes, polio, stroke, and so forth. Also, since he concerns himself with diagnosis, it is fair to assume that he finds some of the people who come to him do *not* have schizophrenia and will therefore not benefit from the particular regimen described in this article. And it is clear that he does not regard schizophrenia as a metaphor. It would be possible, then, for Hawkins to write a book called *The Sixth Patient*, in which he could describe the diagnosis, treatment, and prognosis of a schizophrenic patient in the same terms and even in the same style as Crichton describes the five patients in his book.

Since one can describe a medical model which can be used both in general medicine and in psychiatry, it seems unnecessarily confusing to call much of what goes on in psychiatry "the medical model." The hodgepodge of other models, mixed in with bits and pieces of the medical model, which passes for standard practice in psychiatry could not be used in general medicine without causing an immediate outcry, if not legal action. No one would place much confidence in a surgeon who announced that the appendix was a metaphor, nor in an orthopedist who believed that people claimed to have broken bones in order to conceal their real problems.

Through the eyes of our Martian spy, we have seen what the medical model looks like behaviorally from the outside; there is still the question of what it is analytically. This more complex question we will take up in Chapter IV, where we will show that clinical medicine consists of a very special kind of authority invested in the doctor, Aesculapian authority,[4] and a very special set of reciprocal roles held by doctor and patient, the sick role.[5]

The Moral Model

Viewed from the outside, a mad person's behavior is most often construed as "bad" or "sick." The "bad" role can be granted on the basis of observable behavior alone, what the person "does";

one need not infer what he "is" or "has." When mad, a person may engage in behavior which others find irritating, troublesome, disgusting, frightening, eerie, and so forth. Those who set about to correct this behavior and bring it within acceptable limits (usually without too much concern for its origin) may be said to be using a moral model of madness. The friends and relatives of the mad person, and the attendants at mental hospitals, most often use a moral model which consists of the same repertoire of positive and negative sanctions that they use in any other circumstances. In addition to this amateur version of the moral model, there is also a class of professionals, principally behavior therapists, who claim to possess and employ a body of expert knowledge in the modification of behavior. They, too, use as their method the application of positive and negative sanctions to undesirable behavoior, and they are also less interested in the origin of that behavior than in its correction. The only difference is that for the behavior therapists, the reinforcement schedules have been demonstrated experimentally to be effective, whereas the basis of the amateur moral model is conventional wisdom.

The moral model has certain advantages. First, as the behavior therapists are fond of pointing out, we are all continuously engaged in modifying each other's behavior anyway. It is natural and inevitable that we should respond to crazy behavior by attempting to change it. The second great advantage is that behavior modification is quickly and easily demonstrated. This comes as a breath of fresh air after years of the highly inferential psychoanalytic model. In one of the earliest applications of operant conditioning theories in a clinical setting, a well-known behavioral psychologist [6] induced a patient who had not left his bed in a mental hospital for many years to do so by a simple expedient. The psychologist noticed that the elderly man much enjoyed his food, which was always served to him in bed because he refused to budge from it. Without warning or explanation, the patient's meals were served at a table some distance from his bed. The nurses, believing the old man would starve to death, required much moral support to undertake this harsh procedure. They were assured he would not be allowed to die for lack of food. Nevertheless, the new arrangement was begun with an apprehensive and almost hostile staff. The result of the first meal served at the table confirmed their fears. The old man did not get out of bed and missed his dinner, which was cleared away without comment. He did not however miss another meal, for when supper appeared he got out of bed, sat down at the table and ate heartily. Once he had begun to leave bed, he became more and more ambulant. Years of fruitless exhortations and discussion of his motives were soon forgotten. Dire predictions that other and worse symptoms would supervene proved untrue.

There are, however, some disadvantages to the moral model. Take the simplest one first: the amateur version of it often does not work. Those closely involved with a mad person often find to their dismay that sanctions which work perfectly well most of the time have no effect in this new and unfamiliar situation. Since people tend to believe that the everyday sanctions *should* work, they may persevere for years before calling in the experts. We differ in this way from the residents of Samuel Butler's *Erewhon*,[7] who called in the "straightener" at the first sign of immoral behavior, much as we call in the doctor for illness.

Another disadvantage of the moral model is that even when used most expertly, it still does not work with some mad people. It is fairly easy, with behavior modification techniques, to get someone to give up a few bizarre quirks or to perform routine tasks. But with schizophrenic or autistic children, the sheer number of normal behaviors to be learned and peculiar behaviors to be unlearned is staggering. It is extremely gratifying and a great relief to get a child who does nothing but hit himself and scream to stop this and learn to talk instead. But there is a huge gap between a child who has been made more tolerable to himself and others and a child who is normal. As a very minor poet (Edgar A. Guest) once said:

It takes a heap o' living to make a house a home.

Well, it takes a heap o' behavior modification to make a psychotic child appear normal, and the heap is simply too big. The computer English which some autistic children have been fortunate enough to learn does not result in anything remotely resembling a real conversation with a well child. Isolated bits of normal behavior, painfully learned with behavioral techniques, do not add up to the stream of spontaneous normal behaviors which persuade us that we are talking and relating to another human being like ourselves. In the long run, normal behavior must be generated by normal experience.

From those mad people whose behavior is easily modified, either by themselves or by others, a fresh danger appears. They are somewhat in the position of an ill person who for some reason does not run a fever or feel pain. Both fever and pain are undesirable, dangerous, and even fatal in themselves, but they also serve as warnings of other events, less obvious, which should not be ignored. We know of an incident in which something of this kind occurred. A lady who had made several suicide attempts was readmitted to a mental hospital. This time, she was brought to a new, open, community-centered ward, in which suicide prevention was low on the list of priorities. Taking a look around, she said: "I think I would be safer in X Building."

No notice was taken of the woman's opinion, for her behavior was quiet and composed. That evening, on the basis of her "good" behavior, she was allowed to go across the grounds with a group of patients to take a psychological test. After the test was completed, she slipped away from the group and drowned herself in a nearby lake. The next day her test was scored and it showed that although externally calm, she reported massive perceptual distortions and suicidal impulses. Had she ranted and raved upon arriving at the ward—that is, had she behaved in a way that was appropriate to her inner state—she would have been watched more closely and might still be alive. She was fatally endangered by her normal behavior. One might argue that suicidal behavior could have been modified just as any behavior can, but there was no longer any chance to do so, for she was dead.

Another problem with those who use the moral model of madness is that they often fail to uphold the standard of consistency set in *Erewhon*, where illnesses were treated as crimes and crimes as illnesses. The Erewhonians tried and sentenced those who were ill and punished them according to the severity of the illness. People called physicians were forbidden to practice openly and could be consulted only with the gravest risk. People who confessed to moral failings, however, were treated quite differently:

But if a man forges a cheque, or sets his house on fire, or robs with violence from the person, or does any other such things as are criminal in our own country, he is either taken to a hospital and most carefully tended at the public expense, or if he is in good circumstances, he lets it be known to all his friends that he is suffering from a severe fit of immorality, just as we do when we are ill, and they come and visit him with great solicitude, and inquire with interest how it all came about, what symptoms first showed themselves, and so forth—questions he will answer with perfect unreserve. . . .[8]

Our moral therapists are a long way from such exacting standards of practice, however. W. Glasser,[9] for example, says: "There is no such thing as mental illness; there are only responsible and irresponsible people." But he calls his irresponsible people "patients" and discusses psychiatric residency as the proper training for his "reality therapy." He hopes that his readers will try to substitute the terms "responsible" and "irresponsible" for "mental illness" and its many subcategories, but then he says that it would be "artificial and misleading" to abandon the old terms in his book. This suggests that Glasser is not entirely serious about using the moral model. Neither is Thomas Szasz,[10] a professor of psychiatry, who says that a mad person who murders someone has the right to be hanged for it, rather than be seen as ill. Henry Davidson, commenting wryly on this, said: "If he is hanged by the neck until dead, he will have the satisfaction of knowing that he hangs with his civil liberties scrupulously preserved." [11] So far as we know, Szasz has not yet sent a single "patient" to the gallows or the electric chair.

Another problem which appears to bedevil all kinds of moral therapy is that those who use these methods have an occupational disinterest in test cases and limiting conditions. None of those experts whom we have read profess to being Christian Scientists, so all acknowledge that illness and disease are causes of altered behavior, and those who are *really* sick should get the sick role. If this is so, then it is difficult to see how one can omit detailed discussions of how to avoid treating, by moral means, such conditions as pellagra psychosis, general paresis, cortisone and amphetamine psychosis, alcohol psychosis, lead poisoning, epilepsy of various kinds, cerebral arteriosclerosis, cerebral tumors, and toxic psychosis. This would seem to us a vital requirement for the successful behavior therapist, but we have never seen it debated in these terms; indeed, moral therapists show little concern with those errors in diagnosis which occur even in the best circumstances.

A further difficulty with the moral model is that it is not homogenous as nearly everyone assumes at first, but consists of five submodels, each of which has different rules. The submodel we have been discussing is the rehabilitative moral model, which focuses on techniques for bringing the erring person back within the fold. The deterrent moral model requires that one punish the person either to deter him from misbehaving again, or to deter others from attempting the same thing. One sees this in some mental hospital wards, where treatments such as electro-shock have deteriorated into punishments (because of the absence of the sick role) and are used to deter "patients"—who are really prisoners—from misbehaving.[12]

An even worse feature of the deterrent model is that it works just as well or better if the person punished is not guilty, but has been chosen arbitrarily, e.g., in the shooting of hostages. In the retributive moral model, in which the punishment fits the crime, fixed punishments follow certain infractions inevitably and mercilessly. Thus, young Michael Wechsler[13] was "sentenced" to sixty days in the security ward for a suicide attempt. In a true hospital one measures the degree of the patient's illness, not the period of confinement. The retributive moral model differs from the deterrent moral model in that the person punished must be demonstrated to be guilty, and therefore admission of guilt is especially valuable, while refusal to admit guilt generates uncertainty and sometimes rage in the moral authorities. In the preventive moral model, the moral training of the young is said to prevent later insanity; a case in point is the prohibition of masturbation, once thought to cause insanity.[14] The restitutive moral model, in which a person pays society back in some manner for the injuries he has inflicted, plays a small part in most schemes for the mentally ill, but is included in Mowrer's model.[15] Mowrer believes that mental illness can be equated with sin and should be treated by confession, expiation, and restitutive acts, such as various forms of charity.

There does seem to be a kind of Gresham's Law operating among the moral submodels, so that "bad" ones drive out "good." That is, programs which start as rehabilitative often drift toward being retributive and deterrent if the initial hopes are not upheld, the personnel change for the worse, or the inmates prove to be tougher cases than anticipated. David Rothman [16] has documented this process in American penitentiaries. Those subscribing to a moral model must be careful to specify exactly which one they mean, and provide measures which will avoid devolution into other moral models.

The moral model of madness, then, has many drawbacks. Yet the behavior modification techniques are demonstrably useful. Does the effectiveness of behavioral techniques exclude a biogenetic basis for the psychoses and so invalidate the medical model and the sick role? Some behavior modification experts, according to Begelman [17] believe that the "cause" of severe behavior disorders is the reinforcement of deviant behavior by the environment. Begelman sees no reason why the initial deviant behavior might not be biogenic. He concludes that the success of behavioral techniques tells us nothing about the origin of the difficulty and cites the use of this knowledge with the retarded, many of whom have demonstrable organic defects. In terms of our models, we see no contradiction between the use of the medical model and the use of behavioral techniques. Behavior therapy has much the same relationship to medical treatment as does physiotherapy, speech therapy, or any other rehabilitative measures. These therapies usually, although not always, lie outside the doctor's competence, but they are frequently used in conjunction with medicine and surgery, so there is nothing unusual about their being used in the medical model of psychiatry. The moral model, however, *is* contradictory to the medical model, as Glasser, Szasz, Mowrer, and others have made clear.

There is an understandable but unnecessary reluctance on the part of those using a moral model to accept as "real" what they cannot see. The behaviorist says, in effect: I can see what a person *does*. I can measure what I can see. And I can change what I can measure. But, happily, one can also measure experience, both one's own and the reported experience of other people. A behaviorist, for example, could record each day how he felt about the progress of his work. On Monday he might feel very optimistic about his new experiment, on Tuesday half as optimistic, on Wednesday fairly pessimistic, on Thursday more optimistic again, and so forth. He could then make a graph which showed the ups and downs of his morale about his work, which might not be evident to someone watching him from the outside. A behavioral account of the same time period might not correspond at all with his inner experience. Similarly one can use experiential accounts of mad people,[18] both current and retrospective, to measure the occurrence, frequency, and severity of certain bizarre inner experiences. These might not, often do not, correlate with behavioral accounts of the same person, as we have shown in the case of the Lost Lady who drowned herself in the lake.

In *Erewhon,* Butler described a group of people ("malcontents") who do not believe that illnesses should be seen as criminal. He says:

They believe that illness is in many cases just as curable as the moral diseases which they see daily cured round them, but that a great reform is impossible till men learn to take a juster view of what physical obliquity proceeds from. Men will hide their illnesses as long as they are scouted on its becoming known that they are ill; it is the scouting, not the physic, which produces the concealment; and if a man felt that the news of his being in ill-health would be received by his neighbours as a deplorable fact . . . which might just as easily have happened to themselves, only that they had the luck to be better born or reared; and if they also felt that they would not be made more uncomfortable in the prison than the protection of society against infection and the proper treatment of their own disease actually demanded, men would give themselves up to the police as readily on perceiving that they had taken smallpox, as they now go to the straightener when they feel that they are on the point of forging a will, or running away with somebody else's wife.[19]

Translated into our terms, people suffering from madness, if they were sure they would be treated with the same care and consideration as if they had a physical illness, would not conceal their symptoms as they do now, but would seek psychiatric (medical) help just as readily as they now go to a doctor for an infection or a virus. The problem as we see it is not that mad people exhibit too much "bad" behavior, which should be extinguished, but that they conceal far too often the strange and terrible experiences which generate that behavior and drive them to despair.

The Impaired Model [20]

Of the patients who enter a general hospital, some will respond to the treatment offered to them and return home, either cured or improved, and some will fail to respond, worsen, and die. But what of those who remain too ill to take up their normal lives again, but who do not die? Normally such patients return home, to be cared for by their families, or else they go to live in nursing homes or other institutions for the impaired. Thus the hospital remains a place where acutely ill patients can be treated. Let us suppose that a hospital allowed all those patients who neither died nor recovered to live there permanently. Little by little such a hospital would begin to change its character as it "silted up" with impaired persons. Within a fairly short time, despite its medical personnel and vocabulary, its doctors, nurses, tours of duty, wards, and its diminishing population of real patients, it would become a home or community for the impaired. This new, hybrid institution would appear strangely familiar to us, for that is how our state hospitals came to have their present characteristics.

At a time when most general hospitals were disgusting places where the poor often went to die or, if not already dying, to acquire a fatal illness, there were psychiatric hospitals, the so-called moral treatment hospitals, which used the medical model and the sick role in an exemplary way.* Worcester State Hospital, founded in

---

* In addition to using the medical model, those using the "moral treatment" also sought to maintain the moral behavior of the patients by treating them kindly and decently, which was a kind of behavior therapy.

Massachusetts in 1833, was such a place, and we have a portrait of the first superintendent, Samuel Woodward, which illustrates this:

His intercourse with the sick was so gentle, cheerful and winning that he soon gained their confidence and love. He nourished their hopes of recovery, by holding up the bright side of their cases. They anticipated his visits with pleasure, as their physician and their friend. He recognized the influence of the mind over the physical functions, and by his relation of agreeable stories and successful cases of a similar kind to theirs, he animated their hopes.[21]

So wrote Chandler, Woodward's successor. Woodward spent his day encouraging his patients to get well, using all the means at his disposal, as good doctors have always done. The hospital was so successful that it was soon enlarged far beyond its original 120 beds, and it became impossible for the second superintendent, Chandler, to fulfill these basic medical functions:

I confess my inability to do justice to my feelings in its management. I cannot sufficiently keep myself acquainted with the various departments to act understandingly. I cannot know the daily changes in the symptoms of 450 patients—the operations on the farm and in the workshops—the domestic operations—direct the moral treatment—conduct the correspondence with friends—wait upon such visitors as demand my personal attention and various other things which are daily pressing upon the attention of this Superintendent. . . . The patients expect and desire frequent intercourse with the Superintendent, for it is in his care that they are placed.[22]

One man cannot supervise a hospital that has more than one hundred patients, Chandler said. Within less than twenty years, the hopeful new hospital was well on its way to becoming a custodial institution. It became increasingly difficult for one physician to sustain so many patients in the sick role, and so they gradually came to be perceived as people who lived at the hospital rather than as people who had come into the hospital to be treated and sent out again. Those who did not respond to the available treatments (including new arrivals who had in fact been ill for many years) were "silting up"; meanwhile, the burden of housing and providing for the large number of residents occupied more and more of the superintendent's time. Thus the patients were slowly but surely shifted out of the sick role and into the impaired role.

The sick role and the impaired role are both called forth by the same events: those situations in which a person can no longer do that which is normally expected of him. But the two roles are very different and in some ways mutually exclusive. Gordon [23] first noticed this difference when he discovered the impaired role empirically while attempting to validate Parson's sick role. In his study, Gordon found that the two roles form two clusters of behavioral expectations which have little relationship to each other. Of the twelve illness states which he described in his study, those cases where the person was described as physically impaired by a past illness (handicapped) were *least* often identified as sick. Gordon says:

> The supportive behavior associated with what I have termed the "impaired role" is, on the basis of the evidence, distinctly different from, and not related to, the behaviors associated with the "sick role." In the case of the impaired role, the social pressure serves to aid and maintain normal behavior within the limitations of a given condition, while in the case of the sick role, social pressure serves to discourage normal behavior. Therefore, in terms of function, the two roles are opposites . . . .

According to Gordon's study, sick and impaired persons share a common obligation to see a doctor and to report changes, if any, in their condition. Possibly this obligation derives from the importance of ensuring that the impaired person is truly impaired and not sick. But, unlike the sick person, the impaired person ought to try to do things for himself, and he ought to try to find some useful work. He ought *not* to bother others with every ache and pain.

In addition to these differences between the sick role and the impaired role, there are broad differences between the two models. In the medical model, diagnosis is very important and must be as specific as possible because treatment and prognosis follow from it. In the impaired model, the name of the condition is far more general and tells us what misfortune makes the impaired person different from others: terms such as blind, crippled, paralyzed, insane, and retarded are used. It is the degree of impairment that is measured, for that will tell what the person will or will not be able to do. Treatment is important in the medical model, even if its efficacy is unknown, for it helps to sustain the person in the sick role and keeps up his hopes. There is no treatment for an impairment, although there may be rehabilitative measures, e.g., if blind, learning to use a Seeing Eye dog.* Prognosis in medicine is very important because death is always a possibility and re-covery always a hope. As Gordon showed, the worse the prognosis, the more certain is the conferral of the sick role. In impairment no change is expected, for either better or worse. Hospitals are places where ill people—patients—are treated for their illnesses. Patients *stay* at the hospital, they do not *live* there. They never work *for* the hospital. Institutions for the impaired may serve as pro-tection for the impaired (e.g., colonies for the retarded), protection for the community (e.g., leper colonies), places to live, to work, and to learn reabling skills. In the medical model, physicians are the key personnel for treating the sick. Nurses and aides care for the sick. Physiotherapists, psychologists, and social workers rehabilitate the sick. For the impaired, the key personnel are re-habilitative; medical skill is not necessary since there is no treat-ment. Above all, those who care for the impaired must be kind and humane.

When the moral treatment hospitals began to expand and "silt up" with those who did not respond to treatment, a gradual shift occurred from the medical model to the impaired model. This change in expectations occurred subtly and invisibly in patients, families, and the medical and nursing staff, and gradually spread through the community. Because it was insidious and recognized by only a few perceptive people, nothing was done about it until

* With advances in medicine, an impairment may become a treatable condition. However, it is an immoral move to treat a true impairment as an illness, and the classic case of this is to be found in *Madame Bovary:* Hippolyte, a club-footed boy, is persuaded to submit to an operation to straighten his foot. He is promised that he will be able to please women after his deformity is corrected. After Bovary operates, gangrene sets in, and another doctor is called in to amputate the whole leg. The second doctor rails against the unnecessary operation: "We are practitioners; we cure people, and we should not dream of operating on anyone who is in perfect health. Straighten club feet! As if one could straighten club feet! It is as if one wished, for example, to make a hunchback straight!" Yet today, the same operation might be permissible.

far too late, long after all concerned had become dispirited and demoralized. Finally, even those cases which would have responded readily went untreated, at first because of the press of the large number of patients, and then because the presence of increasingly large numbers of unsuccessful cases changed the image of the illness from highly treatable to nearly hopeless. Had it been possible to send the unsuccessful cases back to their home communities, the image of the psychiatric patient might have remained more positive. Superintendents faced agonizing decisions on this score, since many patients would have gone back into the jails and almshouses from which the hospital rescued them.* On the other hand, had the shift toward the impaired model gone the whole way, treatment would have been abandoned altogether, the medical staff would have been replaced by those with a vocation for helping the impaired, and some efforts might have been made to make these homes for the impaired truly homelike. But the medical model did not disappear; instead, a demoralized and deteriorated version— what one might call the "immoral treatment"—developed. Doctors and nurses are not at their best in nonmedical enterprises, and medical arbitrariness is endurable, indeed legitimate, only in situations defined as medical.

Persons who work in mental hospitals are, on the whole, moral people, as are the patients and their families. Confronted with the task of behaving morally in the presence of two or more conflicting models, they struggle as best they can to do the right thing. But there are moments of truth when the contradictions are so glaring that even the most unobservant can scarcely fail to notice that something is awry, although they do not necessarily recognize what it is. Thus, Miss La Rue Weed, R.N., a psychiatric head nurse at Arizona State Hospital, said:

Somehow, everything had been loaded onto nursing, from clerical work to bed-making and linen-counting. The morning that I got a telephone call asking for nurses to select and supervise a group of patients who were to dig a grave for a patient who had died . . . well that did it! I really started up full steam.[24]

---

* For a fuller discussion of this issue, see David J. Rothman, *The Discovery of the Asylum* (Boston: Little, Brown and Co., 1971).

But Miss La Rue Weed choked on the gnat while swallowing the camel. If grave-digging is a misuse of nurses, what can be said of it as an activity for patients? In a general hospital, such as the one described in *Five Patients*, what would one say if a nurse came around to whistle up a group of patients to dig a grave for a patient who died? This is so inconceivable that it sounds like a sick joke. However, in a community of the impaired, those occupying the impaired role can be expected to do those tasks which regularly arise in the course of community living: cleaning, laundering, dish-washing, snow-shoveling and grave-digging—provided, of course, their impairment allows them to do so. So different are the two models with respect to the rights and duties of the role-holders that what is a reasonable request in the one is an outrage in the other.

It is true that in the moral treatment hospitals of the nineteenth century, agricultural labor was highly esteemed as an activity for mental patients. Chandler mentions the farming operation. How can this labor be subsumed under the sick role? The answer is that the agricultural labor which the patients performed was prescribed for them by their physicians, with whom they were in constant, often daily, contact. Woodward,[25] in a lawsuit over charges for a patient's upkeep, specifically argued that the patient's services could not have been performed out of the hospital with safety and that they were part of his therapeutic regimen. Agricultural labor was a medical treatment because the doctors believed it to be a medical treatment, and they used their medical authority to persuade patients of this. We do not know whether it was an efficacious treatment, but that is seldom known with any certainty in medicine. In the history of medicine many strange and peculiar treatments and regimens have been prescribed by physicians, and while these sometimes kill patients, they do not damage the sick role or the medical model. Even grave-digging might be a medical treatment if some physician believed it to be so and prescribed it for his patient. But Miss La Rue Weed did not believe that burial therapy had been prescribed by a doctor for the benefit of particular patients. A doctor may prescribe work therapy, play therapy, psychotherapy, behavior therapy, burial therapy, or any other therapy that he and his patient believe might be beneficial; but he may *not* use any model other than the medical model. It was the presence of the impaired model, and not the use of any particular activity or therapy, which demoralized the once good moral treatment hospitals. Criticism of state hospitals often takes the form of an attack on the medical model, as if these hospitals represent the best efforts of "medicine" to care for the mentally ill. The appropriate criticism to be made of these institutions is that they contain many very ill people who have not been awarded the sick role, and that the medical model has been replaced by a particularly unfortunate, unacknowledged mixture of the medical model and the impaired model, in which the residents, much to their detriment, receive the full rights of neither.

While one cannot use the moral or the impaired model as the primary frame of reference for schizophrenia, these two discontinuous models can be related in an appropriate manner to the medical model. Once the schizophrenic person has been installed in the sick role and brought under the protection of the medical model, techniques derived from the moral and impaired models can be brought to bear on the secondary effects of the illness. The longer the person has been ill, the more likely that he will need help in sustaining, repairing, and learning the social and psychological skills which are so often damaged by this complex illness. Because these three models are discontinuous and do not claim to explain or solve everything, they can be related to each other by carefully delineating where one stops and the next begins. Discontinuity has another consequence: used properly, these models have a lesser potential for harm than the continuous models and thus they fulfill the first rule of medicine—to do the sick no harm.

3

The Continuous
Models of Madness

FIVE OF OUR MODELS—the psychoanalytic, family interaction, psychedelic, social, and conspiratorial—are continuous in nature. They appear to be derivatives or variations on those religious or cosmological models which offer an inclusive global view of human destiny in which our various misfortunes play a large part. In all the continuous models there is the implication that unseen but potentially understandable forces control the lives of us all. However, only the expert can decipher these conundrums. A properly trained expert who had all the data and used any one of these five systems would be able to explain everything. Thus, if one knew everything that had ever happened in a particular family, one could then reconstruct the origin of a patient's madness. If one knew exactly how a malfunctioning society impinged on a particular person, one would then know just how it drove him mad and by implication be able to prevent and, perhaps, reverse this misfortune. Although frequently implied, this requires some scrutiny, for in at least some cases it becomes implausible on closer examination.

In these continuous models, measurement is unwelcome and even slightly indecent—how can one quantify the anguish of a child driven mad by his family's unkindness, and how should one calibrate the insight of a mad person whose soul is shattered when he recognizes the evasions and dishonesty of all those around him? Where measurement is used, as in epidemiological studies, it is often employed to prove some moral point, e.g., that society is vicious and unregenerate, working in every way to harm the poor, the young, and the innocent.

In consequence, the affect of those using continuous models is usually serious and even gloomy. Its tone is fundamentally religious, in contrast to the secular cheerfulness of those employing the discontinuous models. Those who hold to the continuous models believe that the sins of the fathers are visited on the children from generation unto generation; determinism, rather than free will, prevails. Since blame has to be widely distributed, those who use these models soon get into the habit of attempting to make almost everyone feel guilty, including, of course, themselves. However, practice differs somewhat from theory, for although everyone is guilty, including past generations and doubtless those still to come, relatively few people are actually available for censure, and blame tends to fall unevenly upon these scapegoats, such as the mothers of schizophrenic children.

The continuous models, then, tend to be unfair and generate gloom, but their great strength derives from their capacity to satisfy our need for a cosmology, a way of putting it all together. For orderly minds continuous models provide a certain melancholy pleasure.

The Psychoanalytic Model

Were it not for the emergence of the psychoanalytic model within psychiatry, this book would never have been written. The three models—medical, moral, impaired—which prevailed in psychiatry until the psychoanalytic model made its presence felt were all discontinuous. Although the internal contradictions among these three models made life far from pleasant for many psychiatric patients, it is the virtue of discontinuous models that they do not attempt to explain everything. The evolution of a continuous model, soon to be followed by other continuous models, did much to create the exquisite anguish that now exists among patients and their families. For the psychoanalytic model was offered as a panchreston (explain-all) and what it explained was that patients were no longer to be seen as suffering from a disease, but were, rather, to be seen as victims of grièvous errors of child-rearing. This antimedical view was backed up by medical authority, against the express wishes of the founder of psychoanalysis, Sigmund Freud. How did such a tangle ever come about?

Seen through the lens of the models, psychoanalysis has a very odd history. Initially it began as a medical treatment for hysteria, for which it was not notably successful. By 1910 it had settled down as a relatively brief treatment for neuroses. The people who became Freud's patients believed themselves to be ill and were installed in the sick role; indeed, there was at that time no other role which the patient of a doctor could occupy. As with most medical treatments, there were contra-indications; psychoses in particular were excluded. The goal of this new treatment was the relief of symptoms; psychoanalysis was not considered a good thing in itself. Freud clearly subscribed to the medical model, for he wrote Ernest Jones in a letter in 1911:

We are to withstand the big temptation to settle down in our colonies, where we cannot but be strangers, distinguished visitors, and have to revert every time to our native country in Medicine, where we find the root of our powers.[1]

The theory of psychoanalysis itself had undergone some curious transformations during this initial period. Freud had gradually come to believe that his hysterical female patients were suffering from the trauma of having been seduced by their fathers. This theory was put forth in several papers dated 1896,[2] but in 1897 Freud wrote to Fliess [3] that he had a "great secret"—he no longer believed these stories were true. He gave four reasons for this: his therapeutic failure with these cases; the unlikely frequency of these events; the realization that there is no indication of reality in the unconscious; and the consideration that even in psychoses the unconscious memory does not break through. Less than a month later, Freud wrote Fliess about his new theory, the Oedipus complex. In the book in which the Oedipal theory is first introduced, *The Interpretation of Dreams*,[4] Freud was less definitive than he might have been about his error in regard to the seduction theory,* but later he acknowledged it on a number of occasions.[5]

Gradually the new Oedipal theory supplanted the old seduction theory, and by 1907 Carl G. Jung was being sworn to the new dogma, at about the same time he was being installed for his brief reign as the Crown Prince of psychoanalysis.† In terms of the models, the importance of this shift is that the seduction theory is in principle verifiable. Either the fathers did seduce their daughters or they did not. But the new theory was not verifiable except within the analytic process that generated it. It has to do entirely with invisible and internal events, the analytic interpretations of which cannot in principle be refuted. This is to say, it is not a scientific theory within the definition of Karl Popper [6] and others. Thus a brief treatment based on a refutable theory was replaced by an increasingly lengthy treatment based on an irrefutable theory. The model was now a continuous one and thus already at odds with the medical model.

The second phase began when psychoanalysis came to be used with two classes of people who were not ill: artists and writers of various kinds and analysts-in-training. According to Freud's own account of the history of the movement,[7] artists and writers were included in his circle from the beginning. After World War I they arrived in greater numbers, especially from America, to engage in psychoanalysis as a means of liberating creative energy. They were not medical patients and so did not occupy the sick role.

---

* On pp. 322-323 of *The Interpretation of Dreams, op. cit.,* Freud makes the following remark, in parentheses: "(The interpretation of the dream did not itself show us that what were thus represented in the dream were phantasies and not recollections of real events; an analysis only gives us the *content* of a thought and leaves it to us to determine its reality. Real and imaginary events appear in dreams at first sight as of equal validity; and that is so not only in dreams but in the production of more important psychical structures.)" The editor, James Strachey, adds this footnote: "Freud is probably referring here to the discovery which he had recently made that the infantile sexual traumas apparently revealed in his analyses of neurotic patients were in fact very often phantasies." Freud's letter to Fliess, which was more candid, was of course never intended to be published.

† Freud had not read English history of the Georgian period or he would have known how quickly becoming Prince of Wales (Crown Prince) poisoned son-father relationships, an error for an Anglophile as well as for a psychoanalyst!

The other important group of nonpatients were the analysts themselves. Ernest Jones [8] describes Eitingon's walks and talks with Freud in 1907 as "the first training analysis." In 1918 at the meetings in Budapest, Hermann Nunberg proposed that analysts themselves be analyzed. This was not adopted as a rule until 1925.[9] Meanwhile, in 1921 Hanns Sachs became the first official training analyst, and Franz Alexander his first analyst-in-training.[10] That the rules of this new arrangement had yet to be worked out was made clear by the tragic case of Victor Tausk.[11] When Tausk asked to be analyzed by Freud, he was sent instead to Helene Deutsch, a young analysand of Freud's. Tausk's unexpected suicide raises the question of whether he had been perceived as an ill person in need of medical help or as a colleague in need of further training. In either case, it was a strange and perhaps unethical move to send him to a younger, inexperienced person.

It goes without saying that artists and writers do not flock to orthopedic surgeons, internists, or other medical specialists in search of enlarged creativity or enlightenment. It is just as true, although perhaps less obvious, that training analysis has no parallel in medicine. A young surgeon does not have to have his appendix removed by his senior in order to prepare for performing the same operation on his future patients. The mere presence of all these nonpatients in psychoanalysis indicated that some unusual and nonmedical enterprise was under way. More specifically, neither the artists and writers nor the analysts-in-training, including the unlucky Tausk, occupied the sick role, that hallmark of the medical enterprise.

The question then arises: what role did they occupy? And what were its specifications compared with those of the sick role? It appears to us that they occupied the role of those who have or say they have psychological, spiritual, or creative problems for which they desire expert counsel. We have come to call this the "psych" role,[12] in order to distinguish it from the sick role with which it is so often and so easily confused. The two roles resemble each other in that the sequence of events in both is roughly similar, although there may be great differences in the way in which they are deployed in time. In both cases a suffering, troubled, or needful person undertakes to find help and seeks out a person known to give such help. The two meet, and some sort of contract, usually implicit (except for fees), is agreed upon. A transaction occurs, in one meeting or many, which may be verbal, physical, or both. If the relationship is satisfactory to both, it runs its course and the applicant leaves the relationship subjectively changed in some way—one hopes for the better.

The two roles differ along a number of dimensions, including Parsons's four original postulates of the sick role. *First*, a person in the sick role has both the right and the duty to be exempt from some or all of his usual social role responsibilties, according to the nature and severity of the illness. A person in the "psych" role has far more limited rights and is rarely told that he must desist from his usual responsibilities lest they make him sicker. *Second*, a person in the sick role is not held responsible for having the illness, nor for failing to improve; he is only held responsible for being a good patient insofar as he is able. A person in the "psych" role may or may not be held responsible for being the way he is, but if he fails to improve, the question is raised whether he really wants to get better (i.e., whether he has an unconscious resistance to getting better and an attachment to his neurosis). In the "psych" role the degree of improvement or change is held to be related to a person's will to a much greater extent; whereas in the sick role a person may die in spite of his best efforts. *Third*, it is held to be undesirable to be sick and the sick person is enjoined to get well as fast as possible. In the "psych" role people are not expected to get well quickly; the phenomenon of resistance is held to be central to the therapeutic process. *Fourth*, the sick person is supposed to seek appropriate help, usually that of a physician, and cooperate with that help toward the end of getting well. A person who does not seem to appreciate the seriousness of an illness may be taken more or less against his will to a hospital by his own family or even by complete strangers, for there is general agreement that someone may be too unwell to make decisions for himself. This view is reinforced every time a recovering patient admits that others acted in his interest, although not in accord with his wishes. The sanctions against anyone refusing to enter the "psych" role are far less severe; people are encouraged to get such help if they feel they need it, but they are rarely forced to do so, as Szasz has emphasized.

In addition to the differences in the Parsonian dimensions, there are other related differences. The sick role deals with what one "has"; the "psych" role with what one "is." The sick role encourages a search for the specific organ in which the illness resides; the "psych" role deals with the "whole person." If one pretends to have an illness, one is called a malingerer; if one pretends to be disturbed or unhappy, it is often taken as evidence that one really is. The sick role is highly cross-cultural and can be conveyed in pantomime, as missionary doctors have often demonstrated; the "psych" role is extremely culture-bound, and forms of therapy acceptable in one culture or subculture may be regarded as immoral in another. As Francis Schrag [13] has pointed out, the goal of the sick role is extrinsic: it is to relieve suffering and restore health, if possible; the goal of the "psych" role is an enlarged self-understanding, which is intrinsically good whether or not it relieves suffering. In the sick role the nature of the doctor's authority is highly impersonal, which accounts for its cross-cultural acceptance; the role of the psychoanalyst, therapist, or guru is far more dependent on the individual personality of the role-holder. The direction of the two roles is different: the need for the sick role becomes more self-evident the closer one comes to death; the "psych" role picks up momentum as one acquires enlightenment.

The "psych" role, then, is markedly different from the sick role and the substitution of the one for the other was a critical step in the abandonment of the medical model. Freud, who was nothing if not logical and consistent, became slowly convinced that psychoanalysis was not a medical specialty but, rather, a unique new scientific-educational-research system. He hoped that the future training of analysts would include elements from psychology, the history of civilization, sociology, anatomy, biology, the study of evolution, the psychology of religion, mythology, and the science of literature, but would omit much of what is usually taught in medical schools.[14] He himself had never wished to practice medicine and he lacked what he called the "furor thera-peuticus." Had Freud's wishes been respected, psychoanalysis would indeed have become a field of inquiry completely separated from medicine. But this did not happen; instead, by a very unlikely series of historical accidents psychoanalysis was swept back again into medicine in spite of its founder's specific instructions.

At the Innsbruck Congress of the International Psychoanalytic Association in 1927, the question of lay analysis was hotly debated.[15] The Viennese and Hungarian groups were most strongly in favor of it, the American group uncompromisingly against it. In 1926 the New York legislature had passed a bill declaring lay analysis to be illegal, and in 1927 the New York Society had passed a resolution condemning lay analysis. The deviant American group was treated leniently by the International Association, partly because of the fairness of Anna Freud, who argued that each member society had the right to decide this question for itself. But even more significant was the fact that the American group was small and unimportant; no one dreamed that within a decade the European analytic societies would have disappeared. According to Ernst Federn,[16] the single factor which most changed the course of the psychoanalytic movement and its position toward lay analysis was the rise of Adolf Hitler. In the late 1930s European analysts began to arrive in America as helpless refugees and the American Psychoanalytic Association gained an importance out of all proportion to its original minor role in the development of the psychoanalytic movement.

By 1927 Freud was absolutely clear about abandoning the medical model. In the postscript to his book, *The Question of Lay Analysis*, he wrote:

It will not have escaped my readers that in what I have said I have assumed as axiomatic something that is still violently disputed in the discussion. I have assumed, that is to say, that psychoanalysis is not a specialized branch of medicine. I cannot see how it is possible to dispute this . . . . The possibility of its application to medical purposes must not lead us astray.[17]

In a letter to Paul Federn, also in 1927, he said:

The battle for lay analysis must, at one time or another, be fought to the finish. Better now than later. As long as I live I shall resist that psychoanalysis be swallowed up by medicine.[18]

Against Freud's express wishes, American psychoanalysis remained ostensibly part of medicine. However, instead of employing the well-known and self-limiting sick role to define the reciprocal rights and duties of patient and doctor, the "psych" role with its much vaguer specifications and a tendency toward being self-perpetuating rather than self-limiting was used. It is questionable whether Freud, had he lived, would have ever accepted this strange hybrid as being psychoanalysis. As this peculiar variant of both medicine and psychoanalysis developed during the 1940s and 1950s, it became increasingly arbitrary, as anyone acquainted with the history of medicine would predict, for those who used it were physicians endowed with Aesculapian authority. However, that authority was not limited within the usual confines of medicine. One example of this omnicompetence and overconfidence deriving from the hybrid psychoanalytic model can be found in the spread of psychoanalysis to the treatment of schizophrenia. This was done in spite of Freud and other early analysts such as Paul Federn[19] giving explicit advice against the use of psychoanalysis as a treatment in this illness. This change was made by psychoanalysts in the United States without producing any new data showing that their predecessors were mistaken. No evidence was produced showing either the technical or the theoretical errors which Freud and his colleagues had made or demonstrating new developments which extended both theory and practice. No one so far as we can discover has refuted the warnings of fifty or sixty years ago: they have simply been ignored.

Drastic changes occurred within the theory itself without any explanation as to how they were to be related to Freud's original formulations. One of the great unsung revolutions of our time occurred when the castrating father was deposed by the schizophrenogenic mother. How did this happen and where are the Oedipus complexes of yesteryear? Those stern and frightening Victorian fathers on whom Freud based his theory have vanished without a trace and have been replaced by the bitch-mother who drives her children mad and who resembles, in an almost uncanny way, the witches described in the *Malleus malificarum*,[20] one of the greatest misogynist works of all time. How do the theoreticians account for the disappearance of those psychological traits which Freud held to be universal?

The post-Freudian psychoanalytic model, as developed in America in the 1940s and 1950s, contains the following elements: it is part of medicine in spite of Freud's wishes; it is used for schizophrenia; it uses the "psych" role and not the sick role; and the patient's mother, not his father, is the villain of the piece. Diagnosis has been more and more neglected, for it has no real place in the psychoanalytic model: one treats the "whole person," who is presumably suffering from a universal neurosis.

Even those analysts who wish to avoid treating schizophrenics have lost the tools with which to make the differentiation. Schizophrenics who wish a treatment for their illness find themselves embarking on a voyage of self-discovery; when they attempt to signal to the doctor-analyst that something is terribly wrong, that this "treatment" does not alleviate their symptoms but in fact makes them feel worse, this merely becomes additional material for the analysis. Self-understanding is intrinsically good and, ideally, it is a lifelong pursuit, whereas illnesses are intrinsically bad and are brought to a halt as quickly as possible. This fatal confusion of models sets the stage for a destructive process which goes on until the patient cannot bear it any more, or the psychoanalyst becomes tired of the patient, or the family runs out of money, or the patient commits suicide.

Of all the questions raised by the presence of the psychoanalytic model in psychiatry, none is more mysterious than the meek and submissive behavior of the parents of young schizophrenics in the face of scapegoating which has very few parallels in the annals of medicine. Families are either implicitly or explicitly accused of having driven their children mad, and often of sabotaging the therapy as well; meanwhile, they are expected to pay ruinous fees—"stunning, outrageous fees, out of the Arabian Nights," as Louise Wilson [21] calls them—in order to be slandered and pilloried. Why do they put up with it? They appear to be what Nancy Mitford [22] has called "medically pious": willing to do what the doctor says is good for their sick child however painful it may be. If the analyst were *not* a physician, the parents would never put up with this expensive torture, and indeed, it would not be so expensive, since these are *medical* fees. It is only because they believe they are purchasing an especially valuable medical treatment that this strange situation is allowed to continue.

The first law of medicine is to do the sick no harm. Even when there is no wholly satisfactory treatment for an illness, the doctor can make certain time-honored moves which will alleviate the suffering of the patient and his family. He can give the disease a name and thus reduce its mystery. He can rule out other and worse illnesses. He can reassure the patient and his family that the illness is a natural occurrence and that no one is to blame for it. He can offer the best treatment that is available. He can tell the patient and family that everything is being done which can be done. Although he can never promise a cure, he can usually offer the hope of recovery. Nobody anticipated and very few even noticed that when physicians, trained in psychoanalysis, became the dominant force in world psychoanalysis and a formidable segment of American psychiatry, both patients and their families would lose most of these precious and ancient rights attached to the sick role. Yet we believe that this is just what happened. Since they were being deprived of those rights by physicians who normally accord them, and who indeed were thought to be still doing so, patients and relatives alike did not respond with that justifiable indignation which is the common and almost automatic result of any deprivation of rights. It may be that this is the source of much of the passivity and hopeless resignation found in schizophrenics and their families, who are inhibited from making a natural response because of medical piety.

The Social Model

A chilling phrase, "foreign pauper lunatic," summed up a set of beliefs about the relationship between social change, poverty, and mental illness current among many nineteenth-century American psychiatrists.[23] "Foreign pauper lunatic," as used in New England, referred to someone who had come to public attention because of insane behavior, someone who was not a native of the state where he was now resident, did not belong there, and could not support himself and had no family able to do so. Those professional people who are primarily concerned with this aspect of mental illness may be said to be using a social model, and their field of inquiry has been called "social psychiatry."

The term "social psychiatry" appears to have been the contribution of E. E. Southard,[24] the first director of the Boston Psychopathic Hospital.* Since its appearance in 1917 the term has shifted its meaning several times, sometimes referring to a branch of sociological knowledge, and sometimes to a subspecialty of medical psychiatry.† During the last twenty years or so, the field has expanded greatly, and it is now worth distinguishing two overlapping schools of thought which might be called "conservative" and "radical."

The view of the "conservative" social psychistrists may be summed up, rather crudely, as being: "When society changes too fast, it makes people sick." Stephen Kunitz,[25] in discussing the relation of the Leighton's work to sociological theory, says:

The point is that functionalist theory, which has come to be equated with equilibrium theory, resting as it does on an organic analogy of society, sees change in terms of disequilibrium, dysfunction, and even, at times, pathology. It is in this sense that I would call it conservative. The gemeinschaft-like community tends to be static, unchanging and without history. When it undergoes change, according to this theory, it is likely to disintegrate, and this causes psychiatric problems for its members.

---

* Now called Massachusetts Mental Health Center.

† Social psychiatry is often associated with epidemiological studies, but such studies may be done within the framework of any of the models. We will not attempt to evaluate these studies here, as we are concerned primarily with comparing models rather than with proving or disproving theories, but it should be noted that the epidemiology of mental illness is still in a rather primitive state of development. Mishler and Scotch, in their review article, "Sociocultural Factors in the Epidemiology of Schizophrenia: A Review" (*Psychiatry* 26 (1963), 315-351), have stated: "The amount of useful and systematic knowledge about social factors in the epidemiology of schizophrenia is disappointingly small."

Or, as Alexander Leighton puts it: "Psychiatry enters the picture because rapid sociocultural change can be pathogenic." [26]

What does this group of social psychiatrists offer as a solution to these pathogenic changes? Thomas Rennie [27] sees a greater involvement of the psychiatrist with social institutions. It is his belief that lawyers, judges, ministers, teachers, doctors, and public health nurses, as well as groups of lay people such as the parent-teacher associations and the Traveler's Aid Society, are all clamoring for the advice of psychiatrists about how to conduct their affairs. As he sees it, psychiatrists are bound to respond to this increasing demand for their services.

Paul Roman and Harrison Trice [28] see the need for more structure and security in the lives of poor people. It is their view that creating opportunities for social and economic security will reduce the amount of schizophrenia now apparent at the lower end of the social scale. Seeing some resemblance between the chaotic nature of schizophrenia and the disorganized lives of the poor, they recommend an allopathic remedy: more structure for the lower classes.

The view of the "radical" social psychiatrists may be summed up as follows: if you want to stamp out mental illness, go out and lead the social revolution. If the architectural headquarters of the conservative school is the neo-classical Harvard School of Public Health, then the equivalent building for the radicals is a storefront clinic in the ghetto. This transition was noted unfavorably by Norman Bell and John Spiegel.[29] Their concern is that social psychiatry has become a field of action prematurely and that efforts to develop sound theories have been abandoned in the haste to meet public demands. They feel that the heady wine of social planning has led to inflated expectations for mental health programs and that serious efforts to put the field on a more solid basis have thereby been neglected.

One of the first of the new-look centers to receive money from a federal staffing grant was the Temple University Community Mental Health Center in Philadelphia. The area served by the new center was a densely populated, largely black, urban ghetto. Gardner and Gardner [30] reported the first four years of operation, from 1966 to 1970, which ended with a period of turmoil and the resignation of the director. It appears that the center bit off far more than it could chew. It became involved in an ever growing number of activities, including a community advisory council; a research program to establish a model for evaluation of comprehensive mental health services; another research program to establish a population laboratory to serve a variety of epidemiological and clinical studies; a household census; a survey of psychiatric facilities; an attitudinal survey of 2,400 households; a mental health assistant training program, including a new career ladder; two forty-bed in-patient units at the State Hospital; a six-bed crisis center; seminars for the police; case conferences with public health nurses; a "problem-solving team" for patients needing care for three months or less; an "extended treatment team" for patients needing care for more than three months; a partial hospitalization program, including a day hospital and a weekend program for alcoholics; a patient advocate, or ombudsman, system; and a consultation and education program, including a program for a neighborhood gang and a drug withdrawal program. Like a drunk staggering around a bar and roaring, "I can beat anyone in the house," this center took on any and every need expressed by a very needful community. As the authors put it:

Although we realized the unreasonableness and grandiosity of one mental health center literally accepting responsibility for the mental health of a community and grappling with major societal ills, we also perceived an insensitivity and irresponsibility in completely avoiding the social environment and withdrawing into the security of a traditional clinical program. But what can be done? How completely practical can one remain?

Not surprisingly, the center ran into many difficulties in its far-flung programs. The advisory council was unable to reach consensus about its role and disbanded. The mental health assistant training program saw most of its trainees become more and more isolated from the community, increasingly concerned with better salaries, offices, hours, and other hallmarks of professional status. The career ladder failed to overcome the state civil service classification system, and the senior staff displayed a lack of interest in training. The State Hospital was a thirty-minute ride from the center and the University Hospital, which was closer, did not allow the center to provide staff for its patients. The crisis center proved to be too far from needed medical help and tended to fill up with a backlog of people for whom there were insufficient referral sources, especially geriatric patients. The police proved recalcitrant students and the public health nurses were no better. Reversing the usual order of things, the State Hospital "dumped" chronic patients on the extended treatment team, which quickly became overloaded.

Even their successes were equivocal: participatory democracy in the day hospital worked so well that the clinic staff found it difficult to influence therapy or to maintain any role in the discharge plans for their patients. After three years, the center was still relatively isolated from, and unknown to, most of the community. Community residents and other community agencies complained about the quality of clinical care. The authors state: "We had come to the community much like missionaries and with little understanding of the community's desires." According to the authors, the partial hospitalization program "de-emphasized the sickness model and the usual medical authoritarian structure."

What, then, was the role of the ill person and what were his rights and duties? It is well known that the poor are usually conservative on medical matters and have always maintained that mental illnesses should be treated the same as physical illnesses.[31] They have been the despair of psychoanalysts for this reason and will now, it appears, be the despair of social psychiatrists. But the authors nowhere suggest that any efforts were made to find out how people felt about their doctors abandoning the medical model. The "conservative" social model offers the ill people the role of social victim, a role with privileges but no rights or duties, while the "radical" social model presumably offers the role of social revolutionary. But people suffering from major diseases rarely have much energy left for undertaking social reforms, however politically active they might be if well. In our experience, people who suffer from schizophrenia want exactly what all other ill people want: competent medical advice, preferably in a clearcut, familiar doctor-patient relationship. In the absence of definitive treatments, they want at least to be given the best that is available, told how to keep from getting more ill, and given hope that they may eventually recover. If they cannot find such an arrangement, they will put up with any program that has doctors and nurses in it, no matter how bizarre, with the hope that some medical care may be forthcoming, however strangely it may be presented to them. The test of a program such as the one at the Temple University center would be to run it with *no* medical personnel, *no* hospital and medical school affiliation, and then see if *any* ill person thought it worthwhile to attend. The center had doctors, nurses, in-patients, outpatients, clinics, partial hospitalization, and many of the other earmarks of a medical enterprise. It ran on a hidden medical agenda and was affiliated with a famous university hospital and medical school whose name it bore. In the absence of real consensus about the medical model, attempts to establish consensus about other matters could hardly have succeeded, and they did not.

If the role of the ill person in the social model is obscure, the role of the psychiatrist is even less clear. There is little evidence that the patients, the community, or anyone else has been so impressed with the brilliant performance and diversified talents of psychiatrists that they have rushed to enlist them in plans for changing society. On the contrary, Abram Hoffer [32] has suggested that the psychiatrists are engaged in a flight from the patient. Some psychiatrists write and speak as if they believe that by changing the model, the ill people will disappear, but there is no evidence that this has happened.* Most ill people are not comforted to hear that the illness which they face every day is "just a symptom of a sick society."

In a presidential address to the Royal Society of Medicine, Desmond Curran,[33] a British psychiatrist, had this to say about the expansionist tendencies in psychiatry:

* There is recent evidence, in fact, that patients "dumped" from mental hospitals into the community are finding their way back into the jails and slums from which they were rescued when the hospitals were built. Furthermore, the death rate among these patients seems to be rising. See the report, "Where Have All the Patients Gone?" prepared by the California State Employees Association, January 1972.

. . . when one looks at the vast fields there unquestionably are in the domain of psychiatry and at how much still remains to be done, is it necessary, is it wise, and may it not be rather premature to look for fresh fields to conquer or fail in? . . . I have no yearning to run the world, and I can say with no false modesty I do not believe I could. My own job is quite enough for me. I have called this address "Psychiatry Limited." I understand that a limited liability company is one in which the shareholders, should the company fail or go bankrupt, are not liable for more than they subscribe. The company I have in mind is a respectable company, a large concern with big responsibilities and with a great future before it. The shareholders are quiet, diffident, modest, sober men who have a real pride in their business, but they are vexed when others undermine the reputation of the firm by using the name to float bogus companies, with grandiose prospectuses, backed up by balance-sheets that do not add up to make sense.

The Psychedelic Model

During the nineteenth century, two great illnesses were romanticized: consumption (or phthisis), now called tuberculosis, and madness, now called schizophrenia. Tuberculosis has been thoroughly deromanticized to the great benefit of all those who suffer from it, but schizophrenia still has to be fully accepted and established as a true illness. Meanwhile, it is undergoing a fresh bout of romantic delirium which we call the psychedelic model.

The essence of the romantic, or psychedelic, view of madness is that the mad see things more clearly than the rest of us, that madness is a mind-expanding "trip," and that the burden of the misunderstanding about madness lies at the doorstep of the so-called sane. As Charles Nodier, the teacher of Victor Hugo and Alfred de Musset, said:

Lunatics . . . occupy the highest degree of the scale that separates our planet from its satellite, and since they communicate to this degree with a world of thought that is unknown to us, it is only natural that we do not understand them, and it is absurd to conclude that their ideas lack sense and lucidity, since they belong to an order of sensations and comprehensions which are totally inaccessible to us, with our education and habits.[34]

Or, as R. D. Laing put it more recently:

Future men will . . . see that what we call "schizophrenia" was one of the forms in which, often through quite ordinary people, the light began to break through the cracks in our all-too-closed minds.[35]

Laing, more than anyone else today, has sought to romanticize schizophrenia by confusing it with the natural rebelliousness of young people (who are the chief victims of schizophrenia) and their desire for a new and more exciting world. As young schizophrenics are more likely than their normal peers to feel keenly the desire to escape parental norms and values while still needing parental protection, they are especially susceptible to Laing's view that schizophrenia is a form of enlightenment not available to the "squares" of the older generation.[36]

After the French Revolution, there was a tremendous interest in the romantic aspect of madness. According to Frederic Grunfeld, "The way to the asylum thus becomes a pilgrimage for artists with sketchbooks under their arms." [37] The French painter Géricault set up his easel in the Salpêtrière to do a series of ten portraits of mental patients. His friend Delacroix produced two paintings of *Tasso in the Madhouse*. Blake, Goya, and the Swiss painter Henry Fuseli all did painting and engravings of the madhouse. Meanwhile, exciting mad scenes appeared in operas: Goethe's Gretchen in Gounod's opera *Faust*, and Donizetti's *Lucia di Lammermoor*, based on Sir Walter Scott's novel. The great romantic composer Robert Schumann spent the last two years of his life in an asylum, and the writer Gerard de Nerval killed himself, according to his doctors, "because he saw madness face to face."

Tuberculosis occupied a similar position in the arts, as René and Jean Dubos have shown in their essay, "Consumption and the Romantic Age":

Tuberculosis, being then so prevalent, may have contributed to the atmosphere of gloom that made possible the success of the "graveyard school" of poetry and the development of the romantic mood. Melancholy meditations over the death of a youth or a maiden, tombs, abandoned ruins, and weeping willows became popular themes over much of Europe around 1750, as if some new circumstance had made more obvious the ephemeral character of human life. Instead of singing of the healthy joys of love, poets cultivated the refined sadness evoked by the thought that the beloved might soon depart. For Thomas Lovell Beddoes, whose father had written a famous *Essay on Consumption*, the earth was a "grave-paved star." [38]

Tuberculosis was an ideal disease to use in a literary way, for its symptoms were not loathsome, disgusting or even socially distressing, and the course of the illness was often slow and insidious. The authors say:

Thus a decline could be used at will to render the heroine more attractive, to purify her soul through suffering and resignation, to show the cruel working of an inevitable fate or to deal in fiction with vague problems of heredity and predestination.

Among the literary works which featured tubercular heroines were Dumas's *La Dame aux Camélias*, a story which appeared again in Verdi's *La Traviata*, and Murger's *Scènes de la Vie Bohème*, which served as a play, *La Boheme*, and later as a basis for Puccini's opera. Another of Murger's heroines, Francine, like Mimi, was tubercular; she is described as "pale as the angel of phthisis."

If the mad were said to see things more clearly, then the tubercular were held to have attained more purity than the healthy. Thus Charles Dickens wrote in *Nicholas Nickleby*:

There is a dread disease which so prepares its victim, as it were, for death; which so refines it of its grosser aspect, and throws around familiar looks, unearthly indications of the coming change—a dread disease, in which the struggle between soul and body is so gradual, quiet and solemn, and the result so sure, that day by day, and grain by grain, the mortal part wastes and withers away, so that the spirit grows light and sanguine with its lightening load, and, feeling immortality at hand, deems it but a new term of mortal life; a disease in which life and death are so strangely blended that death takes the glow and hue of life, and life the gaunt and grisly form of death; a disease which medicine never cured, wealth never warded off, or poverty could boast exemption from; which sometimes moves in giant strides, and sometimes at a tardy sluggish pace, but, slow or quick, is ever sure and certain.

In addition to moral purity, those suffering from tuberculosis were held to be more sensitive and creative than ordinary healthy folk. Elizabeth Barrett Browning overheard someone asking her doctor: "Is it possible that genius is only scrofula?" Dumas said facetiously that it was the fashion to suffer from consumption, especially for poets; that "it was good form to spit blood after each emotion that was at all sensational and to die before reaching the age of thirty." The Goncourts believed that Victor Hugo would have been an even greater poet had he not been in such robust health.

But this romantic view of tuberculosis finally came to an end. René and Jean Dubos write:

The attitude of perverted sentimentalism toward tuberculosis began to change in the last third of the nineteenth century. In reaction against the artificialities of the Romantic Era, writers and artists rediscovered that disease was not necessarily poetical, and health not detrimental to creative power. Turning their eyes away from the languourous, fainting young women and their romantic lovers, they noticed instead the miserable humanity living in the dreary tenements born of the Industrial Revolution. In the "tentacular cities" they saw hosts of men, women and children, pale too, often cold and starving, working long hours in dark and crowded shops, breathing smoke and coal dust. Tuberculosis was there, breeding suffering and misery without romance. And, little by little, it dawned on social common sense what a mockery it was to depict consumption as a spiritualization of the being, as a romantic experience detached from the horrid aspects of disease. In the laboring classes consumption was not the aristocratic decline, inspiring works of art and leading painlessly to an ethereal release of the soul among the falling autumn leaves. It was the great killer and breeder of destitution. The writers of the realist school, who visited slums and hospitals that they might observe the sick and the poor, acknowledged in dark words the bodies distorted by cough, the faces livid with asphyxiation, the minds haunted by the thought of death.

Not all illnesses go through this romantic stage. We might ask under what conditions a disease comes to be seen in this light and what qualities of tuberculosis and schizophrenia have lent themselves to this use by a literary public with an appetite for emotional thrills. First, both illnesses attack young adults, and to the extent that people of this age are seen as having a romantic aura, so will the diseases which alter the course of their lives. Second, both illnesses are fatal to some but not all of those who have it, so there is some suspense about the outcome. Then, the insidious onset which often characterizes both illnesses lends poignancy, for some episodes in the story which appear to be happy and normal at the time can later be seen as early indications of the disease. A diagnosis made late in the day greatly adds to the romantic interest. Also, both illnesses are easily confused with other illnesses and with less serious conditions, so that anyone feels he might have it, while only some actually get it. An absolutely clearcut illness, known to be limited to a small and definite population, which can be diagnosed quickly and accurately by a few laboratory tests would not be nearly so satisfactory from a literary point of view. The lines have to be sufficiently unclear so that the hero's or heroine's character, personal choices, and fate can be seen as contributing to the final inevitable outcome. In short, there must be that mixture of free will and inevitability which marks any great tragedy.

As George Vaillant [39] has pointed out, tuberculosis and schizophrenia have more in common than mere "chronicity and a tendency toward poorly explained remissions and relapses." Research on tuberculosis has included twin studies, social class studies, and even studies of double-bind communication in families. Treatments for tuberculosis have included drugs, surgery, a kind of electro-shock therapy, group therapy, and milieu therapy. In *The Magic Mountain,* it will be recalled, psychoanalysis was offered as a treatment for tuberculosis. And what are our expensive, private psychoanalytic hospitals for wealthy schizophrenics if not Magic Mountains? The parallels between the two diseases are such that every model we have constructed for schizophrenia could just as well be applied to tuberculosis. Since tuberculosis has been largely deromanticized, what encouraging signs can one read in its history that might let us hope that schizophrenia, too, will undergo this fortunate metamorphósis?

Tuberculosis, like schizophrenia, was an illness characterized for centuries by what René and Jean Dubos have called "a confusing array of signs and symptoms, bearing no obvious relation one to the other." Most physicians tried to bring order into this chaos by postulating a number of separate diseases, characterized by different types of tubercles, ulcers, and cavities. But in opposition to this, a unified view of the illness was evolved slowly and with great difficulty. The creation or construction of the illness which we now know as tuberculosis was an enormous imaginative effort on the part of many different doctors and scientists, sustained over several hundred years. The Italian school of medicine in the sixteenth century held that tuberculosis was a contagious disease. In 1679 Franciscus Sylvius named the nodules which he found in all parts of the body of phthisic patients "tubercles." In 1722 Benjamin Marten, an English physician, put forth the earliest explicit statement of the germ theory. Auenbrugger invented mediate auscultation in 1761. In 1804 Laënnec gave his famous lecture on the unitary theory of phthisis. The name "tuberculosis" was suggested in 1839 by J. L. Schonlein of Zurich for all manifestations of phthisis, since "tubercles" were always associated with the disease. In 1854 Hermann Brehmer started the first "Magic Mountain" in Silesia. Villemin showed, in 1865, that tuberculosis is inoculable from man and cow to rabbit or guinea pig. In 1882 Koch presented his findings on the presence of the tubercle bacillus in tuberculosis. X-rays were discovered by Roentgen in 1895. In 1952 a new drug, isoniazid, was discovered, which was capable of killing the bacillus. The drama is still not completed, for every year millions still suffer and often die from tuberculosis. If one were to speculate on which elements in this long and brilliant history of medical achievement did the most ultimately to deromanticize the illness, one would probably include the development of instruments of measurement and the discovery of the tubercle bacillus. One would also have to include the extensive public educational campaign to alert those who had tuberculosis of their responsibilities, and the emphasis on the early detection of the illness.

The same process of deromanticization is now proceeding with schizophrenia, R. D. Laing notwithstanding. Techniques are being developed to measure the illness chemically,[40] electrophysiologically,[41] and perceptually.[42] Measurement deflates the romantic balloon as nothing else does. Many laboratories are now engaged in identifying the biochemical lesion or lesions central to the schizophrenic process. The American Schizophrenia Association is beginning to make that series of moves which were so innovative in relation to tuberculosis and are now so familiar and well established: supporting research, educating the public, and pressing for early identification and prompt treatment of the illness.

All diseases are human inventions, and schizophrenia, like tuberculosis, is now being created and constructed from centuries of accumulated observations and insight made by many workers all over the world.* A recent billboard advertisement reads: WHO INVENTED YELLOW FEVER? "Yellow Fever," it seems, is a mixed drink, made with a well-known brand of vodka. It is a joke, because everyone knows that yellow fever is a disease, and diseases are not invented. But in fact yellow fever, tuberculosis, and schizophrenia were all invented. Those who have complained about this "labeling" in schizophrenia have failed to understand that all true diseases are enormous feats of human energy, intelligence, and imagination, and that without this difficult and often slow process of invention, there would be no such thing as medicine. The problem with schizophrenia is not that we have invented it but that the work is still far from completed, and so it can still be,romanticized for a little while longer. Schizophrenia used to be called "dementia praecox"—early, precocious, or half-cooked madness. It is still a half-cooked illness; that is our tragedy.

Romanticizing any illness can become a dangerous entertainment for ill people, their families, and society. It may also be harmful to doctors who are, like others, usually influenced by the social climate in which they live, and so are liable to be carried away by the dramatic atmosphere. They may conclude that their adversary is no longer a mere illness which, however appall-

---

* Sigerist says: "It was only from the Renaissance on that the conception of disease as a morbid entity developed. It was by the strength of Sydenham's work, by the founding of pathological anatomy, and by other results of etiological research." ("Problems of Historical-Geographical Pathology," in *Henry E. Sigerist on the Sociology of Medicine,* ed. Milton I. Roemer [New York: MD Publications, Inc., 1960], pp. 299-307.)

ing, must be fought steadfastly with every available weapon, but something uncanny, unnatural even, and so beyond medical understanding. Such an attitude is not what most of us hope for in our own physician when we are ill. It is demoralizing. A well-known psychiatrist once expressed this exact opinion, saying, "You will never really understand schizophrenia—it is impossible."

A patient is usually better off if his doctor refrains from such global and philosophical pronouncements and, in spite of the limitations of medical knowledge, attends soberly to the task at hand, namely: conferring the sick role and supporting it by making a diagnosis, however crude and inexact; giving the best treatment; and offering a prognosis.

Those members of the public who either want to play at madness or wish to enjoy it as an amusing or enlightening spectacle must recognize their amateur status. In the mid-nineteenth century it was fashionable to appear languid and pale, to brighten one's eyes with belladonna and cough inconspicuously. Many healthy people used to engage in this charming foible, but it did not benefit those dying from consumption, though it gave those who were not an unusual thrill. Everyone is entitled to a hobby, but these romantic poses should not be pursued at the expense of truly schizophrenic people whose professional status in this regard compels them to play for keeps.

The Conspiratorial Model

Madness can be viewed in many ways: as a disease, a moral failing, a result of faulty upbringing, a form of family communication, a symptom of a "sick" society, a permanently lowered status, or a mind-expanding "trip." In addition, there is the logical possibility, which is especially appealing to logical minds, that it may not exist at all. This view, that madness exists only in the eye of the beholder, we call the conspiratorial model. In this model it is assumed that the person labeled as mad is no different from the rest of us, but that for some poorly understood reason, for which a few dark hints are offered in explanation, members of his society choose to call attention to some of his acts, label them as deviant, and move against him in a concerted fashion. Once this process is initiated, it becomes self-reinforcing. As Thomas Scheff puts it:

. . . the more the rule-breaker enters the role of the mentally ill, the more he is defined by others as mentally ill; but the more he is defined as mentally ill, the more he enters the role, and so on. This kind of vicious circle is quite characteristic of many different kinds of social and individual systems.[43]

According to Scheff, a culture provides a vocabulary for categorizing many violations of norms: crime, drunkenness, bad manners, and so forth. After these categories have been exhausted, however, there is a residue of deviant behaviors for which no explicit label exists: these are the norms governing decency or reality which "go without saying." Those who violate these residual rules expose themselves to the possibility of being labeled mentally ill. While most instances of residual rule-breaking are ignored or "normalized," those which are labeled as mentally ill will be continuously reinforced. Thus Erving Goffman[44] writes about the "discrediting" of hospitalized mental patients:

The case record . . . is apparently not regularly used . . . to record occasions when the patient showed capacity to cope honorably and effectively with difficult life situations. Nor is the case record typically used to provide a rough average or sampling of his past conduct. One of its purposes is to show the ways in which the patient is "sick" and the reasons why it was right to commit him and is right currently to keep him committed; and this is done by extracting from his whole life course a list of those incidents that have or might have had "symptomatic" significance . . . . I think that most of the information gathered in case records is quite true, although it might seem also to be true that almost anyone's life course could yield up enough denigrating facts to provide grounds for the record's justification of commitment.*

* This is very odd: would one really expect *any* hospital records to be mainly devoted to the patient's positive achievements vis-à-vis any illness? Even in the case of an Olympic skier with a broken leg, far more space would be devoted to the nature and extent of the fracture, and the resulting disability, than to the patient's Olympic records. These would be seen as irrelevant at that moment. Very little would be recorded about the patient as a walker, dancer, swimmer, rider, leapfrogger, hopper, jumper, hurdler, runner, etc., even though the patient

Scheff, Goffman, and others have described the sequence of events which they believe occurs when someone is labeled "mentally ill." As they perceive it, an innocent victim somehow becomes set upon the downward path to deviant status, stigmatization, persecution, and even death by suicide. But even if one accepts their findings as true, many questions remain unanswered. Walter Gove, in a critique of labeling theory, says: "The societal perspective does not explain why people initially commit deviant acts; it deals mainly with secondary processes that may not always be of crucial importance." [45]

Our first question is: why does the category of "madness" exist at all? Why is it not sufficient to call a deviant person bad-mannered, criminal, radical, and so forth? In spite of vast differences in cultural expectations, the category of madness appears to be world-wide; it has remained remarkably stable over the centuries, and mad behavior, if pantomimed, would probably be understood anywhere in the world. Even quite small children distinguish between someone who is stupid, bad, ill, or crazy. [46] According to David Rothman,[47] the American colonists, while not disposed toward building institutions for deviants of different sorts, nevertheless distinguished carefully between the poor, the ill, the criminal, and the insane person. The Pennsylvania Hospital, founded in 1751, made special provision for those persons "unhappily disordered in their senses." Sociologists write as if there were something very arbitrary about these categories, but it is common observation that these distinctions are and have been well understood for millennia, and therefore have meaning. Everyone apparently, except for some sociologists, has noticed that there is something special about madness.

Another peculiarity of labeling theory is the assumption that those who do the labeling share a set of assumptions about the world and are able to act in concert, whereas their labeled victims, for some curious reason, are thought of as acting entirely alone. Why do they fail to rally friends, family, and co-workers around

---

might be adept at all these and many other forms of healthy leg attainments. It is only when the leg is mended or mending that comparison with the well self helps.

them to combat and confute the malignant labelers? How is it that people allegedly completely normal until caught up in the labeling process so quickly become completely socially isolated? Does even the merest suggestion that someone is mentally ill result in immediate desertion by family and friends? It is true that many people when admitted to the hospital do appear to be socially isolated, but it is possible that the explanation for this lies not in mass desertion but because those who are "unhappily disordered in their senses" have lost that common ground of sharable perceptions which forms the basis of all social interaction. A person whose sensory experiences are highly aberrant cannot combine with other human beings, and therefore his social relationships are almost certain to be damaged or even to break down completely. This is borne out within the hospital as well, for quite unlike all other deviants, mental patients do *not* combine or form a subculture based on their common deviance.[48] There are no riots in mental hospitals, however abysmal the conditions. One psychiatrist, who gave a course on escaping from his hospital, found the patients to be poor students of this particular curriculum,[49] while another, who tried to assist three convalescent patients to make a break from the hospital by means of judicious inattention to their scheme, was disappointed to find that the anxiety of this collaborative effort resulted in all three becoming too ill to undertake their enterprise.[50]

Scheff notes that "psychiatric symptoms can arise from external stress: from drug ingestion, the sustained fear and hardship of combat, and from deprivation of food, sleep and *even sensory experience* [italics added]." He says, further, that even monotonous environments such as long-distance flying or driving sometimes produce sensory distortions. He tells of a pilot flying under such conditions who suddenly felt detached from his surroundings and believed that the plane had one wing down and was turning. He corrected the altitude and went into a dive, from which he was fortunate to be able to recover. When examined, the man was found to have no psychiatric abnormality. Upon being offered an explanation of what had happened, he was reassured and returned to flying. Scheff comments on the importance of reassuring someone who has had a strange sensory experience that his reaction was due solely to the unusual circumstance, that anyone else would have felt as he did. Scheff does not seem aware that the same strategy is open to those who confront a person "unhappily disordered in his senses"; it was used by "mad" doctors like William Battie [51] in the eighteenth century and John Conolly [52] in the nineteenth, and it is used today by psychiatrists who subscribe to the medical model. When a schizophrenic person is told that his senses have been distorted due to some biochemical abnormality, he is just as reassured as if the symptoms had arisen from sensory deprivation, drugs, or posthypnotic suggestion.

Some illnesses, such as leprosy, tuberculosis, and schizophrenia, have had a bad press, and some of those suffering from them have been ill-treated, coerced, or persecuted. Other illnesses, such as cancer, multiple sclerosis, and muscular dystrophy, have been seen as frightful and hopeless, although not socially damaging. Szasz, Laing, Goffman, Scheff, and others using the conspiratorial model have stated or implied that the elimination of the category "mental illness" would end the suffering of those so labeled. But looked at through the lens of the medical model, history reads quite the other way. As each of these illnesses has become better known to the public, and as tests have been developed that enable earlier identification, the stigma of the disease has gradually lifted. In no instance that we know of has any great illness disappeared by abolishing the category, although many treatments and procedures have been abandoned as useless or even harmful. Oddly enough, Scheff uses the example of histoplasmosis to show that early symptoms are usually denied and of transitory significance. This disease, once thought to be rare but always fatal, is now known to be widely prevalent but often benign. Scheff's view is that if we ignore minor symptoms, both physical and psychological, they will go away. While many schizophrenics no doubt live with transitory perceptual anomalies that pass away without comment or medical attention, there is ample evidence that for large numbers of schizophrenics, the illness is not benign or self-limiting. We have talked with schizophrenics who had never before received psychiatric attention or labeling and who had led lives of the most unbelievable misery due to their symptoms. They were tremendously relieved to find that they had an identifiable disease, rather than a "problem in living." They had often assumed that they were "bad" because they were unable to account for their inability to function normally. Of course, illnesses and problems in living are not mutually exclusive categories; as D. A. Begelman has pointed out, "A fractured leg may give an Olympic track star a problem in living." [53] Schizophrenics are perfectly willing to take up their social, psychological, vocational, and spiritual problems once their illness has been brought under control, but they have testified that calling a disease a "problem in living" in no way alters its course or makes it easier to bear.

It seems to us that those using the conspiratorial model, while filled with righteous indignation about abuses to mental patients, have shown very little interest in finding out how psychiatric diseases appear to those who actually have them. We know of only two studies in the literature which deal with this issue, one by Lawrence Linn entitled "The Mental Hospital from the Patient Perspective," [54] and one of our own. [55] Linn found that more than half the patients in his sample wanted to come to the hospital because they felt they needed help. In the numerous autobiographical accounts of these illnesses, there is much evidence of inept or unkind treatment but little evidence that the authors believed they would have been benefited by being seen as normal. What they usually want is more and better medical treatment, and better hospitals should they get ill again. This was certainly Clifford Beers's [56] view, although he was brutally treated in a mental hospital. He started a movement to reform mental hospitals, but he never suggested that his illness was merely a label.

If we have said little about the writings of Dr. Thomas Szasz, the best-known and most widely quoted proponent of the conspiratorial model, this is because they present certain difficulties for the systematic inquirer, which have sometimes led us to question his seriousness. Dr. Szasz is well known for making didactic statements such as "There is no such thing as mental illness," and these ex-cathedra pronouncements have often been accompanied by denunciation of those who disagree with him. His seriousness becomes suspect because he makes little or no attempt to meet those objections which can and have been advanced against his views.* He does not seem to realize that dogmatic affirmation is not enough in a matter of this importance which affects the lives of hundreds of thousands of people and which results in many avoidable deaths due to suicide, accident, or murder.

He seems to belong to a well-known and cherished tradition of medical eccentricity. He is first and foremost a physician and psychiatrist, a discipline so unequivocally a medical specialty that in 1892 Silas Weir Mitchell [57] referred to some of its members, when reproaching them for their unmedical behavior, as being "among the first of specialists."

While nonmedical people have become enthusiastic or angry at Dr. Szasz's antipsychiatry views, his own colleagues have preserved an admirable calm and seem, at worst, mildly puzzled and annoyed by him. This suggests that they consider his antimedical and antipsychiatric writings to be more in the nature of an unusual hobby than a true vocation. However, even a hobby may become so fascinating to the hobbyist that he becomes blind to its dangerous or objectionable aspects.

It is difficult to condense Szasz's copious works, but he seems to believe that, in spite of his excellent psychiatric credentials and his identification as a physician, his assaults upon the concept of "mental illness" are concerned with matters which have nothing to do with medicine but lie outside its domain.

As he himself puts it:

I have tried to develop concepts and methods appropriate to a psychiatry whose problems are not medical diseases but human conflicts;

* Szasz's inability to meet direct confrontation of his views was underscored in a television appearance in England (October 1972). Our informant relates that Szasz was asked whether, if he himself suffered a temporary suicidal depression, he would wish to be rescued from it against his will by psychiatrists, and whether he would be grateful afterward. There was nothing he could say to this. As a philosopher, he is bound to stick to his principles; he must allow the man (in this case himself) to die if he so chooses. As a doctor, or the patient of a doctor, he must place the saving of a life (in this case his own) first. His critic managed to locate one of the points at which Szasz's two models, that of philosopher and doctor, are in absolute conflict, and Szasz was unable to resolve this dilemma. (Christopher Mayhew, M.P., personal communication to H. Osmond, October 10, 1972.)

whose criteria of value are not conformity to social norms or "mental illness" but self-determination and responsible liberty; and which is dedicated to decreasing man's coercive control over his fellow man and increasing his control over himself.[58]

Szasz is far more competent in psychiatric matters than any lay person, for that is his training: he is licensed in medicine and psychiatry. There is, however, no reason to suppose that because of that training he must have acquired any more expertise in resolving "human conflicts" than many other people deriving from a great variety of disciplines. He is using his Aesculapian authority (see Chap. 4) to further a nonmedical approach to psychiatric illnesses by denying their existence. This creates a double bind of the most exquisite ambiguity. It is as if a priest, bent on enhancing his reputation in the church, put forth daring atheistic views. Those seeking spiritual guidance from such a priest would find that if they accepted the priest, they would have to reject the church, and if they accepted the church, they would have to question whether or not he was a real priest. If Dr. Szasz actually treats patients on the basis of his views, he must then force them to choose between accepting his Aesculapian authority, and thereby losing the sick role, or, if they insist on the sick role, defying his Aesculapian authority. This is precisely the kind of behavior which is held by some theorists, such as Bateson, to *create* schizophrenia, and while we do not agree that this is so, it can hardly be helpful to someone already confused and worried.

Szasz does not let sentimental or mere humanitarian considerations interfere with his theory-making. He appears, for instance, to believe that mentally ill assassins and other murderers should be grateful if they are tried and punished only on the basis of their crime, and without any reference to their mental illnesses, which do not, so far as he is concerned, exist. This led him to write of Sirhan Sirhan in terms which appear to urge the authorities to execute the young man in order to preserve his dignity: "We are damned if we accept his offer and execute him, but if we reject it and don't execute him, we are damned a thousandfold more." [59]

We do not know whether Sirhan himself shares Szasz's single-minded approach. Arthur Bremer,[60] aged twenty-one, was tried recently for his attempt upon the life of Governor George Wallace. After he had been found guilty and sentenced to sixty years' imprisonment, he was allowed to address the court. Even though there is much evidence that he suffers from schizophrenia—that nonexistent illness, according to Dr. Szasz—Bremer spoke directly and sensibly. At such a time, and at such a moment of dismal truth so soon after he had heard his fate, he surely had a right to be heeded. This is what he said:

Well, Mr. Marshall [State's Attorney Arthur A. Marshall] tells me he'd like society to be protected from someone like me. Looking back on my life, I would have liked it if society had protected me from myself. That's all I've got to say.

These words give little support for the conspiratorial model. Bremer was seen by a psychiatrist some months before committing his crime, and had the medical model been used more vigorously and imaginatively, two lives would have been saved from a dreadful blighting—the governor's and his own.

The Family Interaction Model

A sick child and a troubled family often go together, and this is the point of departure for the family interaction model. In the medical model, it is usually assumed that the family is troubled because the child is sick. The family may be even more troubled if it contains more than one sick person, as in the case of certain infectious or hereditary illnesses. It is clearly possible to arrange the same data the other way around, and so to claim that troubled families make children sick. It would follow from this premise that the child will get well only if the whole family is "treated," which is the view held by those subscribing to a family interaction model. As W. W. Meissner puts it:

The fundamental insight of family therapy and the basic premise of family theory is that the family is the unit of conceptualization. The patient is thereby only externalizing through his symptoms an illness which is inherent in the family itself. He is a symptomatic organ of a diseased organism . . . .[61]

Those using a family interaction model have sought to treat schizophrenia by gathering together the family members and engaging them in a kind of group therapy designed to reveal the family's underlying patterns of pathological communication. While the theory states that all the members are equally a part of the "sick" family and therefore equally entitled to the sympathetic attention of the therapist, in practice it is almost always assumed that the parents are to blame for making the child sick. A further divergence from theory occurs when it becomes evident that fathers, who usually have full-time jobs, and older siblings, who often have school and other commitments, are not available for endless therapy sessions, and so in practice the family group may come to consist of an embattled and worried mother and her sick child.

Since schizophrenia is not a disease in the usual sense of the word, according to those who use this model,[62] the children who manifest this or other childhood psychoses do not receive the sick role, but rather the "psych" role. The parents typically receive neither the sick role nor the "psych" role, but the "bad" role in a retributive moral model. The absence of the sick role in the face of an extremely serious and evidently crippling illness leaves the door open for a crossfire of accusations and counteraccusations which are likely to grow more heated as time passes without any alleviation of the illness. We propose to examine the consequences of the omission of the sick role by comparing childhood psychoses with other serious childhood conditions.

The purpose of the family is to bear, nurture, and protect children, and to socialize them into the culture of their parents. Therefore it is not surprising that parents feel guilty if their children become ill or injured, die, or fail to become acculturated. Up to a point, such guilt is functional, because it encourages families to fulfill their function. But guilt, like fire, is a good slave and a poor master; it is dysfunctional for families to be guilty about events over which they have no control.

The sick role decreases dysfunctional guilt and focuses the attention of the family on moves which they and others can and must make to increase the child's chances of survival. It is useless to be guilty about the presence of a disease or about death from a fatal illness, but it is extremely useful for a family to be guilty about not seeking appropriate help, not following a prescribed treatment, or not recognizing serious illness as early as possible. It is a matter of importance, then, both for the survival of the child and the well-being of the family, and so for the larger society, whether a sick child gets the sick role or not.

We will now consider four illnesses or injuries which afflict children in terms of the availability of the sick role and how this affects the fate of the child and the family: leukemia, crib death, the battered baby syndrome, and childhood psychoses.

One of the most poignant situations that any family has to face is the death of a child from a fatal illness such as leukemia. Leukemia also distresses the professional people closely involved with the dying child and his family. In order to prepare themselves more fully to support families facing the death of a child, a team of professionals in California [63] undertook a retrospective study of twenty families who had lost a child through leukemia. They found that in eleven of the families, one or more members required psychiatric help, although none had needed such help before. They recommend that doctors be alert to those families which might need such help so that they might have additional attention.

The authors found that the fathers of leukemic children were deeply affected by their children's illness. The fathers tended to cope with their distress by absenting themselves, which had the unfortunate consequence of depriving the mothers of much-needed support. The authors feel that fathers who manifest this method of coping are in need of additional attention and that they should be helped to express their painful feelings.

The siblings of the leukemic children also manifested difficulty in coping with the presence of a fatal illness in their family. Some of the siblings were afraid that they, too, might suffer a fatal illness. Others suffered from enuresis, headaches, poor school performance, school phobia, depression, and other symptoms.

The program of support for families at the University of California San Francisco Pediatric Hematology Clinic [64] includes an initial conference, scheduled shortly after recovery from the shock of learning that a child has leukemia. The doctor makes it clear that he wishes to listen as well as talk and that he is prepared to answer all their questions. Both parents attend this conference, as well as older siblings and grandparents if they wish. The conference is conducted by a staff hematologist and may include a psychiatrist and a social worker, if they are to be part of the clinical team. The conference provides an opportunity for the family and the staff to know each other. The staff hopes to use the conference to develop greater sensitivity to the family, and to let them know that the staff is not only concerned with the illness itself but with the members of the family as human beings in distress.

The first step at the conference is to explain the diagnosis. This is done "without vagueness or equivocation." The family is told what kind of leukemia their child has and that the outcome is probably fatal. They are also told what therapy is planned for the child. They are assured that earlier diagnosis would probably not have affected the prognosis.

Then sympathy and hope are extended to the family. They are assured that neither they nor the child will be abandoned. Examples are offered of once fatal diseases which have been brought under control through research. Current research efforts on drugs for leukemia are mentioned.

Since the family is very likely to indulge in self-blame, it is made explicit that nothing the family has or has not done or could have done is known to have any bearing on the development of leukemia.

The family is then helped to anticipate the problems of telling others about the child's illness. Difficulties that might arise with siblings, grandparents, friends, and relatives are discussed.

In discussing the treatment, the authors make it clear that they are willing to consider any treatment about which the parents might have heard, and also "any press releases, alleged cures or unusual forms of therapy."

After this the child's needs are examined and suggestions are made about what his parents should tell him. Experience has shown that children over four or five years are well aware if they have a fatal illness. A child whose parents try to hide the diagnosis from him is simply forced to add loneliness to his other problems.

The team then begins to raise the questions regarding the likely circumstances of the child's death, because they know from experience that the parents' imaginings about this dreaded and often unspoken-of time were almost always worse than the reality. At this point attempts are made in the conference to assess the strengths and weaknesses of the family, in order to use the former and minimize the latter. The clinical team observes the family closely and tries to identify both sources of support and likely causes of stress. They note whether the family is carrying other burdens besides the leukemic child, and whether there are other serious illnesses in the family. By assessing the vulnerability of the particular family, they learn in what ways the members of the team are most likely to be of help.

These papers show that previously normal families can be gravely disrupted and harmed by the death of a child, which is not surprising. However, in this admirable program, the leukemic child and his family are given the full benefits of the medical model and the sick role, and thus an unavoidable tragedy can become a courageous and even an inspiring enterprise. For tragedy surmounted does not debase and may even ennoble the human spirit.

The next condition we will consider is Sudden Infant Death Syndrome (S.I.D.S.), also called "crib death" or "cot death." In the United States, about ten thousand infants perish each year from this poorly understood condition, which seems to be known everywhere in the world and has been described since biblical times. The syndrome is described as "the sudden, unexpected, inexplicable death of an infant." Typically, the child appears to be perfectly healthy when put to bed (except, perhaps, for minor respiratory symptoms); when the mother next sees it, it is dead. Postmortem findings fail to show the cause of death. According to A. Bergman:

Guilt is universal and pervasive. Whether they say so or not, most if not all the parents feel responsible for the death of their babies. If a baby-sitter is involved, the situation is even more delicate. Blaming neighbors, relatives and friends augments the even heavier burden of self-incrimination.[65]

The burden on the family is so great that it has resulted in its complete collapse:

Marriages have broken up following a crib death . . . because a husband refused to live with a wife who "let a baby die." Older siblings of the victims have become emotionally scarred. (Nightmares and bedwetting are frequent results.) Guilt-ridden mothers have withdrawn from friends and relatives and refused to leave their homes for months. Suicides have been reported. Couples have refused to have further children for fear of another crib death.[66]

Crib death parallels leukemia in its shattering effect on the family, but not in the response it elicits from professional people and law enforcement officers. One mother was asked by a medical investigator how many times she had hit her baby, whether she had let other children abuse the child, and whether her dog had been allowed to bite it. Another mother was distressed by the reaction of her pediatrician, who stopped speaking to her when they met in public. Evidently the assumption of parental innocence which applies in leukemia does not apply to crib death. Why might this be so? Unlike the leukemic child, the baby who dies of crib death was never known to be sick and was therefore never installed in the sick role. The illness does not last long enough to trigger the usual medical response. Doctors tend to be suspicious or perhaps resentful when someone dies without benefit of medical attention. Therefore, the parents of the crib-death baby fail to get one of the chief benefits of the sick role, the injunction against self-blame and protection from blame by others.

Parents who have lost a child through crib death have now banded together to secure their rights. In 1962 they founded the National Foundation for Sudden Infant Death. Dr. Bergman, the president of the organization, said that the foundation will have reached its goal "when a family feels no more guilty about losing a child to crib death than they would if the child died of pneumonia, meningitis or leukemia." Thus, special social efforts have had to be made to compensate for the natural limitations of this too-short illness.

In crib death there is no evidence that the parents have harmed the child, yet they are accused; but in the battered baby syndrome all evidence points in the direction of parental brutality, yet the clues are ignored. Again, the reason for this strange anomaly seems to be related to the presence or absence of the sick role. If a child is beaten by its parents, survives the initial beating, and is brought to a doctor to be treated, it is perceived from then on in the sick role and therefore the parents cannot be blamed. This automatic response is so well learned by doctors and nurses that they require special education to break this particular set. Even when the doctor himself becomes suspicious, he sometimes has the greatest difficulty in convincing other doctors or the police, and children have died because of this. It seems that doctors and police alike are unwilling to believe that a "patient" could also be the victim of attempted homicide. Much can be learned about the power of the sick role to alter our expectations from this unusual circumstance.*

How do the families of schizophrenic or autistic children fare when they seek help from the medical profession, compared with other families we have discussed here? What happens when they seek information about their children's condition? Jacques May, the physician father of twin autistic sons, found that the usual medical courtesies did not apply:

But now, for the first time in my life dealing with a physician, I was made to feel that I was a layman. The general attitude of the doctor made it quite clear that there would be no discussion of the possible causes of the event that brought us to this consultation, no critical review of the methods of treatment at hand, no apportionment of what was known on the subject and what was not. I was made to feel that the doctor knew everything and that I knew nothing, that the problem was really no problem at all, since there was an accepted and unchallenged explanation for our children's condition. As the conversation developed, I had more and more the feeling that my wife and I were finding aloofness instead of understanding, coldness instead of warmth,

* In some cases, the parents of battered babies appear to suffer from alcoholism or schizophrenia. Some of the mothers of battered babies have formed an organization called "Mothers Anonymous," in which mothers support each other in their efforts to curb this particular behavior.

distrust instead of sympathy. Then it became quite clear: to our amazement, it dawned upon us that, in the doctor's eyes, we were being held responsible for the children's situation. This was the accepted view, we found, the official doctrine, the only explanation offered and recognized, the sole basis of treatment. Further, we soon realized that instead of being anxious and desperate people seeking understanding and help, as I had thought we were, we had become culprits hiding something, people with some dark secret whose words were not a simple expression of the facts but a shield to cover our guilt, a way of concealing the truth from ourselves and misleading others.[67]

Jack Wilson, also a physician, and his wife fared no better in trying to find out what was wrong with their son. Tony was ill with schizophrenia from birth, but his parents did not succeed in getting a diagnosis from their various psychiatrists until he was nineteen. In an interview with Tony's latest psychiatrist, Dr. Brewster, Jack Wilson finally decided to insist on a diagnosis and a prognosis.

Dr. Brewster responded:

"Schizophrenia, if you want to label it. The boy is a paranoid schizophrenic."

Suddenly the world went still. *Schizophrenia, if you want a label.* Tony's dark blue eyes, his beautiful, rare smile. And the ugly contortions of rage. Most of all, his fear. Terror and fear. "It's a word, that's all, a word that covers a large, loose category." Dr. Brewster leaned back in his tilting chair and looked at a point on the wall behind us. "It's like saying 'tree.' There are all kinds, firs, elms, pines . . . . There's nothing I can tell you about the way Tony behaves that you don't already know." "I suppose not, except," Jack said, "the course of the sickness, how much better or worse it can get. Of course, I know you can't make any promises. I thought only that, statistically, there might be some indications . . . ."

Dr. Brewster shook his head. "There is so much shifting about on the part of any one patient that it defies prognosis . . . ."[68]

Dr. Brewster's performance is a far cry from that of the doctors at the leukemia conference, where the diagnosis is explained "without vagueness or equivocation." Bill and Jessie Foy had no better luck with their joint conference with a social worker and a psychiatrist:

The sum and substance of the meeting boiled down to the advice that we should work as a team for our son's benefit. What did they think we were trying to do already? There was no explicit information, suggestions—anything we could use to alleviate the child's vacillating emotional disorder. Talk about frustration! It was so thick I could have bitten it! This is how our meeting ended, with two apparently satisfied professionals, and two still-anxious parents.

On the way home, my husband had some comments to make about using the team approach to a problem. He had been a B-17 pilot during World War II . . . . His very life and the lives of others had depended on team work. Each man on the team knew what was expected of him. Each one did his part to insure success for all in the end.

"How can we help him if they don't tell us what ails him?" Bill complained. "I tell you, Jessie, this is the craziest team approach to his troubles I have ever had the misfortune to be involved in. If they can't trust us with the diagnosis, we've been eliminated from their team before the game has started!" He was utterly exasperated.[69]

Clara and David Park, bringing their autistic daughter Elly to a famous "Institute" for diagnosis, had multiple conferences, lasting ten days in all. Then a waiting period of a month and a half elapsed, and finally they were summoned back to the Institute to hear the results:

1. Elly needed psychotherapy.
2. She had performed above her age-level on the part of the I.Q. test she could do, and it was their belief that she had no mental deficiency.
3. "She has many fears."

Of course we asked questions. We had been told we could. But no question we could think of could get the psychiatrist to add anything to those statements. He did not say she was like any child he had seen before. He did not say she was unlike any child he had seen before. We had hoped he would speak from his vast experience of abnormal children, but when we asked about other children at the Institute he suggested, vaguely, that every child was different . . . . He would give the condition no name, suggest not even a possible range of prognoses. I asked if there was any reading I could do. Case histories? I had gotten some ideas from them already. Hesitant before, he was suddenly firm. Case histories would be bad for us. I tried again. I had been impressed by the nursery school. There were, perhaps, books on nursery-school techniques for disturbed children? "Disturbed children? It was hard . . .

very hard . . . in fact it was very hard even to bring up normal children," said the psychiatrist to the mother of four.

No concrete suggestions were made, since the Parks lived far from any place where Elly could possibly get the psychotherapy the institute claimed she needed. Then the interview ended:

We walked slowly down the steps of the homelike building that had turned out to be a model of Kafka's castle. We had come prepared for bad news; we had expected to leave shaken and upset and drive back immediately. Instead we could only laugh helplessly, and went and spent a lovely afternoon in a museum.* It was only gradually that we began to feel angry and resentful, to react as intelligent adults, not as obedient children in the hands of those wiser than we. Our powers of indignation reawakened—indignation at this pleasant, passive, blandly inconsiderate institution, at their incredibly casual scheduling, which multiplied difficulties and intensified anxiety, at the attractive, softly smiling social worker, whom the passage of time had made forget the number of my children, at the cloudy, gently evasive old man who would tell us nothing unless we surprised him into it. We fed information into that computer for ten days. And when we were finally allowed to press the button, the light didn't even go on.[70]

Interestingly, Mrs. Wilson also uses the word "bland": "They blur together in my mind. Bland men, bland as custard, the face behind the desk with a pad and flying pencil, a quiet manner and nothing to say." [71]

One doubts whether the hematologists at the leukemia conference were described by any parents as bland. Kind, yes, but tough and competent, as befits doctors dealing with grave illnesses.

The leukemia team made it clear that they were willing to discuss with the families "any press releases, alleged cures or unusual forms of therapy." How do psychiatrists handle such requests?

The Lorenzes learned about two new drugs, chlorpromazine and reserpine, in an article in the *American Journal of Psychiatry*. They told Ken's (their son's) doctor about it, but he was unimpressed:

---

* Elly's father adds: "A museum was a natural choice. An artist communicates with us, even over time, by being very careful and loving and honest, by revealing all he knows."

Yes, he'd heard of the drug and conceded it might be helpful, but it was new and not sufficiently tested and the hospital had not adopted it.

"What have we to lose?" we persisted. "Perhaps in conjunction with the psychotherapy he's getting he might respond to chlorpromazine . . . . It seems to be our last course, and we will take all responsibility. Won't you agree to an additional stay in order to experiment with this?"

As we spoke, the director was searching through the papers on his desk. He picked up a small booklet and held it up for us to see. "Sure, I know all about these drugs," he said, shaking the pamphlet for emphasis. Then, as if to underscore his answer, he flung it into the waste basket.[72]

The professionals conducting the leukemia conference found it wise to inquire whether there were other stresses in the family, including other illnesses. But when the Lorenzes hospitalized themselves and their teenage schizophrenic son in a famous research institute, they were not so fortunate. In order to participate in this research program (which they hoped would help their son), the father had to take a year's leave of absence from his job, their home had to be rented, and their younger son sent to stay with his aunt. All these moves created new problems, in addition to those created by Ken's illness. At the institute, Mrs. Lorenz's own medical problems were ignored to the point where it nearly cost her her life. Recovering from a severe hemorrhage, Mrs. Lorenz found herself bleeding again, but was afraid to insist that this was so, for fear that this, too, would be the subject of discussion in the "parent group." She says: "In any other setting I might have insisted, but here with every movement recorded, every word dissected, I kept my silence. I could not bear the thought of having so personal an experience slapped clinically into a meeting. There, nothing was sacred; the cold hand of research undressed you for everyone to regard and discuss."

Fortunately, the nurse discovered Mrs. Lorenz lying in a pool of blood, and applied medical rather than family interaction standards to the emergency.

In assessing the strengths and weaknesses of the family, how do psychiatric professionals measure up to the leukemic team in their ability to assess the state of the parents' marriage and their ability to function under stress? Mrs. Eberhardy,[73] the mother of an autistic child, went to a child guidance clinic, where she spoke to a psychiatric social worker: "How did I get along with my husband? Very well. She snapped to attention. 'Why?' she asked. 'Are you afraid to quarrel with him?' Well—we were both in our thirties. We had no serious problems and could laugh at our small differences. Years of separation by the war had made us treasure the ordinary joys of life."

Of the families in the leukemia study, half developed psychiatric problems, in spite of the exemplary behavior of the medical staff. How would these families have fared if instead of being carefully and fully informed and sensitively supported, they had been denied information and accused of causing the child's illness?* One can only wonder how much of the disturbance reported by those using a family interaction model has been generated by the model itself. Living with a schizophrenic or autistic child is surely disruptive of ordinary family life even if all the other members of the family are in perfect health and the behavior of the professionals to whom they turn is irreproachable. But if in addition to the illness itself, the family must cope with professional "help" that ranges from vague, obscure, and incompetent to mischievous, arrogant, and defamatory, it should not surprise us to find that these families are very troubled indeed.

One of the oddest aspects of the leukemia conference is that the services of a psychiatrist were employed, evidently to very good effect. Yet when psychiatrists come to dealing with psychiatric illnesses in children, they seem to forget all the good advice they have given to other doctors and to behave like blundering amateurs instead. It seems to be a case of the shoemaker's children going unshod.

We find it distressing that the family interaction view of child-hood psychosis reflects such a profoundly unbiological view of the family. Living in families has not been a conscious and voluntary choice for all these millennia; we can only suppose that it has been a biological necessity for the preservation of the species.

* We recommend, as an exercise, that our readers try to imagine the sequence of events which would occur if a leukemic child and his family were handled entirely within the rules of the family interaction model. We can guarantee that this will strengthen one's appreciation of the medical model.

The family will probably undergo great changes in the near future, as our relation to our biology and our environment changes, but for the families we have described here, the situation is much the same as it has ever been: sick children are a source of worry and guilt, and the families rally their resources, both within and without the family, to cope as best they can. As Clara Park put it:

Of all the types of success, the most widespread is successful parenthood; the species survives because this is so. It is also the most inconspicuous; it is precisely those millions of parents who successfully pilot their children through illness and crisis who never come to psychiatrists' attention. No one, professional or amateur, should underestimate the immense fund of goodness, knowledge, and resourcefulness possessed by ordinary parents.[74]

Continuous models provide a logical way of ordering psychiatric illnesses, which, combined with their capacity for generating righteous indignation, can be irresistibly seductive. By identifying schizophrenics in particular, and most mentally distressed people by extension, as social rather than medical victims, one can then berate various social and political institutions for these tragic conditions. The families of these patients then become vulnerable to censure, not only because abstract scapegoats are unsatisfactory, for by definition scapegoats should be real, visible, and immediate; but because few find their family of origin so ideal that it can be completely exonerated from having driven them mad, which is what most of these models imply. Since the families of schizophrenics often include more than one sick member, as is found in many other genetic illnesses, the home life of these patients is seldom tranquil and is sometimes chaotic.

Because they aim at nothing less than the recasting of society by reforming major institutions, these continuous models appear to have an impressive potential for good, which attracts adventurous and intelligent people to them. Discontinuous models by contrast are concerned with comparatively modest alleviations of sufferers from sickness, sin, or impairment. While it is true that most of these projected reforms, grand in their conception, remain incomplete, nevertheless according to the patchwork-quilt theory of social change all efforts in the right direction must be encouraged. It is not, however, always understood that should the goals of such massive social changes be mistaken or unattainable, then the greater the effort devoted to these changes, the greater the possibility of harming patients and their families. Some patients and their families have been destroyed or demoralized by the ruthless application of continuous models of schizophrenia. The more grandiose and far-reaching the plans for social change, the easier it is to ignore the damage done by such change, because this can be and frequently is charged against those immeasurable benefits accruing to those who will never become ill in the new and better dispensation. All social changes are accompanied by painful disruption for some people, yet theory-makers however enchanted by great projects should be responsible for assessing their theories, not only in terms of what they might achieve but also for the damage which might ensue.

Mental patients who were ousted from the impaired role found in many custodial hospitals and placed in the "psych" role of the psychoanalysts were transmuted with the best possible intentions. Hundreds of hours often spread over many years were devoted by benevolent psychotherapists attending to the utterances of patients. These sufferers would have otherwise been herded together in wards and dayrooms, or possibly engaged in unrewarded and unrewarding work. However, in spite of these good intentions, psychoanalysis has done little or nothing for schizophrenics, which was what Freud and his colleagues discovered two-thirds of a century ago. There is no convincing evidence that the misfortunes of early childhood play much part in causing schizophrenia. There have been grave doubts about this particular theory since the early twentieth century, and most of these doubts have been voiced openly not only by critics but by the progenitors of psychoanalysis. Yet those who use the psychoanalytic and its derivative continuous models today seem unaware that if, as now seems likely, their theory is erroneous, then they have engaged (unwittingly, no doubt) in cruel and slanderous practices harmful to patients and their families alike. This is a violation of that old and excellent medical precept, *nil nisi bonum*—nothing unless good.

A consensus is developing once again that schizophrenia is a genetic-biochemical illness, a view which has been held widely in various forms for centuries. Will it suffice to say to those parents and families who have been stigmatized during the last few decades with accusations of driving their children mad, and as a form of reparation or penance ruined financially, "We are sorry. We made a mistake"? Those who subscribe to continuous models of madness have a special responsibility to consider what will happen should they be mistaken. This same obligation holds for users of all models, but the discontinuous models are necessarily limited and their scope modest: the continuous models are far grander. Responsibility should surely be proportionate to the extent of the changes imposed by any model. Before employing any model, one must not only scrutinize the etiological theory which it uses, but while weighing the benefits which might derive from it, determine what harm it might do.

It is often claimed today that people are being wrongfully diagnosed (labeled) as ill who would be better off if categorized in some other way. While this sometimes happens, we believe that far more and far greater damage has been and is being done by ascribing schizophrenia to human malice, whether conscious or unconscious, individual or collective. This is an open incitement to witch-hunting, a deplorable human proclivity which erupts from time to time. H. R. Trevor-Roper [75] has noted that once any kind of witch-hunting craze begins, it feeds upon itself and may continue for decades or even centuries. Given certain social, political, or psychological conditions, we can be convinced only too readily that illness and misfortune are the result of spells or evil influences deriving from other people. This is an ancient, convenient, and highly plausible system of explanation. The price for accepting it is to live with witchcraft and black magic. Once a society is infected by the witch-hunting craze, neither intelligence nor morality is immune to its terrible corrosion. It is a universal solvent for decency, kindness, tolerance, humor, and open-mindedness. Only by unremitting vigilance can we avoid this atavism, which has done such harm through the years and even today.

4

The Medical Model

IN THIS BOOK WE HAVE PRESENTED the models in the order they were discovered: first, those used in psychiatry, and in these following chapters, those used within medicine. Since psychiatry itself is a branch of medicine, we might have discussed the medical model and its submodels first, but we decided not to do so for various reasons, the most important being that we ourselves did not become fully aware of the complexity of the medical model until we had explored the models of madness. When it is functioning properly, the medical model appears to be almost invisible because it lies outside awareness and, in spite of its great age, has been an object of scientific scrutiny for a relatively short time. It is only when it does not function properly that attention is drawn to it and often to the other models which it "spins off," like our models of madness. Under what conditions then does the medical model "go wrong?" When does it fail to be self-correcting?

It appears that medicine recognizes certain kinds of events as lying within its purview, and rejects others as being of no concern to it. The ethologists tell us of animals that recognize their own young only if they are a certain shape, have a particular smell, or make a special noise. According to Konrad Lorenz,[1] deaf turkey hens will peck their young to death, for they cannot hear their "cheeps," the only clue they have as to their identity. Similarly, medicine throws out of its nest those illnesses which are not the right "shape": crib death is too short; other illnesses, like tuberculosis and schizophrenia, are too long. Leukemia appears to be "just right": it lasts just long enough to evoke the best medical responses. Some illnesses, like Kanner's syndrome, have too few patients; it takes a special kind of mind to recognize a rare illness rather than misdiagnosing it as something more familiar. Other illnesses, such as the ague (malaria) of the Mississippi Valley in the nineteenth century, are so widespread that they are not seen as illnesses at all. An epidemic disease with a high mortality may be contained within clinical medicine provided those afflicted remain below a certain proportion of the population. When it appears that everyone might contract the disease, as in the case of the Black Death,[2] the clinical model can be suddenly superseded by the public health model, with its heavy legal sanctions and its lack of concern for the individual patient. Leprosy, an illness which fought long to get into the medical nest, is an example of a condition which is both contagious and long-lasting, evidently a bad combination. Some illnesses are too difficult to distinguish from common moral problems: diabetes from gluttony and alcoholism from drunkenness or immoderate drinking; while with venereal disease, it is clear that medicine and morality have often become inextricably muddled. As for etiology, there may be too few suspects, or too many.

Medicine acquires new illnesses slowly, suspiciously, and unwillingly, and it has been from those conditions which have not yet been incorporated within medicine that we learned about the limits of the medical model. Like the dog that didn't bark in the nighttime, in the Sherlock Holmes story, it is the illness that didn't get diagnosed, the relief from pain that wasn't offered, the physical examination that wasn't given, the blame that wasn't withheld, the suicide that wasn't prevented, the family that wasn't treated sympathetically that point to the dimensions of the medical model which would otherwise have escaped our notice. From these cases, we were able to piece together the medical model at its best, why it is important, and what the world would look like without it.

The medical model provides a way of organizing and conserving knowledge about disease and its treatment, and so enables us to save human lives. This undoubtedly has survival value for us as a species. But there is a social aspect to the medical model which is perhaps even more important for our survival: the medical model reduces the social disaster which would occur if all the illnesses of an individual or group were perceived as being due to someone's error or malice. If every time a political leader died, it was assumed to be an assassination and there was not even the possibility of natural death, political affairs and the government of nations would be much more unstable than they are now. If all illnesses were assumed to be caused by malicious intent, whether conscious or unconscious, family and community life would be unbearable. It is difficult for us to imagine the social conditions which would prevail if every illness were seen as an actionable wrong. Even in Samuel Butler's *Erewhon,* the only imaginative attempt which we know in which sick people do not get the sick role, we do not find a sufficiently vivid picture of the accusations and vendettas which would occur if illnesses were seen as intentional rather than as the result of natural causes.*

How does the medical model perform its two functions of treating the ill and ensuring that no one is blamed for illness? First, within the medical model some people are designated as "doctors" (or "witch doctors") and a special kind of authority is attributed to them, which T. T. Paterson has called "Aesculapian authority." [3] Second, this powerful authority is used to persuade certain people that they are "sick" and must submit to treatment and curtail their normal activities, and that neither they nor anyone else is to be blamed for their illness. In order for these two things to happen, the doctor's authority, however derived, must be stronger than any other existing authority—at least for that particular moment and in that particular context. And, as we shall see, it is. In the absence of this authority, few of us would submit to most medical treatments; we would be far too frightened to do so.

* In those cultures where the roles of priest, magician, and doctor have not been differentiated, the medical model runs tandem with the religious model, and some conditions which we would regard as illnesses are held to be the result, directly or indirectly, of human or supernatural malice. But although the scope of the medical model is smaller, or at least different, there is always a body of practical knowledge about treating illnesses and there is always a sick role. In the Western medical model, we behave "as if" diseases always had natural causes, and through religion or some other institution we express our private concerns about why illness has struck us.

Nor, in the absence of Aesculapian authority, would we be likely to suppress that natural tendency to blame ourselves or others for those many appalling misfortunes that attend serious illnesses. Far from considering doctors too "authoritarian" and wishing them to be more "friendly" and perhaps even more human, we should recognize that the medical model—that is, the use of Aesculapian authority to confer the sick role—is one of the greatest human achievements, by means of which we have created an attitude toward unavoidable misfortune in which our usual fears and moral judgments are temporarily suspended, much to our advantage.

From this definition of the medical model—Aesculapian authority used to confer the sick role—it follows that there are two kinds of aberration which may occur: Aesculapian authority may be used without the conferral of the sick role; the sick role may be adopted without the use of Aesculapian authority. Our seven nonmedical models of madness, when used by physicians, are instances of Aesculapian authority without the conferral of the sick role. Instead, a variety of other roles are conferred: the "psych" role, the impaired role, the "enlightened" role, the "bad" role, and so forth.

The other possibility is that a person may confer upon himself the sick role—he knows that he is ill and does not blame himself or anyone else—yet Aesculapian authority may be absent. There may be no doctor available or the illness may be too minor to ensure that one is found. If, however, the illness is serious and lengthy, the consequences of having no doctor may begin to show themselves. Without a doctor, who personifies Aesculapian authority, the self-styled patient does not have available such knowledge as there may be about the illness. Even when so little medical knowledge is available that this is not an issue, it seems to be difficult to sustain the sick role over any period of time without Aesculapian authority. Blame creeps back gradually into the picture when there is no doctor around to prevent this from happening.

A more sinister set of circumstances obtains when the sick role exists without the benefit of Aesculapian authority. This occurs if a patient in the sick role believes that his doctor is employing

Aesculapian authority but, in fact, the doctor is not proceeding according to the Hippocratic oath, and is using the patient as an experimental guinea pig without his understanding or consent. That is, the doctor employs the scientific medical model and not the clinical medical model. Another and equally sinister set of circumstances occurs when the patient in the sick role is being treated by a doctor who is acting according to the rules of public health medicine, not clinical medicine. It might, for instance, be salutary for a whole population to be inoculated for a given disease and yet lethal to a particular individual. Neither scientific medicine nor public health medicine involves the use of Aesculapian authority, as we shall show; yet both of these models employ people called "doctors."

This means that the clinical medical model works only under specifiable conditions, but those conditions have never yet been specified. In the sections that follow, we will discuss in some detail the two crucial elements of the medical model, Aesculapian authority and the sick role, and we shall use the knowledge gained to explore the two other medical models.

Aesculapian Authority [4]

The most important thing about Aesculapian authority is its power, and the oddest thing about it is our failure to notice this. In spite of our intermittent grumbling about doctors and their arbitrary ways, we meekly accept outrages from them that we would not tolerate for a moment in anyone else. Even Hitler, that very symbol of overweening authority, knuckled under just like anyone else when confronted with a display of Aesculapian authority. When Reinhard Heydrich ("Heydrich the Hangman"), the chief of the Security Service, deputy protector of Bohemia and Moravia, was shot, Dr. Karl Gebhardt was called in to treat him. Dr. Gebhardt reports:

In the extraordinary excitement and nervous tension which prevailed and was not diminished by daily personal telephone calls from Hitler and Himmler in person, asking for information, very many suggestions were naturally made . . . . I did not hesitate to take personal responsibility and state my own view, as to which I had no doubts . . . I consider that if anything endangers a patient it is nervous tension at the bedside and the appearance of too many doctors. I refused, in reply to direct demands, to call in any other doctor, not even Morell [Hitler's personal physician] or Sauerbruch. Heydrich died in fourteen days.[5]

Our Martian spy might be surprised that Dr. Gebhardt was not punished for his defiance or for his failure to keep Heydrich alive; but we are not surprised, for everyone knows that physicians may be as adamant as they like on behalf of their patients and that they are not called to account if the patient dies. What kind of authority is this that enables its holder to defy Hitler and Himmler with impunity?

Aesculapian authority was first named and defined by T. T. Paterson in 1957.[6] While investigating problems of hospital administration in Weyburn, Saskatchewan, using a theory of types of authority which he had already developed, Paterson found that none of his five kinds of authority described that of the doctor accurately. He defined the new authority as consisting of three of his types, sapiential, moral, and charismatic, combined in a particular manner; he called it "Aesculapian authority."

By sapiential authority, Paterson means the right to be heard by reason of knowledge or expertness. Such authority resides in the person and not in any position that he may occupy. A person possessing this kind of authority may advise, inform, instruct, and direct, but he may not order. Doctors possess sapiential authority because of their knowledge of the field of medicine. They must know, or appear to know, more about medicine than their parents. Doctors' so-called orders are really advice, for the doctor (as doctor) has no structural authority over the patient and cannot order him to do anything.

If the doctor's authority were only sapiential, then a well-established physiologist would certainly have more authority than a newly qualified doctor. But, in fact, when there is an illness, any doctor is preferable to any physiologist, which makes it clear that the doctor wields something more than sapiential authority.

The second ingredient of Aesculapian authority is moral authority, the right to control and direct by reason of the rightness and goodness according to the ethos of the enterprise. The doctor's moral authority, which is expressed in the Hippocratic oath, stems from the fact that he does what is expected of him as a doctor, and that he is concerned with the good of the patient. As Paterson puts it: "What the doctor is doing is socially right as well as individually good. This is an unbeatable combination. There is no other profession that matches this." [7]

The third ingredient of Aesculapian authority is charismatic authority, the right to control and direct by reason of God-given grace. This element in Aesculapian authority reflects the original unity of medicine and religion which still exists in many parts of the world. In Western culture, the charismatic element in medicine has to do with the possibility of death (which accounts for the seriousness of the enterprise) and with the impossibility of fully assessing the doctor's knowledge. There are too many unknown and unknowable factors in illness for medicine to rest entirely on sapiential authority. For this reason the doctor still retains some of his original priestly role.

The charismatic element in Aesculapian authority accounts for the fact that doctors are not expected to be entirely reasonable; in fact, they are to a certain extent rewarded for being arbitrary. The reason is not far to seek: life and death are arbitrary and so it is appropriate for doctors to have this quality. Extreme rationality and consistency would only raise doubts in the patient's mind, since he knows that medicine deals with powerful and mysterious forces that are not completely amenable to reason.

An example of this quality is to be found in the story of Dr. Schweninger's treatment of Chancellor Bismarck. [8] When Bismarck was sixty-eight, Schweninger was called in for a consultation, and soon confirmed the opinion of the other doctors that Bismarck had not long to live. According to one account:

. . . Schweninger at last imposed moderation on the genius who had imposed it on others, but never on himself. At their first meeting, Bismarck said roughly: "I don't like being asked questions." Schweninger replied: "Then get a vet. He doesn't question his patients." The battle was won in a single round. Bismarck ate and drank less, kept more regular hours. When Schweninger was present, he even kept his temper.

He underwent a slimming diet, which consisted exclusively of herrings . . . it did the trick. Bismarck's weight went down from eighteen to fourteen stone; he slept long and peacefully; his eyes became clear, his skin fresh and almost youthful.[9]

It is important to note that while the charismatic element in the story is evident, the other two ingredients of Aesculapian authority are not missing. Schweninger's regime did in fact work, demonstrating his sapiential authority; and Schweninger's high-handedness was not mere arbitrariness—he had moral authority because of his goal, which was to save Bismarck's life. Schweninger expressed this by saying that he would be responsible to no one but Bismarck himself.

How does a person come to be invested with Aesculapian authority, and what is its natural history? Most people are familiar with the way in which structural authority is conferred. The president, after being elected, takes the oath of office; the king is crowned. What ceremonies turn an ordinary citizen into a doctor? The first thing to be noted is that Aesculapian authority is conferred at an earlier age than most other kinds of authority, certainly than that of prime ministers, judges, senators, presidents, and generals. Occasionally a young doctor who completes his training must wait until his legal majority to be officially registered as a doctor. This early conferral makes it clear that the sapiential element is not all-important, for no one expects that a doctor in his early twenties will have accumulated much wisdom. Yet a twenty-one-year-old doctor is as much a doctor as an eighty-year-old one.

Aesculapian authority seems to be conferred gradually, rather than on a single ceremonious occasion. Toward the end of his medical training, the young doctor is placed more and more in clinical situations which begin to approximate those of a full-fledged doctor. In one medical school we observed that Aesculapian authority was first conferred ironically. Some of the teachers began to address the students as "doctor" in such a way that neither the nurses nor the patients were deceived by the hyperbole. The medical school joke, in which the cadaver of the dissecting room is named "Ernest" so that "we can work in dead Ernest" may also have the function of preparing the student for the day when he will indeed work in earnest.

More important, perhaps, is the gradual conferral of Aesculapian authority on the fledgling doctors by the patients, who gently correct the students' errors in their new role. A mature patient will have accumulated more experience in the role relations involved than a young and healthy doctor.

The conferral of Aesculapian authority is gradual in other ways as well. At one point the student passes his last examinations; at another point he graduates and takes the Hippocratic oath. Then, at least in the United States, he takes other examinations in order to become licensed, sometimes a year or so after he has graduated. At still other points he has a shingle made, opens an office, fills out his first death certificate, and so forth. He becomes more and more a doctor as he passes each of these milestones. The ceremonies involved are unimpressive compared with the investitures and coronations which mark other such transitions. Interestingly enough, many people appear to be uncertain at what point a doctor-in-training becomes a "real" doctor.

Once Aesculapian authority has been conferred, the doctor can take up his main function, the conferral of the sick role, which only someone with Aesculapian authority has the right to do. The first step in this process is to determine whether or not a potential patient is sick. If the answer is affirmative, the doctor then uses his authority to exert pressure on the person to accept the fact that he is sick. The patient often resists, because illness brings with it the fear of death or disablement, the miseries of medical treatment, the loss of personal privacy, the expenditure of money, and other undesirable consequences. Far less often does the doctor have to use his authority to convince a well person that he is not sick.

Once the patient accepts the fact that he is sick, the doctor, usually by implication, absolves the patient and his family from blame for the illness. If he fails to do this, as so often happens in psychiatry, he may find that he cannot gain the cooperation of the patient and his family, which is essential to the medical enterprise. He then lays upon the patient the heavy duties of the sick role, which consist mostly of things he would not otherwise do, of allowing people to do things to him he would normally resist, and of refraining from many normal or even instinctual activities.

The doctor now uses his Aesculapian authority to exempt the patient from such of his normal responsibilities as are disallowed by his particular illness. Without the doctor's authority, the patient might be unable to restrict his activities for fear of appearing irresponsible; the sick role enables the patient to occupy a different, but morally acceptable, social role until he can take up his usual role once again. The doctor's authority must carry more weight than all the other authorities to which the patient is subject or the doctor cannot perform his function of restricting the patient's activities for the sake of his health.

An example of this is provided by the following incident from World War II.

On August 1st [1942] a thick-set Soviet general was arguing with his doctor in a room of a hospital in Moscow, where he was recovering from a leg injury, his second serious wound of the war. He was attempting to persuade the doctor that he was fit to return to duty, and after some acrimonious discussion about the rights of patients versus doctors in deciding when a man was fit to leave, the irate doctor had subjected him to a practical test of his ability to walk without his stick. Half a dozen steps brought out a cold sweat on his forehead, and his leg went numb. "Enough, enough," cried the doctor triumphantly. "Now it is clear, esteemed Colonel-General, who is mistaken about the moment of recovery. There's still fundamental healing to be done." Sheepishly the general confessed that he had already reported himself to Stavka as ready to return to the front. "So much the worse for you," said the doctor. "Without a note from the doctor in charge they won't even look at your report." Bluff having failed, the general resorted to an emotional appeal. "Tell me, Professor, hand on heart, if you were suffering from an illness like mine, in its present stage, could you sit calmly on one side, knowing that hundreds of people were dying from wounds and waiting for your help, yours, Professor, no one else's?" The Professor thought about this, but gave no direct answer. In the end he said, "All right, then, if you give me your word of honor to follow strictly the regimen I prescribe, I won't object to your discharge." [10]

Thus General Yeremenko, one of the victors of Stalingrad, gained his doctor's permission to end his stay at the hospital and take up his duties once again.

When the doctor takes the step of prescribing treatment on the basis of the diagnosis, he is employing the sapiential part of his authority, but that alone would not be sufficient to ensure that the patient would accept the treatment. For medical treatments, if they are not sanctioned by Aesculapian authority, might be and have been mistaken for torture. Both Charles II of England and Louis XIV of France said as much. The same procedures not done by medical men would be perceived as dangerous and horrible assaults. Much of the history of torture can be more or less faithfully reproduced in the history of medicine. If the doctor believes that the patient's life is at stake, he has permission to do almost anything he thinks fit that the society will tolerate and the patient accept. In practice this means and has often meant pain, mutilation, and even unnecessary death for the patient. With a few exceptions, almost everything that can be done has been done in the hope of saving life.

The patient's drive to survive is one of the principal levers which the doctor uses to enforce the acceptance of medical treatment. The doctor's charisma derives to a great extent from the possibility of death and the patient's willingness to pit himself against it. On one occasion, when Sir Winston Churchill had pneumonia, his doctor, Lord Moran, called in Dr. Geoffrey Marshall as a consultant. Lord Moran writes:

While his mind was busy conjuring up possible complications of his illness, Marshall, a genial but offhand physician, told him that he called pneumonia "the old man's friend." "Pray explain," said Winston. "Oh, because it takes them off so quickly," Marshall answered unabashed. He was soon established high in the P.M.'s favour.[11]

In this case Dr. Marshall's willingness to use Churchill's drive for survival to control his patient enhanced his Aesculapian authority.

Eventually all patients leave the sick role in one way or another.

Ideally they recover, and then the doctor must use his authority to ensure a smooth transition back to normalcy. The doctor must inform the patient when he is well, for it may not always be obvious. If the patient shows some reluctance to depart from the sick role, the doctor must pronounce him cured, sometimes in no uncertain terms.

Some patients leave the sick role by dying, which is perfectly satisfactory from a medical point of view so long as the doctor can say that everything that can be done has been done. But to die of an illness without benefit of the sick role is to incur grave medical displeasure. In the United States this constitutes a medical examiner's case, and at the autopsy the sick role is conferred retrospectively. In Molière's play *The Physician in Spite of Himself,* the sick girl's father says that he should be heartbroken if she should die. Sganarelle, the medical impostor, retorts: "She'd better not! She can't die without a doctor's prescription."

In some illnesses, such as polio, the patient may leave the sick role but still not be able to reenter his old social role because of permanent impairment. The doctor's role ends when the illness ends, for Aesculapian authority does not cover the state of impairment. Since there is no further hope of improvement, treatment is not warranted; and there is no fear of death from the impairment, consequently the drive to survive which is so central to Aesculapian authority is absent.

Aesculapian authority is conferred early in the doctor's life and it usually lasts until he dies. This may be as long as seventy years. A ninety-year-old doctor may be too feeble to see patients, but he still has Aesculapian authority and will be treated accordingly. No other authority is so handy, so effective, so permanent, and so lacking in danger to the holder. Society is most indulgent to those who employ Aesculapian authority well; their little foibles are quickly and readily forgiven, whether these are religious (Christian and Jewish doctors, although infidels, were appreciated by the Moslems), political (Hitler had no hesitation in getting advice from non-Aryan doctors), or personal (Dr. Palmer the Poisoner had a successful practice, even though there were rumors abroad about his murderous, drunken, gambling, and lecherous ways). Doctors do not need social charms or graces, they need not be witty or wise, they do not even have to be very rich, competent, or experienced, but they must give their patients the sick role and they must show real determination to preserve them from death. That the struggle may be badly planned, ill conducted, and end fatally is of less importance than that it should not only occur but be seen to occur.

Another important aspect of Aesculapian authority is the relation that it creates between doctor and doctor. The doctor's Aesculapian authority is enhanced if he sustains other doctors in their role. It is true that one doctor might gain a temporary advantage in enlarging his own merits at the expense of other doctors, but in the long run the charismatic component of Aesculapian authority demands that doctors close ranks. In Molière's play *The Hypochondriak*, Dr. Diaforus's opinion of the patient, Argan, differs in every respect from that of the previous doctor, Purgon. But he cleverly covers up the differences:

DR. DIAFORUS: He orders you, doubtless, to eat roast meat.
ARGAN: No, nothing but boiled.
DR. DIAFORUS: Ay, yes, roast, boiled, the same thing. He orders you very prudently and you can't be in better hands.

So Dr. Diaforus simultaneously enhances his own Aesculapian authority and that of Dr. Purgon, who will no doubt return the favor.

The realization that Aesculapian authority is enhanced if doctors agree to support each other has now been incorporated into most of medicine and most medical specialties, with the notable exception of psychiatry. As Richard Hunter and Ida Macalpine put it:

How far psychiatry is still behind medicine is shown not only by the survival of therapeutic principles long since discarded from the parent science, as for instance treatment by shock, but also by the persistence of schools of psychiatry, not to mention psychology or psychotherapy, the like of which vanished from the medical scene one hundred years ago with the scientific developments of the nineteenth century.[12]

Psychiatrists of different "schools" compete with each other, each claiming to have more Aesculapian authority than the other and not noticing that they are in this way damaging psychiatry as a whole. Doctors in most branches of medicine today are, to a certain extent, interchangeable parts, and patients who move from one part of the country to another typically find "another doctor" to replace the one they have left. But psychiatric patients sometimes decline to make geographical moves that might otherwise be advantageous because they do not believe that their psychiatrist can be replaced. In one instance that we know of, the death of a psychiatrist was followed by the suicides of a number of his patients, who evidently did not believe that their illnesses could be treated by any other psychiatrist and so lost hope.

If doctors can defy *Führers* and send generals, prime ministers, kings, popes, and presidents to bed, then why don't they rule the world? The answer is that although they can at times overrule any other authority, there are, happily, some limitations to the privileges which they enjoy. Aesculapian authority must be used in relation to a particular sick person who believes himself to be the patient of that doctor. Lord Moran had no right to send the prime minister to bed, but he did have the right to send to bed his patient, Mr. Churchill, who happened also to be the prime minister.

Another way to look at the limitations of Aesculapian authority is to ask what our Martian spy would have to do or avoid doing in order to be a medical impostor. He would have to display sapiential authority about medicine, demonstrating that he knew more about an illness than the patient or his family. He would have to persuade both patient and family that he was doing what was right as a doctor and that he was acting in the best interests of the patient. And he would have to display just enough eccentricity and arbitrariness to show that he was in touch with powers greater than mere reason and technical competence. These are exactly the moves made by Sganarelle, the impostor in Molière's play *The Physician in Spite of Himself*. No one doubts for a moment that Sganarelle is a real doctor, but when he attempts to use his Aesculapian authority to gain access to the breasts of the beautiful wet-nurse, Jacqueline, he is unsuccessful, for she never agreed to become his patient. She declares that it is not "right" that he should examine her breasts.

Dr. Gebhardt, as quoted in our first example, appeared to understand perfectly just what his Aesculapian authority would allow him to do on behalf of his patient, Heydrich. But his efforts to extend this authority to a group of people who were not his patients—concentration camp prisoners—and to perform experiments on them which were not for their benefit led to his trial at Nuremberg and his eventual execution. Doctors make many mistakes (it is said that they bury their mistakes) for which they are forgiven, but they are not forgiven the sin of using Aesculapian authority for some purpose other than that for which it was intended: the benefit of a particular patient.

The Sick Role [13]

The sick role shares with Aesculapian authority both potency and invisibility. It is even more difficult to study, for when we are well we are not interested in studying it and when we are ill we are too preoccupied with our own misery to study it. Talcott Parsons somehow avoided this particular dilemma and to him we are indebted for naming and describing this valuable sociological entity.[14]

Parsons describes four essential aspects of the sick role, sometimes called "Parsons's postulates." First, depending on the nature and severity of the illness, the sick person is exempted from some or all of his normal social responsibilities. Second, the sick person cannot help being ill and cannot get well by an act of decision or will. Third, the sick person is expected to want to get well as soon as possible. Fourth, he is expected to seek appropriate help, usually that of a physician, and cooperate with that help toward the end of getting well.

There seem to be no cultures which have not developed the sick role,* and there is anecdotal evidence that a prototypic

---

* We know of only one culture which does not have the sick role, although they did have it in the recent past, the Ik of northeast Uganda (Colin Turnbull,

form of it occurs in some animal societies, although without the corresponding "doctor" role. According to Lilly,[15] a sick or injured dolphin will emit a distress call which will bring other dolphins to his aid. There are many instances of the rescuing dolphins pushing the sick dolphin to the surface so that he can breathe.

Elephants, too, appear to protect and care for ill or injured members of their group. Jean-Pierre Hallet reports on a trunkless elephant whose trail he followed in Uganda:

> . . . I watched the trunkless elephant stand idly while the herd tore at the trees, gathering twigs and leaves, None of them ate so much as a single leaf but moved instead toward their handicapped companion, bearing bundles of food, as they must have done for several years. He opened his mouth expectantly. Eager to feed him first, two of the elephants jostled each other. The rest waited their turns patiently. In all, they brought their trunkless welfare case so much food that he hardly had time to chew it; he gulped furiously for a while, then closed his mouth tight and shook his head from side to side, rejecting any more leafy bundles. Only then did the other elephants move away and at last start to feed themselves.[16]

Archeological evidence suggests that in human societies, too,

---

The Mountain People [New York: Simon and Schuster, 1972]). The Ik are a disintegrating culture in the process of losing not only the sick role but the family and religion as well. Instead of caring for the sick, the Ik now steal food from those too weak to defend themselves. When Turnbull found that his chief informant was begging food from him for a supposedly sick wife who was in fact already dead, he was so revolted by this misuse of the sick role that he wanted to leave the field at once and would have done so except that the road down the mountain was blocked. Turnbull, a seasoned field anthropologist, was ready for all kinds of unusual and even repugnant behavior among the people whom he studied. Nevertheless, he was so distressed by what he found in the Ik that at first he refused to believe what he saw. When he was unable to deny his own observations, his intention was to leave at once because he felt the Ik were devoid of humanity and so by definition hardly suitable for study by an anthropologist. According to his narrative it was not his professionalism which saved him from demoralized flight but mere accident. For a well-trained and experienced scientist, his intention was analogous to a general deserting on the battlefield. That he reported his failure of nerve is a high tribute to his integrity as a scientist, but admiration for courage may obscure something of even greater significance. Gross exploitation of the sick role for personal gain was perceived by him as a violation and negation of essential universal humanity. That Turnbull found this so aberrant underscores the importance of the sick role in human affairs.

injured and incapacitated individuals were cared for by others and thus survived when they could not have cared for themselves.[17] This valuable social role is evidently both very old and universal; but human children are not born knowing it, so it must be taught and learned. Yet how this early instruction occurs is very obscure; so far as we can make out, there are few if any studies regarding the acquisition of the sick role in the young. A printout from the National Clearinghouse for Mental Health Information using the key words "sick role" and "children" yielded only three articles, none of them bearing on our concern here. One can find articles on the psychological impact of illness on children, but these deal with the "psych" role and not the sick role. In an early paper by Anna Freud [18] on this topic, it is explicitly denied that the child distinguishes between being ill and being in the sick role:

The child is unable to distinguish between feelings of suffering caused by the disease inside the body and suffering imposed on him from outside for the sake of curing the disease. He has to submit uncomprehendingly, helplessly and passively to both sets of experiences.

Yet later on she says:

It is the psychological meaning of pain which explains why doctors, and other inflictors of pain, are not merely feared but in many cases highly regarded and loved by the child. The infliction of pain calls forth passive masochistic responses which hold an important place in the child's love life. Frequently the devotion of the child to doctor or nurse becomes very marked on the days after the distress caused by a painful medical procedure has been experienced.

Miss Freud implies that it makes no difference to a child whether the person inflicting pain is a doctor who is known to be doing it in the sick child's interests, or some "other inflictor of pain," say, a neighborhood sadist. We can hardly imagine this to be true.

Owing to the dearth of relevant literature, we must fall back upon personal observations. Here is a report from our files regarding a small child receiving the sick role for the first time:

Our eldest daughter received her first lesson in this role when she was only about one year old. She was a tiny ebullient red-head, who was very lively and active. However, one morning instead of leaping around in her pen in the usual way, she lay down flushed and inert. Noticing this, my wife became very worried, and I was not unconcerned myself. We examined the quiet, sweating child with solemnity and apprehension. Suddenly she began to sneeze, and we decided that she must have a chill. By the evening, she was suffering with a running nose, and coughing a little, but clearly feeling much better, for she was no longer keen to lie inert in her mother's arms, but wanted to be scrambling around and playing. By the next morning, she was ready to abandon the sick role, but discovered that she couldn't do this until we had decided that she was indeed better.

This was her first lesson in acquiring the sick role, which had been given before she could speak more than a few words and when she had only just learned how to walk. After this, she was very skilled in the sick role but much later discovered that it was wrong to feign illness to avoid unpleasant school work. She tried this once or twice, but it was impressed upon her that this was immoral.

We have observed a two-year-old-child who not only announced that she was sick when she was, but also quickly grasped the advantages of malingering. Lying on the floor one evening, she was obviously very tired but did not want to admit it. When her older sister asked if she was ready to go to bed, she said, "No, I sick," while rolling her eyes seductively around as she tried to gain our sympathetic attention. She evidently believed that the sick role had more dramatic potential than merely being an overtired two-year-old.

One way of teaching children the sick role is through the books they read. An example is to be found in one of a series of popular books for small children about Babar the Elephant.[19] Pom, the baby elephant, tells his father, Babar, that his stomach hurts. Celeste, his mother, calls the doctor:

"My child," says the doctor, "you have eaten too much lobster. That's all there is to it." Pom has to take bad-tasting medicine, and he grumbles a little. But he wants to get well, so he does what he is told.

One of the most striking features of the "improving" Victorian literature for children was its preoccupation with serious illness and death, subjects which rarely appear in children's books today. A counting rhyme goes:

> Mother, mother, I feel sick,
> Send for the doctor, quick, quick, quick.
> Doctor, doctor, shall I die?
> Yes, my dear, and so shall I.
> How many carriages shall I have?
> One, two, three, four, . . .[20]

In a story called "Don't You Cry for Me, Kitty,"[21] the "kind doctor" tells a boy named Jamie that he is going to die. When he asks how soon, the doctor says: "Not for a little while. I think you may yet live some weeks, perhaps even longer. But you will never be strong and well again, I am afraid, little Jamie."

Such stories are clearly functional in a society in which the death of children from illness is a frequent occurrence. By contrast, a recent book called *My Friend the Doctor*,[22] written in cooperation with the Menninger Clinic, deals only with trivial illnesses and could not be used with a child who was seriously ill. There is no discussion whatever of the possibility of death in this book of instruction for modern children, or even any suggestion that the child might be ill for any length of time or experience great pain. This is in marked contrast to the vivid descriptions of grave illness in the Victorian children's books, whose function was exactly similar—to prepare children to meet life, sickness, and death.

Although the sick role is an old and universal property of the human species, its acquisition in any individual case may be uncertain and is often fraught with difficulties. Ideally, every sick person should be offered and should accept the sick role, relinquishing it gracefully when well, and no well person should occupy the sick role. But there are many variables in the situation of illness which make this perfect fit elusive. It makes a great deal of difference whether or not the illness in question is safely within the medical model, for different illnesses command the sick role to a different extent, as we have shown with leukemia and schizophrenia. The history of the individual is important too, for some people learn the sick role properly in childhood and others do not. Some people are skillful in communicating that they are ill and in need of medical and nursing care, while others are clumsy or reticent about this, usually to their own detriment. It often matters whether one's family is sensitive and knowledgeable about the sick role, for one may be too ill to take action oneself. Doctors vary, too, in their ability to recognize illnesses in the early stages and in their expertise in conferring the sick role. One's status and social class may also have a bearing; some people are not recognized as being ill because their status is too low, others because it is too high. If one has a job which provides "sick leave," it may be easier to get the sick role than if one is a mother of small children at home. We might say that the sick role "works" for the species as a whole, and to a greater or lesser extent for each human society, but whether it benefits a particular individual or not is much more problematic.

Some people, for reasons of temperament perhaps, or of personal history, have difficulty accepting the sick role at all. Here is an extreme case:

A physician, in middle age, sustained an acute coronary heart attack. His professional colleagues, who diagnosed his illness, advised immediate and absolute bed rest, quiet, and heavy sedation, all of which the patient stoutly refused on the grounds of his heavy schedule of work with his own patients. He persisted in his medical work and died suddenly in his office twenty hours later.[23]

Although few people reject the sick role so completely, many cannot make peace with their altered status. One class of people for whom the sick role is particularly onerous consists of those for whom life is primarily verbal rather than physical. Such individuals ignore their own bodily processes as much as possible, and sometimes develop a style of locomotion which implies that if they were only able to move quickly enough, they would be able to abandon their bodies altogether. An example is to be found in Herr Settembrini, one of the characters in Thomas Mann's great novel of the sick role, *The Magic Mountain*. Settembrini, an Italian humanist, is one of the patients encountered by the hero, Hans Castorp, at the International Sanitorium Berghof. Settembrini regards disease as a degradation and sees no possibility of dignity in the sick role. When Hans first meets him, Settembrini pours out a stream of malicious gossip and slander about doctors and patients of the Berghof. He tells Hans that he must not suppose that the rooms are unheated for medical purposes; it is only to save the management money. Settembrini reserves his greatest contempt for the other patients, who use the excuse of their illness to indulge in a life of idleness and flirtation. He tells Hans:

"I would urge it upon you: hold yourself upright, preserve your self-respect, do not give ground to the unknown. Flee from this sink of iniquity, this island of Circe, whereon you are not Odysseus enough to dwell in safety. You will be going on all fours—already you are inclining toward your forward extremities, and presently you will begin to grunt—have a care."

Hans and his cousin Joachim, who are trying each in his own way to be good patients, find Settembrini's mocking attitude seditious and distasteful. It makes them uneasy to talk with someone who is so lacking in medical piety. But, on one occasion, Settembrini goes too far and is revealed as a crypto-patient. He sets out to reduce their faith in the accuracy of the X-rays. Are they aware, he wants to know, that some patients have no spots on their X-ray plates, but die of tuberculosis anyway? And with others, who have spots on their plates, it is found at the autopsy that they really had some other disease. Hans says:

"Can you see spots on your plate, Herr Settembrini?"
"Yes, it shows some spots."
"And you really are ill too?"
"Yes, I am unfortunately rather ill," replied Settembrini, and his head drooped. There was a pause, in which he gave a little cough. Hans Castorp, from his bed, regarded his guest, whom he had reduced to silence. It seemed to him that with his two simple inquiries he had refuted Settembrini's whole position, even the republic and the *bello stile*.

Settembrini is the Coriolanus of the sick role, the Roman general who refused to show his battle wounds to the populace, although that was the time-honored way of establishing his right to rule them. Settembrini refuses to give the others visible evidence that he is a tuberculosis patient like themselves, although there could be no other explanation for his residence at the Berghof.

In both cases, the reason is the same: the unwillingness to give the body its due. But Settembrini, for all his mocking, is no fool; he occupies the sick role no less than the others, for he knows that his life is at stake, and his beautiful philosophy must be housed, however unwillingly, in a fragile and mortal human body.

It is one of the privileges of the sick role to be exempted to varying degrees from one's normal social responsibilities. But this is conditional on taking up the responsibilities inherent in the sick role: trying to get well, seeking help, accepting treatment, and so forth. In many illnesses, the duties of the sick role are sufficiently dreadful that no one is likely to prefer them to those of his normal life. But in some slowly developing illnesses, such as tuberculosis, it is possible to claim the privileges of the sick role without being overtaxed by one's duties as a patient. If the space-time released by the abandonment of one's usual duties is not entirely taken up by the duties of the sick role, a moral vacuum occurs. The person may now be both "sick" and "bad."

We see this possibility illustrated in Frau Chauchat, a resident at the Berghof. Frau Chauchat slams doors, comes late to meals, bites her fingernails, rolls her bread into little pellets and gazes at the male patients in a direct and shameless way. The patients at the Berghof are fascinated by her because she does what many would like to do but dare not: she openly uses her illness as an excuse for badness. In fact, her sickness and badness are so thoroughly intertwined that her occupancy of the sick role becomes a disputed issue among the other patients:

If she was ill—and that she was, probably incurably, since she had been up here so often and so long—her illness was in good part, if not entirely, a moral one: as Settembrini had said, neither the ground nor the consequence of her "slackness," but precisely one and the same thing.

Because of this possible abuse of the sick role, most people are reluctant to grant it to another if there is any suspicion that it may be used in this way. Fred Davis,[24] in his study of polio victims, found three families in which the parents suspected their children of malingering. However, they soon abandoned this hypothesis when their children became rapidly sicker; and while no one wishes to give the sick role to someone who is "bad," it is even worse to give the "bad" role to someone who is sick. Any real or supposed failure to recognize that a child is seriously ill is almost certain to make the parents guilty. It is not just that treatment may be delayed, although this can occur, but rather that our expectations of other people's moral responsibility hinges on their being capable of doing the "right" thing. A sick person may not be unwilling, but unable, to do what is expected of him. It is significant that in our most protective and ethically sensitive relationship, that toward children, we incur the greatest guilt if we do not confer the sick role as soon as it is needed. To deny a sick child the sick role is a particularly inhumane act.

In some illnesses there is a tendency for the ill person to oscillate between the sick role and the "psych" role. Today schizophrenia is such an illness; in the nineteenth century tuberculosis was similarly ambiguous. One of the treatments offered for tuberculosis at the Berghof was psychoanalysis, for, as Dr. Krokowski put it: "Symptoms of disease are nothing but a disguised manifestation of the power of love: and all disease is only love transformed." Our example here is provided by the fatal illness of the poet John Keats.[25] Sometime during the year 1818, Keats came to believe that he had only a thousand days—three years—to live. At the end of this year he nursed his younger brother, Tom, through the final stages of tuberculosis. Judging from the regimen he then adopted, it now seems clear that he believed that he might be developing the illness himself. A few months later, Keats coughed up blood for the first time. Seeing that it was arterial blood, he knew from his medical training as well as his personal experience with the illness that he was fatally ill. Having confirmed for himself his worst doubts and fears, Keats then had a short period of serenity. He was for the moment safely esconced in the sick role. "How astonishingly does the chance of leaving the world impress a sense of its natural beauties on us," he wrote to a friend.

Soon, however, he became worse and a specialist was called in. After examining Keats, he said that there was "no pulmonary affection and no organic defect whatever." He told Keats that his illness was "all on his mind" and recommended fresh air and exercise. Keats was now evicted from the sick role and soon began to share his doctor's view that it was "all on his mind." He began to hate the reviewers who had been unfavorable to his poems and who had ruined his chance of success. Deprived of the blame-free sick role, he cast about for some other explanation for his illness.

When Keats's health began to deteriorate further, his friends decided to send him to Italy, a standard course of action for English consumptives. His physician in Rome, Dr. James Clark, also believed that the cause of his illness was "mental exertion"; his prescription was fresh air, moderate exercise, and avoidance of worry. Keats was bitter and lonely in Rome, feeling that the voyage had been to no purpose and that he was cut off forever from his betrothed, Fanny Brawne. Finally he gave up both the thought and the hope of recovery, and this gave him a brief period of peace. Keats died in February 1821. The autopsy showed that his lungs were entirely destroyed. Then began a series of disgraceful quarrels among those who had loved him, each accusing the other of having caused his death. Charles Brown wrote Joseph Severn that Keats's brother George (who was in America!) would have to answer for Keats's death. The poet Shelley believed that Keats's final hemorrhage had been brought on by an unfavorable article in the *Quarterly*. Fanny Brawne, Keats's beloved, was not spared in this free-for-all; it was said that Keats had been killed by her cruelty and that she was not fit to have become his wife.

Describing this series of events in terms of the sick role, it falls into four stages. First, Keats was relieved when the doubts and fears which had been gnawing at him were swept away by the certainty that he had tuberculosis and he had a period of calm, although he now knew that he had a fatal illness. Second, his physician's insistence that it was "all on his mind" sabotaged his occupancy of the sick role and caused him to look for the source of his illness in his personal relationships. Third, when he knew that he was ill beyond any hope of recovery, he reentered the sick role and put aside his preoccupations with the state of his relationships. Fourth, after his death he was retroactively removed from the sick role by his friends, who took to quarreling among themselves as to which of them was to blame for his death. Even if nothing further could have been done for him medically, the firm insistence that the illness was due to natural causes rather than inadequacy and malice could have prevented enormous suffering, both on the part of Keats himself and later on the part of his friends and relatives. Unfortunately, tuberculosis was not at that point sufficiently well organized as an illness to command the sick role for its sufferers in an unequivocal way. Today it would be unthinkable for the friends and relatives of someone who had died of tuberculosis to behave in this fashion.

It is interesting to contrast the reaction of Keats's friends to his death with the reactions produced by the death of seventeen-year-old Johnny Gunther, son of the writer, who died of a brain tumor after an illness of fifteen months.[26] Letters poured in to the Gunthers, describing Johnny as a gallant and heroic soul. Dr. Wilder Penfield, the famous neurosurgeon, who had been a consultant on Johnny's case, wrote to his parents: "You two, by your restless effort, kept him alive a year longer than should be expected. You could have done no more. It was worth while."

The sick role requires of its occupants that they try to get well as soon as possible and that, to this end, they cooperate with whatever treatment has been prescribed for them. In other words, they must be "good" patients. But unfortunately there is no guarantee that one will be rewarded for this goodness by improving health. Yet the patient who has a serious illness is sorely tempted to make this equation, for being a good patient may be the only thing that he can do to exert control over his situation. John Gunther describes this response in his son, Johnny:

Hoping with such vehemence to recover, yearning with such desperation to be all right again, refusing stalwartly to admit that his left hand, too, was showing a little weakness now, he became heartbreakingly dutiful about everything the doctors asked. He was still limited as to fluids; drop by drop, he would measure the exact amount of water he was permitted. All he wanted was to obey, to obey, and so get back to school.[27]

Joachim, Hans Castorp's cousin, is another obedient patient. At first he is very reluctant to take up the sick role because he is eager to begin his career as an army officer. But, having agreed to stay at the Berghof until he is pronounced cured, he tries to be an exemplary patient. He absorbs much technical information about his illness and impresses his cousin with his knowledge. He carefully obeys all the rules of the treatment regimen and refrains from using his position in the sick role for other purposes. Unlike the other patients, who use their enforced idleness to indulge in endless flirtations, Joachim devotes himself entirely to getting well. He appears to be the ideal occupant of the sick role, but Dr. Behrens, with his experienced eye for these things, recognizes that this is not so, and tells Joachim that he has no talent for being sick. Behrens proves to be correct, for Joachim cannot tolerate the unpredictable fluctuations in his illness; he is implicitly expecting to be "promoted" step by step, as he would in the army. Joachim finally leaves against medical advice, tastes his new career briefly, and then gets sicker and returns to the Berghof to die. At the end, when it is courage that is required, rather than submission to the fickleness of the illness, Joachim comes through with flying colors; he dies like a soldier.

In contrast to those patients who believe that by being "good" they will be rewarded with rapid recovery, there are other patients who come to abandon the idea of recovery altogether. They are willing to give up their normal responsibilities, they do not blame themselves or others for the illness, and they cooperate with the treatment; their difficulty is with the third requirement of the sick role, the duty to try to get well as quickly as possible. Instead they settle permanently into their illnesses, as most of the patients at the Berghof did. It would be a mistake to see these patients as wanting to stay in the sick role; rather, they have abandoned the sick role for the impaired role. In general, the impaired role has a lower status than the sick role, but life at the Berghof is so luxurious for these wealthy patients that they do not care. It is true that no one takes them seriously, and their life is ordered for them by the resident physicians, but in return for this childlike status, they are allowed to spend their days as children do, playing card games, taking up hobbies, having meals served to them, "playing" with each other, or, most often, doing nothing at all. In order to enjoy this particular variant of the impaired role, one must have a docile temperament, a great deal of money,* and an illness, like tuberculosis in its early stages, which lends itself to such a life.

In the sick role, the patient has the duty to cooperate with the treatment insofar as possible. In many illnesses this is not much of a problem, either because the illness lasts only a short time, or because the nature of the treatment is such that not much is required of the patient. But in some illnesses which last a long time and have a complicated regimen, the patient must know a great deal about the illness in order to cooperate. Betty MacDonald [28] noted the lack of cooperation among the patients at The Pines, the tuberculosis sanitorium where she spent a year, and attributed it to the patients' ignorance of the illness. Some information of a general kind was gradually forthcoming in the form of printed lessons. But the critical information for maintaining the sick role is the progress of the patient's own illness, and this was completely lacking. Mrs. MacDonald says: "Of this progress we were told nothing. The only way we could tell if we were getting well or dying was by the privileges we were granted."

In the tuberculosis sanitoria described by J. A. Roth, a sociologist who himself contracted tuberculosis, all the patients were preoccupied with the system of privileges that prevailed in their particular hospital. When the hospital did not provide such a system, the patients noticed the regularities themselves, and then if they did not get the privileges at what they believed to be the proper times, they felt that they had been cheated. Roth says:

Physicians are frequently annoyed because patients are always thinking in terms of the class they are in or the privileges they have rather than about the improvement that has taken place in their lungs. . . . The patients are interested in recognizable steps toward discharge such as are provided in a classification system or in an ordered series of privileges. The physician with experience in reading X-rays and in interpreting other diagnostic indices can also keep in mind a rough series of steps toward discharge and thus provide himself with another basis for

---

* Or, in the absence of a private income, privileges at a Veterans Administration Hospital. See Braginsky, Braginsky, and Ring, *Methods of Madness: The Mental Hospital as a Last Resort* (New York: Holt, Rinehart and Winston, 1969). The V.A. hospitals seem especially prone to confer the impaired role.

categorizing patients and making decisions concerning their treatment. The patients, however, do not know about the finer points of interpreting the diagnostic tests to enable them to do so, and the staff does not supply them with the information needed to make such interpretations even if they did know how. They therefore stick to those clues that are more readily understandable to them, namely the privileges and the classification system. Physicians will probably be successful in getting patients to focus on their clinical improvement only if they are able to reduce such improvement to a series of ratings or classifications similar to those now in use in many hospitals for designating the patient's permitted level of activity.[29]

Interestingly enough, the patients found it quite reasonable to be "held back" if they had a cough, weakness, or a fever. But it should be noted that while a cough and weakness are directly observable, it is only the use of the thermometer which makes a fever observable. An instrument which measures how sick the patient is at a particular time is the best possible aid for keeping him in the sick role. It will be remembered that the point at which Hans Castorp challenged Settembrini's mockery was the point at which the latter cast doubt on the accuracy of the X-rays. This was a serious blow to aim at the sick role, for the X-rays were one of the few means of objectifying and quantifying the illness. As we have seen with John Keats, it is difficult to sustain the sick role in the absence of measurement.

The sick role appears to be a highly unstable social role. Far from being adhesive, as some people fear, it is very difficult to keep people in the sick role even when the illness in question falls undisputedly within the province of medicine. The sick role is like a narrow, slippery path that one must traverse from the inception of an illness until its conclusion. At every point one may lose one's footing and slide into some other role. The consequences of these sudden departures from the sick role are often serious and sometimes fatal. They are of three general kinds. First, the failure to occupy the sick role may result in a prolongation of the illness or even in death. If a person fails to give up his normal social role when necessary, if he tries to get well too fast or not fast enough, if he does not cooperate with the treatment, he may jeopardize his life. Oddly enough, we do not have a term for people who do this, although we call those who demand the sick role when they are not sick "malingerers." When Joachim is on his deathbed as a result of his failure to comply with the demands of the sick role, Dr. Behrens calls him "crazy."

Second, the failure to occupy the sick role may result in the deterioration or destruction of one's most vital relationships. Those who blame themselves or those around them for their illness cut themselves off from the practical and emotional support that they need until they are well. Blame of any kind has a corrosive effect on the relationships of the patient and his family, and good morale in the sickroom cannot be maintained in the face of accusations and counteraccusations.

Third, a person who fails to maintain the sick role may find himself in the impaired role. Unlike the sick role, the impaired role is easy to maintain and difficult to leave, for it is meant to be permanent. But it carries with it a loss of full human status. It is true that the impaired role does not require the exertions of cooperating with medical treatment and trying to regain one's health, but the price for this is a kind of second-class citizenship.

Death or prolonged illness, destruction of vital relationships, loss of full human status—these are the costs of not having the sick role when it is needed. Put the other way around, the function of the sick role is to save the life, maintain the vital relationships, and ensure the full human status of the sick person until he gets well or dies. This makes it quite clear that a person occupying the sick role is not deviant; in fact, the chief function of the sick role is to prevent deviancy. Deviance means a departure from the norm, either statistical or social, and while few people are sick all the time, there is hardly anyone who does not occupy the sick role at some time in his life. Social deviance is behavior which runs counter to one's social group; or, in the case of social roles, it means a failure to perform an assigned role in an acceptable manner. A person in the sick role is deviant only if he fails to perform the functions assigned to that role. The sick person who refuses to go to bed, refuses to take medicine, does not accede to every kind of invasion of his bodily integrity and mental privacy with readiness and good will is deviant. The sick person who conforms to the role may be seen as unfortunate, heroic, a bit of human wreckage, but not deviant. It therefore comes as a shock to find that Talcott Parsons, who invented the concept of the sick role, perversely stigmatized it with the unnecessary and inaccurate adjective "deviant." [30] This error crept into psychiatry via medical sociology and grew in the rich muddlement of that confused specialty. It is not clear to us why Parsons decided that a universal role learned so early in life should be categorized in this way, but in our opinion it has been harmful for many if not most psychiatric patients and has damaged the relationship between medicine and sociology. This is a high price to pay for a misused adjective.

Neither doctors nor patients are likely to give serious heed to a science which describes the sick role, one of the least deviant of human and prehuman activities, as deviant, abnormal and, by implication, immoral. This fundamental error, which has stood for over twenty years without, it seems, any open disavowal by sociologists, must be corrected; for only then will both medicine and society be better disposed to give medical sociologists the hearing they deserve. This discipline could and should add much to medicine's self-understanding, to society's grasp of the complex nature of an ancient craft, and ought to play a large part in medical education. Perhaps the fact that it does not yet do so is owing to the apprehension by doctors and medical students that there is something gravely wrong with this basic premise of medical sociology. Medicine's reluctance to welcome the sociologists may be a kind of dumb and protective prudence which should be discarded once this fundamental error is corrected. This mistake is in no way essential to Parsons's concept of the sick role and does not alter the importance of his notable contribution, but its existence has ensured that the sick role would have minimal appeal to those practicing medicine, for whose enlightenment it must have been invented.

T. T. Paterson's concept of Aesculapian authority, on the other hand, has been neglected for very different reasons. Like many aristocrats, physicians are so accustomed to their massive authority, which they wield so deftly, that they consider any examination of it both boring and gauche. It is a fact of life for them and a pleasant one. Those who are comfortable with their high prestige and status and who enjoy the deference accorded to them by others have little motive for inquisitions into the origins of so excellent a state. Indeed, there might even be disadvantages, resulting in not exactly discomfort, but perhaps unease. Aristocrats usually avoid unease. Intellectual curiosity of an introspective kind has rarely been characteristic of those exemplary craftsmen who are the backbone of clinical medicine; nevertheless, in times of great social and technical change such curiosity is essential for survival.

Aesculapian authority was derived in the context of medicine at a psychiatric hospital and conforms unequivocally with the requirements of the medical model, even though its discoverer, T. T. Paterson, formulated this concept almost a decade before we had constructed our earliest version of the medical model. Parsons's sick role, however, is somewhat equivocal, as it seems to be compounded of elements from two different models, the medical and the psychoanalytic. Parsons confused the sick role and the "psych" role. While the sick role is so well known as to have been invisible until Parsons observed and defined it, the "psych" role, especially in its purer forms, is unfamiliar, and those who hold this role are probably deviant. Nearly everyone in the world has been treated by a doctor or some cultural equivalent, while hardly anyone has been treated by a psychoanalyst. Parsons evidently grafted the deviancy of the "psych" role onto the sick role. However, our everyday experience from our earliest months of life underscores the fact that the sick role is not deviant, which must make it harder to accept and recognize Parsons's very important concept. Unluckily, without a sick role which is accepted and whose qualities are understood, it becomes much harder to grasp the peculiar significance of Aesculapian authority. We believe that the models link these two concepts whose proper use is so essential for both medical practice and medical education.

Since the roles of doctor and patient are a reciprocal pair, it may seem pointless to ask which is more important. However, one patient offered an opinion on this issue: "Of course Guy's Orspital is a very fine Orspital, I know it well . . . . And there are some very good doctors—I knows 'em . . . . But what I want to know is this—What would Guy's Orspital be without the patients?" [31]

There is some evidence that the sick role is primary: while some animals have the sick role, none has the doctor role. Also, in minor illnesses and sometimes even in major ones, the sick role can be conferred on oneself or on another member of the family. Mothers often confer the sick role on their children without the aid of a doctor or anyone acting in that role. If these speculations are correct, then we might say that Aesculapian authority exists in order to confer the sick role, and not the other way around. Doctors exist because there are patients, not patients because there are doctors. The reason that this is important is that doctors without patients are far more likely to "go wrong," to use their authority improperly, than patients without doctors. We have seen doctors in administrative posts, trying to run a structural system on the basis of Aesculapian authority—and it is a disaster. Neither doctors using the scientific medical model nor public health doctors have patients, and while both of these submodels are as old as clinical medicine, it is only recently that they have become powerful enough to matter, and this has greatly increased the model-muddle both in general medicine and in psychiatry.

5

Medicine and Its Submodels*

The medical model, as we have described it, has at its core a pair of reciprocal roles, doctor and patient. This clinical medical model has so completely dominated the other two forms, public health medicine and scientific medicine, that even today when we speak of doctors we generally mean those who treat patients for illness, not those who track down and contain epidemics or those who study disease processes in the laboratory. If we are correct that Aesculapian authority and the sick role are the critical dimensions of clinical medicine, what of these dimensions in the two other models?

Public health medicine appears to have derived, at least in the West, from the cult of Hygeia.[1] It has as its goal the prevention of disease and the promotion of health for a given population. The central roles in this model are not doctor and patient, but public health official and citizen. If public health medicine worked perfectly, clinical medicine would wither away; but it doesn't and its failures march every day into the offices of clinical doctors to be converted from "citizens" into "patients."

What of the authority of public health doctors? Although invested with Aesculapian authority due to their medical training and apprenticeship, public health officials cannot operate on that basis because they have no patients. The basis of their authority

---

* A somewhat different version of the material in this chapter is to be found in our paper, "The Three Medical Models," *Journal of Orthomolecular Psychiatry*, Vol. 3, No. 2 (1974).

is structural, not Aesculapian. T. T. Paterson[2] defines structural authority as "the entitlement to command, stemming from a legal or other contract, vested in a position in the enterprise, and so in the person occupying that position, in ordering and coordinating functions pertaining to other positions and to expect obedience in that ordering and coordinating." Unlike "doctor's orders," which are really advice, a public health official can give true orders, as when a restaurant is "closed by order of the Board of Health." But unlike the clinical doctor, whose advice covers such drastic actions as radical surgery, the public health official can usually order citizens only within very narrow limits and with reference to those actions about which there is widespread social agreement and understanding, such as the closing of public facilities to prevent the spread of dangerous contagious diseases.

The public health official also has sapiential authority because of his knowledge of public health; he is expected to advise citizens how to maintain and safeguard their health on the basis of this knowledge. An example of this is the Surgeon-General's well-known report on the dangers of smoking. Citizens have the right to expect this information and concern from their public health officials, and public health officials have the reciprocal duty to provide it.

Since public health deals with illnesses that cannot be controlled on a private basis, the public health official has the right to expect that occurrences of contagious diseases will be reported to him and that citizens who become "carriers" of a disease will submit to quarantine or whatever measures might be deemed necessary. In general, the public health official has the right to expect that his orders will be obeyed, and the citizens, in turn, have the right to determine the limits of the official's authority. When a public health system is working properly, we take it completely for granted; we are rarely moved to go to the office of our local official (if indeed we know his or her name, or the location of that office) and offer our thanks for the fact that we have not contracted the plague or cholera lately.

In the scientific medical model, a doctor wields neither Aesculapian nor structural authority. His authority is only sapiential; it derives directly from his knowledge of the field of medical research. He occupies the role of scientific investigator, which in principle is no different for a medical doctor than for a biologist, physiologist, biochemist, or any other scientist who happens to be investigating matters of human biology. In practice, however, there is a difference, which is our only justification for speaking of a "scientific medical model" as distinct from any other scientific enterprise. The difference is that while the sick role is not adhesive, Aesculapian authority is extremely so: once a doctor, always a doctor. Anyone who is known or even thought to be a doctor carries the halo of Aesculapian authority with him, even if his daily work does not involve its use and even if he does not have a single patient. Since both the doctor himself and the research subjects he sees (some of whom may also be patients; if not his, then of some other doctor) may be confused about this, it is of the utmost importance to differentiate the two situations in terms of rights and duties, in order to provide guidelines for both. Otherwise there is almost certain to be some violation of expectations, usually, although not always, those of the subject.

The corresponding role in this model, then, is neither patient nor citizen, but experimental subject. This role is significantly different from that of patient or citizen in a number of respects. While the patient pays the doctor in one way or another, and the citizen provides a salary for the public health official through tax money, the experimental subject expects to be paid or otherwise compensated by the investigator. Although some individuals feel a broad social duty to participate in experiments for the good of future patients, the imperative to do so is much less strong than that of the citizen to obey the public health official or the patient to follow his doctor's advice.

In addition to the right to be paid, the experimental subject has the right to know that the investigator will take every possible precaution in order to protect him from harm. He also has the right to know that the experiment is necessary, worthwhile, and well designed. The investigator, in turn, has the right to expect that the subject will honor the special commitments, if any, necessary to carry out the research procedure.

If the sick role is learned very early, as our preliminary inquiries seem to indicate, at what age is the role of experimental subject learned? We know of only one study to date which investigates children's concepts of research hospitalization.[3] The author studied thirty-six children, most of them hospitalized because of short stature. The purpose of the research was to determine whether they might benefit from human growth hormone when it became available. The children ranged in age from four to seventeen years old. The author states:

In spite of careful preparation, none of the 17 children under and only six of the 19 over the age of 11 showed awareness during admission that their hospitalization had anything to do with research. Five of the six who showed some awareness of research presented symptoms of overwhelming anxiety. This study suggests that even after careful preparation the child subject most often is not aware of the research nature of his hospitalization. It further suggests that only after 11 years of age may a child be aware of being a research subject and that such an awareness may result in overwhelming anxiety.

From this study it appears that the subject role is not learned as early or as readily as the sick role. We know of no book designed to teach this role which is comparable to *My Friend the Doctor*. Indeed, if there were such a book for toddlers, it would have to be illustrated by Charles Addams and would presumably contain such sentences as "My friend the doctor does not give me real medicine because he wants to see what will happen if I don't get it." In short, the idea of teaching two- and three-year-olds that it is a good thing to be a research subject verges on the monstrous, and only emphasizes how much we take for granted the morality and acceptability of the sick role.

The goal of the scientific medical model is neither to treat individual patients for their illnesses nor to promote the health of a given population, but to acquire knowledge about human anatomy and physiology and about the cause, prevention, and treatment of diseases, so as to provide a rational basis for the practice of medicine. This being the case, scientific experiments which have as their only goal the acquisition of knowledge must be the province of informed adults, and are not an appropriate activity for children.

The three medical models are different in their goals, in the roles of their principal actors, and in the rights and duties which make up the reciprocal relationships of these roles. One might then ask if they have anything in common, beyond the fact that all three employ doctors. What they do have in common is the dimension of etiology. That is, all three medical models rest on the assumption that diseases have natural causes and are not the result of supernatural forces or human malice. In addition, the three models are not distinguished by their *methods*, for all three use observation and experiment. In fact, as P. B. Medawar[4] has pointed out, the clinical doctor intuitively using the hypothetico-deductive method may be more "scientific" than a laboratory scientist who is superstitiously attached to methodological procedures which may be little more than magic formulae. However, these common elements serve to keep the three models just close enough together so that frequent collisions are almost inevitable.

The awareness of the profound differences among the three medical models is very old. In the writings of Celsus[5] in the first century, the differences between scientists, or Dogmatists as he calls them, and the clinicians, or Empirici, are described:

They, then, who profess a reasoned theory of medicine propound as requisites, first, a knowledge of the hidden causes involving diseases, next, of evident causes, after these of natural actions also, and lastly of the internal parts . . . . They hold that Herophilus and Erasistratus did this in the best way by far, when they laid open men whilst alive—criminals received out of prison from the kings—and whilst these were still breathing, observed parts which beforehand nature had concealed, their position, colour, shape, size, arrangement, hardness, softness, smoothness, relation, processes and depressions of each, and whether any part is inserted into or received into another . . . . Nor it is, as most people say, cruel that in the execution of criminals, and but a few of them, we should seek remedies for innocent people of all future ages.

He then goes on to describe the clinical point of view:

On the other hand, those who take the name of Empirici from their experience do indeed accept evident causes as necessary, but they contend that inquiry about obscure causes and natural actions is superfluous, because nature is not to be comprehended. That nature is not to be comprehended is in fact patent, they say, from the disagreement among those who discuss such matters, for on this question there is no agreement, either among professors of philosophy or among actual medical practitioners. Why, then, should anyone believe rather in Hippocrates than in Herophilus, why in him rather than in Asclepiades? If one wants to be guided by reasoning, they go on, the reasoning of all of them can appear not improbable; if by method of treatment, all of them have restored sick folk to health: therefore one ought not to derogate from anyone's credit, either in argument or in authority . . . . That such speculations are not pertinent to the Art of Medicine may be learned from the fact that men may hold different opinions on these matters, yet conduct their patients to recovery all the same. This has happened, not because they deduced lines of healing from obscure causes, nor from natural actions, concerning which different opinions were held, but from experiences of what had previously succeeded.

The scientific model is concerned with *future patients,* that is, with hypothetical patients. The clinical model is concerned with "restoring sick folk to health" and "conducting patients to recovery." These are not hypothetical patients who might exist in the future, but real patients who exist in the present and who need to be treated with whatever treatment is available. Both are legitimate concerns, but the rules governing them are very different.

An early instance of a satisfactory relationship between investigator and subject is that of Dr. Beaumont and his patient-subject, Alexis St. Martin.[6] As C. J. Wiggers [7] has pointed out, Dr. Beaumont met all the criteria for a responsible experimenter. He studied the available literature on gastric functions, he was persuaded that animal studies were insufficient, he planned the experiments so as to elicit the maximum information from each, he obtained the consent of his subject, even entering into legal contracts with him, he discontinued the experiment whenever it distressed his subject, and, finally, he brought the experiments to an end at St. Martin's request. Beaumont also served as clinical doctor to St. Martin, thus demonstrating that it is not inherently impossible for the same person to fulfill both functions satisfactorily.

Evidence that the two roles of patient and subject can be managed by one person is to be found in Renee Fox's *Experiment Perilous*.[8] So far as we can determine, this book marks the first systematic attempt to tap the actual experiences of patient-subjects. She found that patients with serious metabolic disorders were pleased and proud to make a contribution to scientific knowledge. For example, one patient wrote:

. . . If you need any details as to my symptoms, let me know and I will report to you so you can keep your records up to date . . . . My case is the reason Dr. T. started doing adrenalectomies. I had high blood pressure for many years, you see. And when I got Addison's disease, that cured it. It was my case that gave him the idea of doing an adrenalectomy to relieve hypertension. . . .

Another study of human volunteers in clinical research, by D. C. Martin *et al.*,[9] points in much the same direction. Asking a wide sample of potential volunteers about their attitudes toward clinical research, they found that their respondents believed that they had an obligation to help improve life. This view was expressed most strongly by those in relatively low socioeconomic groups, by women, and by those responsible only for themselves. It was expressed least strongly by those of more privileged status, particularly men, which is disturbing, for those who conduct clinical experiments are most likely to come from this reluctant group. The authors have this to say:

We strongly recommend that the discussion of human participation in medical research be taken to the public. The usual procedure for seeking solutions to perplexing ethical questions often fails to sample vast segments of public opinion. The findings of these studies strongly suggest that the decisions of professional men do not necessarily represent the intent and will of the larger community.

It is evident from the examples mentioned above that the scientific medical model has real social support, both from potential healthy volunteers and from patient-subjects. It is also clear that the scientific medical model and the clinical medical model can be used simultaneously without untoward consequences. But the two models do not always coexist in such harmony, and it seems to be a matter of chance whether a doctor who uses both models becomes aware of crossing the line from one to another. Here is an example of a Massachusetts doctor,[10][11] practicing around 1800, who did not seem to be aware of the implications of changing models. Dr. Benjamin Waterhouse, of Cambridge, Massachusetts, and Harvard University, was the first in America to introduce Jenner's method of vaccination with cowpox serum as a protection against smallpox. He received the vaccine serum directly from Jenner himself. He started by vaccinating his own children, ages five, three and one, and some servants. After they had passed through the mild cowpox disease, they were inoculated with smallpox and, as Dr. Waterhouse predicted, they did not get smallpox.

About two and a half years later, Waterhouse decided to perform a decisive experiment in order to establish full faith in the new inoculation. After adopting and rejecting a number of plans, he applied to the Boston Board of Health to do such an experiment. He says: "I . . . thought it proper to take a broader ground than that of a private practitioner; hence I addressed them as the public teacher of the practice of physic in this Commonwealth . . . ." (Note, here, that he has shifted quite explicitly from Aesculapian authority to sapiential authority.) A board of six Boston physicians was formed, and the experiment began. On the sixteenth of August 1802, nineteen children were inoculated with the cowpox. On the ninth of November, twelve of these children, plus one more who had had the disease previously, were taken to a hospital on Noddle's Island, in Boston Harbor, and inoculated with smallpox. The same smallpox matter was inoculated into two other children who had had neither disease in order to prove that the matter used in the experiment was indeed active. These two boys soon came down the smallpox. The thirteen inoculated children were kept in the same room as the two boys with smallpox, so that if they were susceptible to this disease they would get it, if not from the inoculation, then by direct contagion. They did not get the disease, and so, from Waterhouse's point of view, the experiment was a complete success.

As a private practitioner, operating within the framework of the clinical medical model, Dr. Waterhouse was justified in inoculating his own and other children with cowpox serum in order to protect them from smallpox. (This is provided, of course, that the children were his patients.) We can see this by applying Claude Bernard's [12] rule to the situation, namely: among the experiments that may be tried on man, those that can only harm are forbidden, those that are innocent are permissible, and those that may do good are obligatory. Jenner had shown that vaccination did not fall into the first category of experiments which can only harm, and there was reason to believe that it might do good. But Dr. Waterhouse was not justified in inoculating the vaccinated children with smallpox, or in exposing them to the children who had smallpox, for while it might not harm them, it could not conceivably do them any good. As Claude Bernard put it: "It is our duty and our right to perform an experiment on man whenever it can save his life, cure him, or gain him some personal benefit." The two children who were given smallpox were harmed without being benefited in any way; their lives were endangered and they were used as experimental animals, for they were not volunteers. It should be clear by now that Claude Bernard's rule applies only within clinical medicine; it tells us nothing about which experiments might or might not be done within the scientific medical model.

Dr. Waterhouse may have been confused about which model he was using, but not so the German doctors on trial at Nuremberg for performing experiments on prisoners. They were perfectly clear that they were using the scientific medical model, as the language of their reports indicates. The report on the low pressure experiments begins:

The object is to solve the problem of whether the theoretically established norms pertaining to the length of life of human beings breathing air with only a small proportion of oxygen and subjected to low pressure correspond with the results obtained by practical experiments.

The report goes on to describe the various experiments:

It was a continuous experiment without oxygen at a height of 12 km. conducted on a 37-year-old Jew in good general condition. Breathing continued up to thirty minutes. After four minutes the VP * began to perspire and to wiggle his head, after five minutes cramps occurred,

---

* VP means *Versuchsperson*, in this case the human experimental subject.

between six and ten minutes breathing increased in speed and the VP became unconscious; from eleven to thirty minutes breathing slowed down to three breaths per minute, finally stopping altogether. Severest cyanosis developed in between and foam appeared at the mouth . . . .[13]

When questioned by the judges as to whether doctors (i.e., clinical doctors) ought to have conducted such experiments, the defendants cited as precedents the experiments of Goldberger on pellagra and Strong on the plague. They believed themselves to be operating within a well-known tradition of scientific experiment, which to a certain extent was true. Their error, if one may refer to this disaster as such, lay in another dimension. Their authority over their research subjects was structural, not sapiential. They were able to give orders, backed by brutal and inexorable force. In the scientific medical model as we have described it the investigator must woo his subjects by describing the experiment as being of great humanitarian importance and beautiful design; he must coax the subject with the promise of fame, money, or other blandishments; he must court the subject by promising to take good care of him. The subject, like one being courted, is free to reject the proposal at the outset, or to display fickleness by leaving the experiment at a later time, perhaps even for the more alluring experiment of another investigator. In the experiments which came to light during the Nuremberg trials, there was no courtship, just rape.

In addition to the impropriety of using structural authority in the scientific medical model, the subjects had no rights and no duties, that is, they had no role. Without a role they were reduced to mere objects. The experimenters did not have their consent, for to give consent means to accept the rights and duties of the experimental role.

The appropriate criticism to be leveled at the German doctors is not that they failed to uphold the Hippocratic oath. They did not consider themselves bound by the standards of clinical medicine either at the time of the experiments or at the time of the trial because they perceived themselves as scientists. The code of behavior governing doctors who are scientists was very poorly understood at that time and, indeed, it is largely because of the Nuremberg trials that attempts are now being made to construct such a code. In terms of our models, the appropriate criticism of the German doctors is twofold: first, they used structural rather than sapiential authority; and second, the subjects did not occupy the experimental role.

Lest one think that such abuses of the scientific medical model lie only in the past, or only in some highly aberrant state like Nazi Germany, there are many examples of current research which illustrate in principle if not in degree the same difficulties highlighted at the Nuremberg trials. At a meeting held to discuss human experimentation and informed consent in relation to research grants, one applicant wished to place a special capsule in the arterial circulation to measure certain enzymes in a not very original manner. It was a rather mundane business; what drew attention to his grant application was that although his animal studies showed a 35 percent fatality he stated that his procedure was ready for immediate use in humans provided that he received his money. The granting agency considered his application premature, but in this researcher's mind the goal of benefiting future patients outweighed the dangers to actual people living now. Needless to say, no informed subject would agree to such an experiment.

At the same meeting another study was described, using student volunteers. The study was of some kind of antigen-antibody reaction, and for reasons which were obscure some of the students developed overactive thyroids. One clinician protested that since this complication had been observed in previous studies this particular one should never have been undertaken. None of the three hundred researchers present supported his protest, but about twelve people did speak on behalf of the researcher. All of them emphasized how essential it was that this sort of work should be done. The students were apparently being perceived as test animals whose well-being "must" be hazarded for these "essential" results. It was not clear just why the results were of such vital importance that the students' health and careers should be endangered. Examples such as these could be multiplied many times.

Just as difficulties and conflicts arise at the convergence of clinical medicine and scientific medicine, so they arise in relation to public health medicine. An illustration of the differences between clinical and public health medicine is provided by the famous case of Typhoid Mary,[14] a cook who rivaled some of the country's most notorious mass murderers in the number of victims who died unusually slow and painful deaths, while others suffered grievous injury. She was not perceived as a mass murderer because diseases, within the medical model, are held to have natural causes and therefore no one is to blame for them. Mary herself never accepted that she was a carrier of typhoid, which is not surprising, for this was a new idea at that time. She did not believe that she was ill because she did not have any clinical signs of the disease. However, public health officials, using structural authority, apprehended Mary and took her to an island hospital for quarantine. She was confined there for three years and was then released after promising she would never cook again. She broke her promise, started several new outbreaks of typhoid and was again taken to North Brother Island by officials of the Health Department.

Examining the career of Typhoid Mary in terms of our models, the first thing to be noted is that the goal of the public health officials was not to benefit Mary, but to preserve the health of a particular group of people by preventing her from spreading typhoid among them. The authority which captured and quelled Mary was structural and could not have been otherwise, for she was deaf to Aesculapian authority and disinterested in sapiental authority. Since she had failed to carry out her duties as a citizen voluntarily, structural authority had to be used to prevent her from harming others. Public health officials prefer not to use force to ensure obedience to the laws, but it must be available to them in cases such such as this, for people are reluctant to have their personal freedom curtailed unless there is some direct benefit to themselves. The patient may hope to regain his health, the experimental subject may hope to gain pride and prestige for contributing to scientific knowledge, but poor Mary, who is said to have been a very good cook, was faced with the loss of her chosen occupation and no gain at all—except that of being a good citizen. Evidently the joy and satisfaction of being a good citizen was not presented to Mary with sufficient force or drama. Perhaps she could have been made a kind of public health heroine, sacrificing herself for the good of the community, but for whatever reason, this did not happen.

An interesting fictional presentation of this theme is found in Sinclair Lewis's *Arrowsmith*.[15] The carrier in this case turned out to be, unfortunately, a frail, gentle, virtuous spinster who was ashamed to be examined. Dr. Arrowsmith, after failing to persuade her that she was a danger to others, returned with the police officer and forcibly confined her. But unlike the urban public health officials who apprehended Typhoid Mary, Arrowsmith did not have the full support of the rural and somewhat backward Dakota community where he worked. Without such support, public health laws are almost useless. The problem was solved by Arrowsmith's wife, who suggested that they all take up a collection and send the poor lady off "to some big hospital where she can be treated, or where they can keep her if she can't be cured." This subtle move enabled the community and the spinster to see the situation in a more dramatic and noble light, and Arrowsmith, who had been accused of persecuting the poor woman, was now seen as doing a good job.

Perhaps Arrowsmith's major problem was that he was primarily a clinical doctor and occupied a public health position only on a part-time and semiofficial basis. To the townspeople, for whom he was a doctor who helped sick people, his snooping into garbage cans and poking into manure piles was an affront. When sick people are in need of a doctor, the last thing they want to be confronted with is a public health official. This is borne out in a newspaper article reporting discontent in the Soviet Union about medical care.[16] The writer, Mr. Dyagilev, charged that too much Soviet medicine was cold hearted and bureaucratic. He believed that the problem stemmed in part from "the heavy burden of paper work resting on doctors, half of whose time is spent in filling out forms, compiling data and making reports." The complaint about paper work tells us that the public health, rather than the clinical health, model is in use. The true clinician requires only modest notes to jog his memory when the patient comes again. The sick role is not conferred by pen and paper, but in direct verbal and physical exchanges between doctor and patient. In the public health model, the individual patient is not the focus of attention, and thus, if he is sick, he is likely to be quite dissatisfied with the kind of attention he gets from a public health doctor. To rephrase Mr. Dyagilev's complaint in terms of our models, it would read something like this: "Soviet citizens are displeased to receive the attentions of public health officials when they are ill and wish to have the services of clinical physicians." It may be, of course, that public health medicine represents a better use of scarce resources than clinical medicine; many countries have made such a choice. But there would be less complaining if the choice were made explicit to the consumers of medical services.

Even when a country makes the choice to put its scarce medical resources into public health programs rather than into clinical medicine, the decision is not as permanent as one might think. This is already evident in Cuba,[17] where a vigorous program for improving sanitation, controlling epidemic diseases, providing a pure water supply, and so forth has been so successful that the Cubans have already begun to run into the health problems of the richer countries. Heart disease and cancer are not nearly so amenable to administrative control as tuberculosis and malnutrition. Only clinical medicine can meet the basic human need to be cared for, cherished and understood when one is ill. There is no culture so poor that it does not provide this in some form or other. Whether a culture can afford the Western version of the clinical medical model is quite another matter. But much of what makes Western clinical medicine so expensive—its inefficient distribution, for example—is not intrinsic to the model itself. And nowhere in our model does it say that the patient must have private financial resources equal to the cost of his medical needs. Public health medicine must be publicly supported—there is no such thing as a "private" public health doctor—but clinical medicine may be supported either privately or publicly.

One of the problems with the public health model, then, is that it may be seen, incorrectly, as a substitute for the clinical model. Another is that its goal, which is to create healthful conditions for a whole population, is dangerously open-ended. Who is to say what way of life we should all follow in order to have a sane mind in a sound body? People who reach their one-hundredth birthday are often questioned about their formula for longevity, and the answers vary from total abstinence to drinking a quart of whiskey a day. Many individuals and social groups have worked out for themselves a way of life which they believe keeps them healthy. The Christian Scientists have evolved a formula for leading a disease-free life, as have the nudist groups, the health food groups, and others. In *Arrowsmith,* Dr. Almus Pickerbaugh, the health officer for the city of Nautilus, believed that he had the key to good health for all, as was amply demonstrated by his bevy of eight healthy daughters. Not content with preventing specific diseases such as tuberculosis, he broadened his program to include increasing church attendance, encouraging pure-mindedness and denouncing all forms of alcohol. The cults of Hygeia are many.

With an open-ended goal, plus structural authority, it sounds at first as if the public health model would inevitably lead to tyrannical abuses. But a safety device is built into the model: the structural authority applies only to laws for which there is overwhelming public consensus. Dr. Pickerbaugh, with all his plans for improving the citizens of Nautilus, actually proceeded with the greatest caution, for he would not and could not budge without real social agreement. In spite of his apparent legal power and immense personal authority, he was unwilling to close down a block of tenements believed to harbor unusual quantities of tubercle bacilli. When Arrowsmith burned down the tenements after succeeding to Pickerbaugh's position, it was the beginning of the end of his career as a public health officer.

But this safety device does not always work. In Nazi Germany, the goal of improving the health of the society was present, as was the structural authority to enforce this goal, but the feedback from the general public was absent, for plans were made in secret. Without informing or consulting the families and communities involved, German doctors began in 1939 to exterminate their aged, mentally ill, and mentally retarded patients. The medical personnel involved in the so-called "euthanasia" program were sworn to secrecy and told there was a death penalty if they told others about the program. The secrecy began to break down immediately, however, for as in all bureaucracies, mistakes were made. One family was sent two urns; another family was told that their patient had died of appendicitis, when he had already had an appendectomy before entering the hospital; and another family was told that the patient had died of a spinal cord disease, when the family had found him in good health the week before. The local children quickly learned to recognize the buses used for transporting the patients to be gassed, and called out: "There they go again for gassing." Hitler was sufficiently impressed by the growing public alarm that he ordered Dr. Karl Brandt, commissioner of state for public health, to stop the program. By this time, about one hundred thousand patients had been killed.

Interestingly enough, it was apparently possible to refuse to join the euthanasia program: Dr. Schmidt, a witness at the Nuremberg trials, remained quite unmolested after telling Dr. Brack, his superior, that he would not cooperate. Brack insulted him, but only because he had not been notified earlier. This suggests that public health programs which do not really rest on public consensus are extremely vulnerable to dissenting opinions. This, plus our knowledge of the proper limits of the public health model, ought to give us the courage to protest when such a program comes to our attention.

Since the differences among the three medical models are so profound, and the consequences of confusing them are so serious, one might expect that doctors would be deeply concerned about these issues and that debates would ring through the halls of medical schools. But while some lawyers, philosophers, sociologists, and a few atypical doctors have started to concern themselves about these ethical issues, the venerable old craft of clinical medicine sails on, its crew unperturbed as always by the worried looks and gloomy prognostications of the passengers. What is the source of this remarkable certainty?

Clinical medicine has been guided for centuries by the wonderfully successful automatic pilot of custom. So good has that pilot been that there has been no need until recently to look for any other. The sick role and Aesculapian authority rest on a solid foundation of species-wide homogeneity which is sunk well below cultural and linguistic levels. So well known is the complex of behaviors required to sustain clinical medicine that doctors and patients require far less cultural similarity for it than for any other human activity, with the possible exception of casual sex. One may arrive ill at a foreign airport, be taken to a doctor who speaks a language different from one's own, and be installed in the sick role within, say, fifteen minutes, with little or nothing being said by doctor or patient. Although usually conveyed by speech, the essence of the sick role is so universally understood that it can be communicated by pantomime, as missionary doctors have long known.

What need, then, for doctors to discuss and write about something that has endured for such a very long time without any conscious effort at all? Indeed, if one goes through the vast medical literature, the textbooks, the journals, the indices of articles, all of which doctors have come to feel essential to the practice of medicine, one finds virtually no discussion at all of the central medical event, the conferral of the sick role by someone with Aesculapian authority.* Conspicuous by their absence are spirited disputes about how the sick role should be accorded, how it should be withdrawn, how it relates to adjacent roles, what the consequences are of not getting or not sustaining the sick role, and all the other issues which one might have thought essential for doctors to hammer out among themselves.

It is only on the fringes of medicine, where matters are uncertain, with illnesses whose status is unclear, or with procedures which may be novel and not culturally acceptable, that trouble arises. It is in psychiatry, with its uncertainties about role and authority, that the models have proliferated, each one offering a solution to some part of the problem while making the rest of it

---

* Our perusal of the medical and psychiatric literature included five general medical texts, and ten years each of the *New England Journal of Medicine*, *The Lancet*, and the journals of the American Medical Association. In the *Index Medicus*, the sick role is mentioned for the first time in 1971, and is absent from the previous nine volumes. In psychiatry, seven textbooks had no reference to the sick role, while three referred to it in a minor way, suggesting that it was not particularly important. One comprehensive textbook of psychiatry, 1,666 pages long with an index of thirty-five pages ranging from Abreaction to Witzelsucht, did not refer to the sick role at all.

worse. Thus it was in psychiatry that we first noticed the dog that didn't bark.

But these models have importance beyond psychiatry because of the huge expansion of medical technical competence, which has not been balanced by any increased understanding of the nature of medicine, the relationships involved, and the social, economic, and historical importance of these relationships.

Such academic advances as have been made have had little or no impact on the teaching of medicine, for they have been either anthropological, and thus remote from everyday affairs, or psycho-analytic, reductive, and obscure. Neither of these approaches throws much light on the sick role, Aesculapian authority, or the doctor-patient relationship. The complexity of present-day medicine, which deflects at least some doctors from their most essential, unique medical functions connected with the sick role, requires us to teach, demonstrate, and examine what was once acquired by apprenticeship. In addition, the enormously expanded possibilities for medicine has itself produced new moral and ethical issues in medicine and surgery which did not exist before.

Ironically, it is the primitiveness of psychiatry, with its passé "schools" which are no longer found in other branches of medicine, that makes the whole matter of models so clamant; but it is not in psychiatry where the models are most needed. True, psychiatry should benefit greatly from discussions of models and model-making, and this may assist it to disengage itself from the folly of the schools and those schoolmen who are always to be found in such stagnant places; but the greatest benefits may well accrue to the rest of medicine. It is in medicine generally, far more than in psychiatry, that the three great models of medicine are lurching to and fro, wielding their powerful weapons with formidable nonchalance. As for psychiatry, its problems will be understood only when those of medicine are understood, for the alternate models of madness are not truly separate from medicine, but are mere aberrations on the poorly understood medical model.

It is not only great increases in technical and scientific knowledge which pose problems for medicine and so for the social aspects of medical education, but complex changes in doctor-patient relationships have occurred which have still to be explored fully. During the last two hundred years, the status of doctors seems to have improved considerably, although not always evenly all over the world. This has been partly due to increased competence, much of it deriving from the intricate and ever-growing relationship between medicine and many sciences. Especially in the United States, but also in western Europe, doctors have increased their status by becoming wealthy as a profession. Not only has their status grown but their prestige as well. The doctor is considered to be one who acts for the public good and whose actions affect individual people in the most personal way—by saving their lives, for instance. In spite of the grumbles of satirists, medical prestige has been high for centuries. Moreover, two and a half millennia ago, the writer of the *Odyssey* observed in the seventeenth book of that epic "who, pray, of himself ever seeks out and bids a stranger from abroad unless it be those that are masters of some public craft, a prophet or a healer of ills or a builder, aye or a divine musician . . . for these men are bidden over the boundless earth . . . ." A great medical craftsman is clearly considered an international asset. However, in the past there have been other competing groups who had both high status and high prestige, such as the clergy, the aristocracy, the military, some scholars, occasional poets, lawyers (especially judges), a few teachers, scientists and savants, occasional artists and philosophers. Until the mid-nineteenth century the doctor, at least in England, was on the same social level as most tradesmen. He did not always have commissioned rank in the armed services and was of a much lower status than most clergy or members of the aristocracy. This situation has changed in England, and in North America physicians have risen steadily in both status and prestige. There is little evidence that doctors themselves are greatly concerned by such matters, though they are worried by the increasing number of lawsuits against them, which might indicate that in their fairly recently acquired position of noblesse, they may be expected to make some rather strenuous efforts to oblige. Our inquiries into the medical literature and among doctors themselves suggest that their interest in the relationship between themselves and the public who are their patients, their patrons, and their paymasters is usually of a modest, super-ficial, and sporadic kind. Their curiosity about the nature and consequences of their massive and unique authority which Pater-son named Aesculapian, seems to be almost nonexistent. Such facts alone should cause concern to theoreticians of medicine, who do not abound in so pragmatic a craft, but there are other problems deriving from the existence of a literate and sophisticated public.

Matthew Baillie, John Hunter's nephew, president of the Royal College of Physicians of London and the last holder of the legend-ary gold-headed cane, introduced a startling innovation well over 150 years ago. When dedicating a memorial to him in the 1820s after his death, his eulogist described this discovery thus:

His manner of explaining the disease, and the remedies recommended, was peculiar to himself, and singularly happy. It was a short com-pressed lecture . . . in such simple unadorned language as was intelli-gible to his patients, and satisfactory to his colleagues. Before his time, it was not usual for a physician to do much more than prescribe reme-dies for the malady, and to encourage the patient by such arguments of consolation as might present themselves to humane and cultivated minds. But as . . . a more curious anxiety began to be observed on the part of the patient to learn everything connected with his complaint, arising naturally from the improved state of general knowledge, a differ-ent conduct became necessary in the sick room. The innovation re-quired by the spirit of modern times never could have been adopted by any one more fitted by nature and inclination to carry it into effect than by Dr. Baillie.[18]

It seems this "innovation required by the spirit of modern times" has not been widely recognized or celebrated by the pro-fession, at least in recent years. We have yet to discover books or papers expounding the extraordinary importance and practical application of Baillie's great invention; so far as we know it is not taught in most medical schools, nor is it a regular subject of ex-amination. It would be a safe bet that most doctors have never heard of it. Yet what he was advocating was that the patient should be treated as a responsible person who should be actively and intelligently engaged in the struggle against the illness. Other great physicians have understood this, but Baillie seems to have been one of the first to link increased education to a change in doctor-patient relationships. "The improved state of general knowledge," both formal and informal, due to newspaper, radio, television, and general education has increased logarithmically, so that it would appear unlikely that the same doctor-patient relationship inherited from our Stone Age forebears in the misty distance of prehistory could continue more or less unchanged over the centuries. Yet with few exceptions this is what seems to have happened. If anything, the human, nonspecific, general aspects of medical training have narrowed in recent years because of a vast increase in the so-called basic sciences from which some medical educators seem to believe medicine itself was engendered, although the reverse is true. Added to this has been a steady increase of specialization, much of which favors the technical rather than the general approach to patients. Doctors start their medical careers in their late teens, work very hard to acquire their professional status, yet receive little information about how to behave appropriately once that remarkable status has been acquired or accorded. Most of the instruction they get is implied rather than explicit. It is therefore miraculous that, on the whole, things go so well. This must be ascribed to the fact that being inducted into the sick role is a skill gained early by nearly all of us, if not with our mother's milk, then at her knee. However, even the most indulgent public finds it hard not to resent the arrogant and overbearing behavior not infrequently found in the profession upon whom it has lavished so much money, trust, and admiration.

It seems that the legal profession in the United States, after the distressing events of Watergate, is becoming worried about the nature and quality of the moral and ethical aspects of legal education.[19] It might be prudent for medicine to emulate its great sister profession and, taking heed from its painful soul-searching, inquire zealously and determinedly into the moral and ethical roots of medicine with the intention of using this knowledge to improve medical education. Our inquiry into the three models of medicine suggests that a greater understanding and a clear recognition of the nature of Aesculapian authority and the sick role will do much to reduce unnecessary and often harmful friction between the public and the profession. It seems to us that these matters should be taught early in undergraduate education and continued throughout the later years into specialization, with attention being paid to the problems of particular branches of medicine.

In the past there have been many attempts to teach courses of medical history to students, and in recent years this has been extended or sometimes changed to medical sociology and a sort of comparative anthropology. The intention has been to prepare students not only for the current problems of medicine, into which they will be plunged after graduation, but also to serve them for the rest of their careers. Those who teach these courses hope to give students a grasp of the historical and social background of medicine to carry with them into the future. The hopes or doubts expressed by those using or exposed to this approach appear to be largely a matter of temperament. Only the most ardent advocate of medical history would suggest that it appeals greatly to most medical students, and even then its appeal is not intrinsic but due to especially gifted and inspiring teachers. Perhaps the reason for this is that most medical schools tend to select practical, energetic, and active students for whom the social and historical aspects of medicine are likely to seem far less urgent than the clinical curriculum. The unimportance of these subjects is recognized in a practical way; they play a very small part in medical examinations. Yet in spite of this apparent indifference, such magazines as *M.D.* indicate that there is a wide general interest among doctors in the history of their profession. Correspondence in that excellent magazine is full of evidence for this, but for some curious reason enthusiasm for these subjects is seldom shown by undergraduates.

In recent years, medical students have begun to grumble about what they call the irrelevancy of their courses. During this century, possibly due to the increasing status of the profession, neither its students nor its practitioners have been noted for political zeal, although there have been times (especially in Europe) when, excited by liberal professors such as the great Virchow, they have played an important, even revolutionary part in politics. Students, like most of their elders, find that learning to practice medicine and to do it well leaves little time for other activities, however worthy. In our opinion, the three models of medicine can be used to illuminate those profound social relationships which inhere in the practice of medicine and so are likely to foster better communications with patient, relatives, the public, and our colleagues of various disciplines. Using the models, these relationships can now be understood and explored by a combination of simple principles, case studies, illustrations, and role-taking. For centuries, students who were apprenticed to physicians learned the art of doctoring by trial and error, constantly supervised by their masters. During the last thirty or forty years, with the rise of scientific medicine, there has been a tendency to sneer at the so-called bedside manner which was once so highly regarded. Those who have ever watched a great physician using the bedside manner will recognize that this is the proper employment of Aesculapian authority with its full graciousness, irrespective of the age, sex, class, race, religion, or caste of the patient. It is not only a good way of acquiring information from patients to speed diagnosis and treatment; it can sometimes be life-saving. Here, for instance, is a description of one of the greatest clinicians saving the life of a sick child:

One remembers a young brother with very severe whooping-cough and bronchitis, unable to eat and wholly irresponsive to the blandishments of parents and devoted nurses alike. Clinically it was not an abstruse case, but weapons were few and recovery seemed unlikely. The Regius, about to present for degrees and hard pressed for time, arrived already wearing his doctor's robes. To a small child this was the advent of a doctor, if doctor it in fact was, from quite a different planet. It was more probably Father Christmas.

After a very brief examination this unusual visitor sat down, peeled a peach, sugared it and cut it in pieces. He then presented it bit by bit with a fork to the entranced patient, telling him to eat it up, and that he would not be sick but would find it did him good as it was a most special fruit. Such proved to be the case. As he hurried off, Osler, most uncharacteristically, patted my father on the back and said with deep concern,

"I'm sorry, Ernest, but I don't think I shall see the boy again, there's very little chance when they're as bad as that." Happily events turned out otherwise, and for the next forty days he put on his doctor's robes in the hall before going to the sick room.

After some two or three days, recovery began to be obvious and the small boy always ate or drank and retained some nourishment which Osler gave him with his own hands. If the value of personal approach, the quick turning to effect of an accidental psychological advantage (in this case decor), the consideration and extra trouble required to meet the needs of an individual patient were ever well illustrated, here it was in fullest flower. It would, I submit, be impossible to find a fairer example of healing as an art. This kind of inspired magic, independent of higher degrees and laboratory gimmicks, is given only to a doctor with a real vocation, and the will to employ it.[20]

Some students are naturally gifted to be good doctors, but many are not. Teachers need not worry about those with natural skills, but they should be concerned about those who do not have them and who therefore need encouragement and instruction to acquire the art of relating to patients in an appropriate manner.

We believe that our models provide a scheme which can be employed to show that if one uses the clinical model, one must avoid those approaches which smack of either the public health or the scientific model; it goes without saying that one must also avoid approaches which are completely nonmedical and do not involve the proper exhibition of Aesculapian authority. This is of particular importance today because during their early years of medical education many students are taught by those who use the scientific medical model and who are not apt or even well acquainted with the clinical model. These great skills on which the practice of medicine depends should be taught explicitly rather than implicitly, as in the past, if for no other reason than that explicit teaching will encourage interest and attention. Furthermore, if these skills are taught and are then discussed, students and doctors will discover that both chiropractors and impostors know a great deal about doctoring that is not taught systematically in medical schools. Jim Parker, one of the most successful chiropractors in the United States, advises his students to "dig for chronicity." [21] His approach seems to be to persuade patients who are almost resigned to the impaired role that they have a chronic and hence treatable illness, which might become worse at any time. As for impostors, the usual medical response is a combination of moral indignation and embarrassment; thoughtful study is very rare. Yet medical students and their teachers would do well to study the careers of impostors such as the Bronx carpenter who posed for six months as a physician at Parkchester General Hospital,[22] the Pennsylvania cab driver who doctored a community of Tangiers Island fisherman for ten days,[23] and a California laborer who treated eighty-seven patients while posing as a heart specialist,[24] and that nonpareil, the greater impostor Demara,[25] who posed as a surgeon and even undertook chest surgery. Much can be learned from these "doctors," including what kinds of behavior are not permissible in physicians.

There are very good reasons why this skill should be taught by physicians to up-and-coming physicians rather than delegated to a variety of social scientists, however able these may be. It is unlikely that descriptions and discussions of Aesculapian authority by those who do not possess it and are never going to possess it will have much effect upon neophyte doctors. Nor are they likely to be helped by inspirational talks by distinguished physicians, for lacking a suitable language for discussing the social basis of medicine, these talks are often vague and even mystical. We believe that our work, combined with that of T. T. Paterson, provides a foundation on which problems of Aesculapian authority can be discussed and examined in an intellectually respectable manner. This seems to us a more satisfactory approach than those extensive exercises in the social sciences which have recently been suggested by T. Lidz [26] and others. Medicine has a long history of developing and molding sciences so that they meet its particular and peculiar needs, and perhaps this is another example of that familiar phenomenon.

6

Community Mental Health: What Model?

Public health, as we have described it, has as its goal the prevention of disease and the promotion of health for a given population. Its analogue in the field of psychiatry would be mental health, with the analogous goal of preventing mental diseases and promoting mental health.* In order to be successful, a public health program must meet certain requirements, among which the most basic are that the diseases to be controlled are amenable to public health measures, and that the community is entirely agreeable to the intervention of public health officials. The same is true of mental health programs.

As we have noted earlier, public health programs work best with illnesses of certain kinds; their most outstanding achievements have been with communicable diseases. If one lives in a country which has a sound public health program, one may hope to live without contracting cholera, the plague, yellow fever, polio, smallpox, and a host of other diseases which are either caused by known organisms or which can be controlled by ensuring clean food and water and safe disposal of sewage and other wastes. Other illnesses, such as heart disease, cancer, multiple sclerosis—in fact, most of the diseases for which national organizations exist—are not amenable to any public health measures of which we are presently aware. As for mental health, we have no evidence, thus far, that an

---

* Public health really means public *physical* health; mental health really means *public* mental health. In both cases, the redundant word gets left out.

145

assiduous program for improving mental health has any effect whatever on the incidence or prevalence of any particular psychiatric disease. The only psychiatric diseases we know that have been brought under control by preventive measures are pellagra psychosis and general paresis of the insane, and here it is public health, not mental health, which deserves the credit. No amount of child-rearing or mental hygiene information, whether in the form of lectures, pamphlets, or films, can conceivably affect the incidence of pellagra, but the addition of niacin to our bread has done just that. General paresis has been vastly reduced by the development of the Wasserman test and the organic arsenicals such as salvarsan and later penicillin.

As far as promoting mental health is concerned, the problem is that no one has agreed what it is and therefore it is difficult to measure how much of it has been promoted by the mental health movement. However, it is certainly true that in societies where there is rapid social change, parents are eager to get advice from experts on the age-old problems of child-rearing, and therefore lectures, films, discussion groups, etc., on these universal problems are always welcome.

The second requirement of a good public health program is community consensus. This has often proved much more difficult to obtain than one might think. Charles Erasmus,[1] an anthropologist, discussing this problem in relation to technical assistance and medical aid to communities in so-called "underdeveloped" countries, proposed a list of six requirements which such a program must meet if it is to have a chance of success:

1. Empiricism: the community must be able to see changes which they consider desirable;
2. Need: the community, as distinguished from the innovators, must feel that they have a need for the proposed innovation;
3. Cooperation: members of the community must cooperate in the innovation in order for it to succeed;
4. Inducement: the community must feel that even if they do not entirely agree with the proposed innovation, they will get something out of it;

5. Complexity: since many innovations are more complex than they seem at first, the community must often agree to more changes than the innovation itself;

6. Economic feasibility: the community must be not only willing but able to afford the innovation.

Erasmus notes that, ironically, patent medicine salesmen have often proved more sensitive to the community's needs and beliefs than professional innovators. Few community mental health innovators could satisfy the requirements suggested by the above list and, as we shall see, they have often been far too sanguine about the acceptability and feasibility of their programs.

The present mental hygiene or mental health movement got underway as a result of the efforts of Clifford Beers,[2] a Yale graduate who in 1900 had a psychotic episode and was hospitalized in his native Connecticut. After several uncomfortable stays in various mental institutions, Beers decided to form an organization which would be devoted to the reform of mental hospitals. He never suggested that any failure of mental hygiene had been the cause of his illness, nor did he suggest that his loyal and supportive family had been at fault. He seems to have subscribed to a medical view of his illness, and in spite of his poor treatment at several hospitals, he confidently asserted that if he ever became ill again, he would once again seek medical help and, if necessary, hospitalization. He was advised to approach Adolf Meyer with his plans for a reform movement, because Meyer was at that time one of the best-known and most highly regarded psychiatrists in America. Meyer, however, was a very different sort of person from the practical and straightforward Beers, and it was through his suggestion that the term "mental hygiene" was adopted. Mental hygiene is not at all the same thing as hospital reform, and before Beers knew what had happened the new organization was set off in quite a different direction than that which Beers had anticipated.

In order to understand the historical developments which led to the present community mental health movement and in order to answer our question, What model does this movement represent?

we must say something about the remarkable impact that Adolf Meyer had on American psychiatry.

Adolf Meyer [3] was a charismatic and visionary man, according to his many prominent pupils, and his vision was focused upon a new science to be called "psychobiology." During the 1920s and 1930s he dazzled and dominated Anglo-American psychiatry, but his influence faded quickly after his death in 1950; and since then both his critics and his pupils have been equally at a loss to account for it.* It is very difficult to decide, even when one had personal contact with Meyer's own pupils, what exactly his doctrines were, for they are as elusive and mysterious as the man himself now seems to be.

It appears to us that one unusual feature of Meyer's psychobiology arose from the fact that he was a devotee of holism, a philosophy advanced by General Jan Christiaan Smuts and Alfred Mond. When applied to science, this involved a global or holistic approach to phenomena rather than the atomic or analytic one which has been in more general use. It was apparently Meyer's intention to apply this new scientific method to psychiatry; however, as Karl Popper [4] has emphasized, holism happens to be in direct contradiction to the whole methodology of modern science. It is therefore understandable that Meyer's attempt to use it did not work, and even some of his close associates seem to have been uncertain what exactly he was about.

In a sense Meyer was not only using a science model but attempting, via psychiatry, to introduce a new kind of science. In addition to the internal difficulties of Meyer's theories, which contributed to the obscurity of his puzzling writings, the timing of his effort was inopportune. When he first came to Worcester State Hospital in 1896, the moral treatment was long since dead and buried. Most patients there, and no doubt in other hospitals, had come to occupy the impaired role, and Quinby, the superintendent, was only too happy to concentrate on administration, turning

---

* Desmond Curran, one of Meyer's most distinguished pupils, wrote to us: "I am afraid you are right about Adolf Meyer. No 'heuristic value' as E. S. would say—but he never came under the spell of the magician as I did. He was a most remarkable personality." (Personal communication, 1973.)

clinical responsibilities over to Meyer. But Meyer seems to have been mainly interested, at least at this time, in patients as experimental subjects for his new theories and his new kind of science; he does not seem to have perceived them as clinical patients. Thus, in spite of the exhilaration which he generated among the staff at Worcester, Meyer left the patients very much as he found them. This has been interpreted as showing that scientific interest in psychiatric diseases leads to a lack of interest in the treatment of patients.

Thus Grob writes: "The continued insistence by psychiatrists that their profession was truly scientific, however, exerted a profound, though negative influence over the character of the mental hospital. As we have seen, the assumption that mental disease was somatic in character invariably led to therapeutic nihilism." [5] If correct, this is surely one of the greatest medical enigmas. Why was it only in psychiatry, of all medical specialties, that the growth of scientific research had so little positive effect on the well-being of patients, and may even have contributed to the further decline of the already torpid mental hospitals?

In all the rest of medicine, the increasing presence of scientific research became a source of therapeutic optimism; doctors and patients alike took heart from the efforts of laboratory scientists to understand the nature of various diseases and to combat them. Even in psychiatry such efforts were not entirely without results: within Meyer's lifetime, two major psychiatric diseases, pellagra and general paresis, were greatly benefited by laboratory science.

Our preliminary investigations, which we hope medical historians will pursue, suggest that this is what may have happened: when Meyer began his career in clinical psychiatry, the specialty was in poor shape. Had this not been so, Weir Mitchell could hardly have made his critical speech of 1894. There was no outpatient psychiatry, the skills of the moral treatment had been lost, and in Mitchell's bitter phrase, psychiatrists who were once "the first of specialists" had become little more than the keepers of "second-class lodging houses." Meyer's scientific medicine, when used with the inmates of these gloomy and demoralized institutions for the impaired, was hardly likely to increase either therapeutic or scientific optimism for long. It was not proper science, as we now understand it, and even had it been scientifically sound, the chemistry and other methods employed for studying the human brain and body were far too crude to quantify what had to be measured. Meyer was using an aberrant scientific medical model which, had it been employed consistently, would have conferred none of the benefits of the clinical model. However, since he was, from all accounts, an unusually humane and kindly man whose philosophy was holistic and therefore opposed to excluding views that did not accord with his own, clinical and other models which had many advantages for his patients crept in. The ensuing muddle, in which initial confusion was worse confounded, became the now puzzling but once revered psychobiological psychiatry.

Grob notwithstanding, this in no way resembled what happened during the era of the moral treatment. Those early American psychiatrists of whom Grob writes so appreciatively had a viable, though crude, medical theory and a workable medical model. They conferred the sick role upon their patients. They assumed that they were dealing with diseases of the brain about which they still knew little; pending further developments, they built, ran, and staffed humane and excellent hospitals. Using this relatively simple but effective intellectual equipment and the methods and general approach which it engendered, they were able to do much more for their patients than the turn-of-the-century doctors, although inspired by Meyer's misleading presence.

Meyer's influence spread far beyond mental hospitals and in his later years did much to encourage outpatient clinics, psychiatric social work, and psychopathic hospitals, especially after his installation in the Phipps Clinic. In accordance with his holistic rather than atomistic views, Meyer managed to convey to at least some of his followers and sympathizers that there existed in his time, or soon would exist, a system of mental hygiene. Exactly what this was, and how it worked, remains unclear to us, but many came to believe, and perhaps Meyer was among them, that this would usher in an era of ever-increasing mental well-being. Since Meyer's writings are notable for their obscure complexity, and his speech, although enriched by his presence, also tended toward ambiguity, it is not easy to be sure whether he really believed that mental hygiene existed and could be put to work, or felt that it would be beneficial for his pupils and the public to be inspired by this article of faith. For Meyer was a man who enjoyed, as indeed his philosophical interests suggested, fine shades of meaning and subtle distinctions, something which is less common in medicine than in law or philosophy. However that may be, his ideas about mental hygiene were in accord with many North American aspirations and were received with enthusiasm. The conditions of the mentally ill worsened during his long dominion, and although it would be unfair to blame him for this, his ideas for all their inspiring qualities did not prevent that worsening.

Meyer's death in 1950 left a tremendous vacuum in Anglo-American psychiatry. What was the prevailing mood in psychiatry at that time? The mental hospitals were in terrible shape, but they had begun to experiment on a small scale with patient government, milieu therapy, and day-hospital programs. It was a far cry from the moral treatment, but it did show a renewed interest in the actual lives of hospitalized patients. As for treatment, the 1949 Nobel Prize went to Moniz for his work on prefrontal lobotomy; the tranquilizers were yet to be, and insulin shock and electroconvulsive therapy stood high on the list of available treatments. On the research front, Manfred Bleuler, summing up the previous decade's work, felt that the heart had gone out of those searching for a physiological basis for schizophrenia. Reading the funeral service over the medical model, he said:

Looking over these and other works on the pathological physiology of schizophrenics, one is forced to make this negative statement: These works have failed to bring us even one step closer to the possibility of finding, behind the "psychological" psychosis of schizophrenia, a definable, specific, pathological "somatic" schizophrenia. We have no evidence of any disturbance of basal metabolism which would characterize schizophrenia and neatly differentiate it from other psychoses, somatic disorders, or the norm. It is possible that, as a consequence of these negative results, the search for a specific somatic basis for schizophrenia will be given up for a long time to come, if not permanently.[6]

What was left? Mental health and psychoanalysis. Although

Meyer had not been interested in psychoanalysis, and Freud had been bitterly opposed to its absorption by medical psychiatry, nevertheless a marriage was arranged between these two children of which neither of their famous fathers would have approved. Psychiatry came to be dominated idealogically, if not practically, by this strange pair, and it is in this context that the present community mental health movement got started.

In 1951 two researchers, a sociologist and a psychiatrist, tried to change the attitudes toward the mentally ill of the citizens in a small Canadian town. Their account of this effort, *Closed Ranks*,[7] became a classic of its kind, and is mentioned wherever there are discussions of community attitudes toward mental illness. In order to achieve their goal, they used an intensive educational campaign, composed of materials from the Canadian Mental Health Association and their own ideas, which were derived largely from psychoanalysis. They assessed their results by measuring the citizens' attitudes before and after the educational program and by conducting a series of interviews. According to their own account, they failed to make any dent in the residents of Blackfoot, except that by the end of the six-month test period, their initial friendly reception had been converted into outright hostility. The Blackfooters had closed ranks against them.

Blackfoot, a town of 1,500 inhabitants, was chosen because it was settled and stable, with a homogeneous population, fairly representative of the southeastern section of Prairie Province. It was small enough to allow questionnaires to be given to the entire adult population and large enough to yield useful data. Although a conservative town, it had a tradition of learning new ideas from itinerant preachers and teachers.

The project's planning committee assumed that although there might be biological and hereditary bases for mental illness, "there was also a causal connection with long-term disturbances of interpersonal relationships." They believed that if the people of Blackfoot accepted the importance of interpersonal factors, then this would result in their being more tolerant toward the mentally ill and so more inclined to cooperate in their rehabilitation. The authors state: "We reasoned that by teaching that there is little difference between illness and health, we would persuade people to behave toward the ill as they do toward the well."

The committee agreed on three working principles as a basis for the educational program:

1. Behavior is caused and is therefore understandable and subject to change.
2. There is a continuum between normality and abnormality.
3. There is a wider variety of normal behavior than is generally realized.

When the educational program began, the researchers found that the Blackfooters, while not enthusiastic, were willing to accept the program and to be helpful. The team began to worry, however, when there was little evidence of any more active interest in the program. Then, in the fourth week of the program, two rumors swept through the town. One was that "the Government" had sent out the research team because "they" were thinking of building a mental hospital in Blackfoot. Second, the survey was said to be a "plot" of the Roman Catholic Church. The team was at a loss to account for these rumors, which were wholly false. Three months after the program began, the researchers started to notice "a pattern of withdrawing behavior." They thought at first that the townspeople were, as they claimed, simply busy with other activities. But this did not seem to be the full explanation. The researchers record: "Toward the end of the program we were beginning to feel that there was something very wrong." During the second survey, the interviewers grew increasingly tense as they sensed the suspiciousness and hostility of the respondents. They contrasted this with the friendly attitude which had prevailed during the first survey. According to the Cummings:

The event which best symbolizes our hostile rejection by Blackfoot occurred during the course of the second survey, when the Mayor of the town approached one of our interviewers, asked him what he was doing, questioned him in great detail about his credentials and his right to conduct such interviews, and finally said, "We have had too much of this sort of thing; we are not interested in it in this town any more. The sooner you leave, the better." The ranks had closed against us. Blackfoot had responded as if to a threat to its integrity as a functioning community.

At the conclusion of the educational program, the Cummings found that the average score of the two scales of their questionnaire had not changed, which they took to mean that the average person in Blackfoot was neither willing to get any closer to a mentally ill person nor willing to take more responsibility for the problem of mental illness than at the beginning of the program.

At this point, it is important to realize that the Cummings did no reconnaissance at all in Blackfoot; they assumed that they knew what the Blackfoot people felt about mental illness. Furthermore, neither the first questionnaire, the second questionnaire, nor the interviews were analyzed until *after* the educational program was over. Thus the Cummings were cut off from feedback of any kind from their respondents. The base line from which the Blackfooters were to be moved was not considered when the educational program was being developed.

How did the Cummings account for their failure to change the Blackfooters attitudes? On examining their data, they discovered that, contrary to their original assumption, the Blackfooters perceived a much broader range of behavior as normal than the mental health workers who were trying to increase their tolerance of abnormality. Their second assumption, that behavior is caused and therefore understandable, was true also for the Blackfooters, who, however, saw very different causes from the Cummings. The Cummings had erred in assuming that lay people wait for professionals to tell them what to think, whereas it became clear in retrospect that most people believe that they understand human nature. With their third assumption, that there is a continuum between normality and abnormality, the Blackfooters did not agree; they saw a fairly sharp cut-off between the two.

Analyzing the Cummings project in terms of our models, we find that there were at least six models in use: the psychoanalytic, the medical, the impaired, the social, the conspiratorial, and a kind of scientific model. The presence of the psychoanalytic model can be inferred from the Cummings bias that behavior should be interpreted symbolically, rather than in some other way. Presenting to the Blackfooters a case history of a phobic and compulsive girl who was afraid to ride up and down in elevators,* the Cummings were surprised to find that "no respondent . . . expressed any suspicion that this might be symbolic behavior or that fear of elevators might protect Mary White from other more disturbing unconscious fears." Another dimension of this model which seems to have been present is that of etiology, which can be inferred from the child-rearing emphasis of the educational program. A weekly radio program called "Junior Jury" offered panel discussions of common childhood problems, such as sibling rivalry, authority relationships with parents, and children's allowances. The dimension of "definition" was present also in the statement that there was a continuum from normal to abnormal behavior. Although one can eke out the rest of the model by combing the Cummings account for relevant statements, the instructions provided by their version of the psychoanalytic model are sketchy indeed. We do not learn, for example, how one is to tell minor emotional disturbances from major ones, nor if the proposed course of action varies according to the severity of the disturbance. If these emotional disturbances are to be differentiated from organic illnesses, it is not suggested how this might be done or who would do it. They do not offer any evidence that the solution of ordinary daily problems, such as those discussed on "Junior Jury," would decrease the number of patients ill enough to be hospitalized. It is not clear what advantage would accrue in interpreting behavior symbolically rather than in some other way. No treatment is discussed for any patients along the proposed continuum, nor is any prognosis offered for people with different degrees of disturbance. We do not learn what is to be done with those currently in the hospital. We are not told what qualifications people ought to have to work with the mentally ill. It is not clear how ill people ought to behave, nor what their families have the right to expect. It is not clear whether society is mistaken in imagining that some mentally ill persons present a danger to themselves or others; indeed, it is not clear whether society has any rights at all under this model. In sum, this model, as

---

* Elevators, other than grain elevators, are not a prominent feature of Canadian prairie life.

deduced from the Cummings study, does not give clear instructions for patients, their families, those treating the mentally ill, or for members of the community in which they all live. However appealingly it might have been presented, it does not tell anyone what to do when actually confronted with mental illness.

In the dimension of "definition," the researchers ran afoul of the Blackfooters. It was the concept of a continuum running from mild emotional disturbance through to grievous psychiatric illness that the Blackfooters could not accept. The Cummings believed that the way to get the Blackfooters to be more tolerant of the mentally ill was by enlarging their understanding of the normal mechanisms of behavior in ordinary life situations. As they put it: "On the basis of the concept of the equilibrating function of prejudice for some people, we decided not to make a direct attack, at least at first, upon the attitudes of the members of the community toward the mentally ill but to approach by way of the more general subject of human behavior." But, as the Cummings noted later, the Blackfooters were already sold on the value of understanding human behavior: "Modern teaching about child development has really 'taken' and become a significant part of people's thinking. The brisk sale of books on this subject and its popularity for discussion at parents' groups further indicates its acceptability." Therefore, the main thrust of the educational program was to teach the Blackfooters something that they already knew. But it does not follow that if one accepts the teachings of modern psychology about normal behavior, one will find that this erases the differences between normal people and the mentally ill. What makes an encounter with a psychotic person such an eerie experience is the disconcerting discovery that one's usual understanding of human nature breaks down in the face of inexplicable behavior: this is the very definition of psychosis. If there is any correlation between a psychodynamic view of human nature and tolerance of the mentally ill, it is an inverse one: people who are alert to psychological subtleties and have high standards for interpersonal relationships are sure to notice that the mentally ill are greatly handicapped where social and emotional flexibility is required. Thus it is not surprising to learn that the Blackfooters proved to be more tolerant of the mentally ill than the more sophisticated Cummings and their colleagues.

The Cummings used a scientific model on one occasion only, when for unknown reasons they attempted to establish their authority in relation to the agricultural scientists in Blackfoot:

A public debate on the subject of whether or not social science is really a science was arranged with the agricultural station group. Although this debate was rather lively in a somewhat incoherent way, it seemed amiable enough; therefore we were surprised to learn from acquaintances that it had raised considerable antagonism among the agricultural scientists present. In content, the discussion seemed innocuous: the speakers for the social science side emphasized the contributions of R. A. Fisher to the art of experimental design, and the agriculturalists insisted that "man is too complicated to be studied scientifically." Which aspects of the debate annoyed the agriculturalists most is still in doubt, though we will suggest in a later section that it was not the content of the debate but the fact of the educational team, by their actions, implicitly calling themselves scientists which was so vexatious.

We do not know why the Cummings felt that a public debate with the agricultural scientists would improve their chances of creating greater tolerance for the mentally ill in Blackfoot. They themselves offer no explanation for this eccentric action. The best guess which we can offer is that, having largely abandoned medicine as a source of authority, they still wished to establish that they were authorities of some kind and tried to present themselves as scientific experts. Psychoanalysis seems to have been a poor source of authority in Blackfoot; such authority as it has, derives from medicine. They did not argue that the psychoanalytic concepts underlying their program were scientific, which might have been a more logical, though perhaps more difficult, thing to do; instead, they tried to show that their method of designing the study was scientific. It is evident that their arguments were not directed at the people of Blackfoot to impress them with their expertise regarding the cause and cure of mental illness. Rather, the Cummings went over the heads of the Blackfooters, so to speak, to address their agricultural scientist colleagues living in Blackfoot on the merits of their research abilities.

The Cummings did not consciously or deliberately use the medical model, but it is implied in the setting of the study, the Psychiatric Branch of the Department of Health in Prairie Province, and in the fact that one of the Cummings was a psychiatrist—that is to say, a medical doctor trained in psychiatric medicine. The study could not have been done without the blessing and active support of the Health Department.

Had the Cummings wished to use the medical model, an obvious step would have been to enlist the cooperation of the doctors practicing in Blackfoot. But, in fact, they moved in exactly the opposite direction. They concluded that it was a mistake to have had any medical person on their team at all:

It is probable that a psychiatrist—as in our case—should not be placed in a position where he is the chief organizer and one of the major contributors to a mental health program. Such activity, to most people, is simply not appropriate to the role of a specialist physician, and this probably acted against acceptance of our program in Blackfoot.

Yet other medically sponsored programs were wholly acceptable to the people of Blackfoot. The Cummings note that:

. . . during the course of our experiment, an outside effort to incorporate the town of Blackfoot into a larger public health unit was made. The proponents of the scheme, Provincial civil servants, entered the community with considerably more directness than we did; they distributed literature, hired a hall, and when people came, told them about the plan. Blackfoot people argued with the proponents of the scheme, but they listened, and when the matter came to a vote, the town, which seemed completely opposed to a change, voted for the formation of such a health unit.

The Cummings use this example to show that the Blackfooters were not suspicious of outsiders. A more useful inference to be drawn from this example is that programs explicitly using a medical model (in this case a public health medical model) can be readily accepted in a town such as Blackfoot. They need not be perceived as threatening, they do not have to be approached indirectly, and it is not inevitable that they will generate hostility.

The Cummings give us one example of the use of the impaired

model. This was the point in the program at which they seem to have achieved the greatest consensus with the Blackfooters:

Probably the most successful event of the program was the engagement of several members of the Blackfoot branch of the Canadian Legion in a project which took them seventy-five miles to visit a veterans' group in a ward of a large mental hospital. These men were given a one-hour introduction to the problem of the chronic ward by the superintendent, and following this, they visited the patients. The Legion members voted at their next meeting to adopt this ward as a continuing project, sending cigarettes, candies and other comforts. It is of particular interest that this Legion group decided not to limit its interest to the veterans when sending comforts to the ward but to include the whole ward in its project. Apparently the governing Legion principle of service to veterans was temporarily replaced by a broader interest in all the patients in the hospital.

It is important to realize the implications of sending candy and cigarettes to hospitalized patients. Normally, people prefer to supply these things for themselves, or, if they are too ill to do so, they enjoy receiving them from family or friends—from someone who knows them and cares for them. The implication of a group of Legionnaires sending candy and cigarettes to a whole ward is that the patients lead a captive and impoverished existence, perhaps permanently, in which they can be expected to be grateful for anything that anyone chooses to do for them. To a patient in a general hospital, one sends fresh flowers, which people do not ordinarily buy for themselves, the implication being that one is getting a special treat because one is sick. We shall know that schizophrenics can command the sick role when they, too, are sent fresh flowers when hospitalized.

If this project does not fit the medical model, it makes even less sense in terms of the psychoanalytic model. If mental patients are just like everyone else, why then are they living in an institutional building seventy-five miles from Blackfoot, depending on total strangers to supply ordinary daily needs such as cigarettes? And what is the relation of this program to "Junior Jury" and unconscious fears? Yet the Cummings found nothing incongruous about a project so far removed from those stated principles which they were trying to teach the Blackfooters.

The social model was represented in the Cummings question-naire by a "social responsibility" scale, which was intended to measure whether the people of the community felt that they were at all responsible, as citizens, for the occurrence of mental illness. They also wished to know whether those who felt social responsi-bility for mental illness also felt responsible for caring for the mentally ill. They did find such a relationship, which they attrib-uted to the Province's long history of radicalism.

In the psychoanalytic model, at least as it is usually interpreted, people *are* encouraged to see the souce of their illness as lying within themselves, and are discouraged from attributing it to out-side forces. In the dimension of etiology the psychoanalytic and the social model are in contradiction. Yet the Cummings seem to subscribe to both. A possible explanation for this may be the vague-ness of the social duties of citizens as described by the psycho-analytic model. They are to be "more tolerant." The Cummings wish to see a more active role for citizens in respect to mental ill-ness, and so they are probing to see if the socially minded Black-footers accept the causes of mental illness as lying within the com-munity.

The Cummings found that those who believed the causes of mental illness to be biological were less willing to feel responsible for doing anything about it. This is strange, for in two models—the medical and the impaired—people have demonstrated the willing-ness to take social action on behalf of the sufferers, although they clearly do not feel responsible for having *caused* the condition, which is something very different. In the impaired model, the blind, deaf, and crippled are all recipients of social concern and aid. Using the medical model, there are many examples of organi-zations founded by lay citizens to further research and treatment for a particular disease: the Cancer Society, the Heart Associa-tion, the National Foundation, and so forth. One does not need to make members of a community feel that they have caused an illness in order to get them to take responsibility for doing some-thing about it. Indeed, the typical stance taken by these organizations is that the causes of the disease in question are unknown, and cannot be determined except for long-term, expensive, and effortful research. People are made to feel that the disease is an external enemy to be fought, rather than an interpersonal problem or the manifestation of a "sick" society. What the Cummings were probably running into here was the notion that hereditary diseases are hopeless, which is a version of the predestination theory. This is really a religious moral model (that is, a continuous moral model) in disguise. We have not included such a model in our system because it is largely out of date, but no doubt it is still lurking around in traditional communities. We are now learning that many illnesses have a genetic basis, and that far from this being a source of gloom, it offers a clue for scientific research.

In 1951 the conspiratorial model was not yet in full bloom; the writings of Szasz, Laing, Goffman, and Scheff had still to appear. In *Closed Ranks* there is just the faintest suggestion of it, but it is worth looking at as a harbinger of things to come. The Cummings were frequently asked by the townsfolk why they wanted to know what the Blackfooters thought about mental illness; why not ask the experts, they wanted to know. To which the Cummings would reply, cryptically but significantly: "Who sends people to mental hospitals?" The Cummings tried to convey the message that some of the patients in the hospital were no more ill then those who remained harmlessly at home. Here we see the germ of the idea that mental illness is *just* a label which some people are unfortunate enough to get pinned on them, while others, in no way different, escape this fate. This model conflicts with the psychoanalytic model in the dimension of "definition," for symptoms in the latter model which would normally go unnoticed are seen as evidence of emotional disturbance, while in the conspiratorial model one is discouraged from labeling anyone as mentally ill since this is seen as a prejudicial act. The conspiratorial model also conflicts with the medical model in this dimension, for in medicine the sooner one notices the early symptoms of a disease, the better the chances of treating it. Consequently, failure to notice symptoms as early as possible is certainly a mistake and may even be considered negligence.

The Cummings presented the Blackfooters with an indigestible brew of six incompatible models, and they did so without finding out in advance or ever really comprehending the models which the Blackfooters held. What were the prevailing models in Blackfoot at the time of the Cummings study?

The model of mental illness which the Blackfooters used was primarily a moral model; it focused on the social behavior of the members of the community. Most people, they felt, behave in a way that makes sense in terms of the way they were raised, the standards of the community, and the particular experiences which they have had. Only a small minority of people cannot be fitted somehow into this normal social existence. Those people who simply cannot be made to fit, or whose behavior cannot be rationalized as normal, must be extruded from the community so that it can continue to function. This minority are crazy, mad, insane. Once they have been extruded, it generates too much anxiety to take them back again because they have already demonstrated their unpredictability and their lack of response to the usual sanctions.

Madness, then, is that residuum of behavior which is left when all known explanations have been exhausted. When we use the word metaphorically, as when we say that some political leader's actions are "mad," we mean that we do not know and cannot even imagine what explanation might be found for them. The Blackfooters managed to keep the number of mad people as low as possible by giving everyone who behaved strangely the benefit of every doubt. This was the best they could do in the absence of information which would describe the inner experience of mad people and so make their behavior understandable and perhaps even predictable.

Once mad people are inside mental hospitals, however, an interesting model-switch takes place. They are no longer seen as mad, unpredictable, and potentially dangerous. Within the hospital, there is an atmosphere of sluggishness and apathy, rather than the atmosphere of anxiety and acute danger which often exists up to the point where someone is taken to the hospital. Within the confines of the hospital, the mad person's behavior usually becomes predictable and therefore much less dangerous. He is now seen as impaired, that is, as permanently occupying a somewhat subhuman role as a damaged or crippled person. The transition from madman in the community to impaired person in the hospital (or rather, home for the impaired) is rather like the transition of a wild animal in the jungle to a sleepy lion in his cage. It should not surprise us, then, that mental hospitals used to charge admission to see the patients, as if the hospital were a zoo. But although the impaired role is not an attractive one, it is at least an improvement over the mad role; the mentally ill person is cared for and can hope to survive until some other role is made possible for him. It is better than being put aboard a ship of fools or simply being driven out from the community to freeze or starve.

As we have noted above, the Cummings and the Blackfooters were able to agree on the impaired model in the instance of the Legionnaires "adopting" a ward of patients at a hospital seventy-five miles from Blackfoot. The impaired model can be made very comfortable, and rich impaired people like the residents of the Magic Mountain live very much better than poor impaired people. To have visitors who bring candy, cigarettes, and their company is surely better than to be impaired without these comforts. The Cummings did, therefore, succeed in improving the lives of some mental patients occupying the impaired role, and both they and the Legionnaires evidently experienced that sense of well-being which accompanies an act of betterment.

If the impaired model were fully adopted by the Blackfooters, they could greatly enhance the lives of hospitalized mental patients by introducing all sorts of luxuries and improvements. After all, people who are cut off from any hope of rejoining the community and leading normal lives certainly deserve our best efforts at compensating them for their ill-luck. But unfortunately it does not seem to work that way. For unknown reasons the status of impaired people always seems to be lower than that of normal people or ill people, and so the efforts to make their lives more bearable usually fall short of this humane and equitable goal.

Although the model used most by the Blackfooters was a moral model, with a mad-impaired annex for those who had to be extruded from the community, the medical model was not entirely absent. When someone is behaving in a non-normative and unpredictable way and the efforts of family and friends to set him to rights do not succeed, the next step is to send him to a doctor. If the doctor is unable to do anything, the afflicted person is then sent to a mental hospital, which resembles other hospitals at least insofar as it has a medical staff and offers some medical treatments. He is not simply extruded or sent to a madhouse, which would be the logical step using the Blackfooters' model consistenly. The medical model has successfully encroached upon the mad model to the extent that there is at least a token effort to regard the madman as a medical patient with the appropriate rights and duties of the sick role.

The Cummings failed to move the Blackfooters from what was mostly a moral model to what was mostly a psychoanalytic model. We can see several possible reasons for this. First, the psychoanalytic model to which the Cummings subscribed was so vague in its formulation that the Blackfooters were hard put to see how this new view would help them cope with the realities of mental illness. The fact that this model, with all its internal shortcomings, was mixed in with bits and pieces of five other models muddled the Blackfooters and reduced their confidence in the Cummings as a useful source of information.

Then, at the outset of their study, the Cummings did not know what model the Blackfooters already held; they guessed, but were mistaken. As nearly as we can make out, the Cummings thought that the Blackfooters believed that some sizable proportion of the population was mentally ill and that what they meant by mental illness was madness. In fact, unlike their mentors, the Cummings, the Blackfooters saw most people as normal and reserved the category of madness for a tiny fraction of their community who could not possibly be subsumed under the moral model. Even then, the mad model was applied only until such person was safely put away in a mental institution; from that point on, the mental patient was seen primarily as impaired—harmless, but socially dead. Since the Cummings also saw hospitalized patients as impaired, rather than ill, mad, or emotionally disturbed, their only positive contribution was to make a slight improvement in the version of the impaired model which the Blackfooters already held.

In trying to discover what went wrong with their educational program, the Cummings made a number of suggestions as to how it might have been improved. The essence of these suggestions is that the Cummings believed they should have acted more slowly and trodden more delicately in moving the Blackfooters from their model to the Cummings own. One possibility that the Cummings did not consider was that their model was useless and that the Blackfooters, realizing this, rejected it on very good grounds. It is never easy to accept that others have not responded to our teachings because those teachings, however carefully planned and well intended, are mistaken. It is more comforting to believe that if only we had been a little cleverer, if only we had put it a little differently, the others would have been won over. To be sure, the Blackfooters model was not ideal, and they knew it; hence their anger at having it exposed to the light. But their model, while unattractive, worked, whereas the Cummings model, which they felt was far more humane and up-to-date, proved to be unworkable and probably harmful. Communities have no choice about mental illness; they must cope with it and they always have done so. Thus it is not surprising to find that Blackfoot, like every other community, had a model which had stood the test of time.

The Cummings violated every known canon of the public health model. They did not know whether the illnesses with which they were dealing were amenable to communitywide preventive measures. They did not have a clear understanding of what positive mental health might be, let alone any consensus with the Blackfooters about this. They had no evidence of any relation between improving mental health and controlling mental diseases. They did not respond to any "felt need" on the part of the community. They were not even curious about how the Blackfooters had coped all those years without their help, or how urgent the Blackfooters felt about those of their citizens who were actually suffering from an acute psychotic disorder at that time, a number which must have been extremely small.* However, there is one treasure to be salvaged from this sorry affair: the Cummings, with admirable objectivity, have preserved for us a complete record of an experiment that failed. If we can learn from it, it will have been worthwhile. Has the present crop of community psychiatrists learned anything from the Cummings misfortunes in Blackfoot over twenty years ago? Or has community psychiatry a penchant for that ill-fated attitude manifested by the Bourbons of having "learnt nothing and forgotten nothing"?

Just twenty years after the Cummings set out for Blackfoot, one of us (Miriam Siegler) attended a meeting at a new community mental health center, one of the first fruits of the changed laws in that state decentralizing mental health facilities. It was very difficult to find the building, because it had no sign. The director later explained that a sign had not been put up because "people don't like to be seen entering a community mental health center." This suggests that the stigma attached to mental illness is in no way diminished by calling a small, locally based psychiatric clinic or hospital a "community mental health center."

Community mental health has no model. It uses a goulash of models, in about the same mixture as the Cummings used, with the probable addition of two new models, the family interaction and the psychedelic, and without, of course, giving up the medical model entirely. Lumping the nonmedical models together, and ignoring, for the moment, the presence of the medical model in that mixture, we might consider the following oversimplified set of possible combinations of personnel and purpose:

   (*a*) Doctors using a medical model.

---

* It should be noted that while the Cummings suggested that there might be an indefinitely large number of mentally ill people, it is quite easy to calculate the number actually in Blackfoot. The gloomiest calculations might suggest that about 10 percent of the population would be ill at the same time. However, thanks to the Blackfooters surprising tolerance, it seems probable that no more than three or four people were residing in the Provincial hospital, and perhaps one or two in the local psychiatric ward at the time of this study. In view of the actual conditions of overcrowding and underfinancing in the hospital at that time, it hardly behooved the educators to encourage the Blackfooters to become less tolerant than they were. There is no evidence that the Cummings concerned themselves with these crude but relevant logistics, which require a medical bias to recognize their importance.

(*b*) Doctors using a nonmedical model.

(*c*) Nonmedical personnel using a medical model.

(*d*) Nonmedical personnel using a nonmedical model.

Of these, only the first and last are permissible. A doctor using a nonmedical model (that is, one with no Aesculapian authority and no sick role) needs to establish his authority and competence on some other basis, for otherwise he becomes a fraud or a quack. What most often happens is that everyone except the doctor involved realizes well enough that he is a doctor, and the result is a covert or clandestine medical model. Unlike romances, which are sometimes greatly improved for being carried on sub rosa, the medical model merely comes out tattered and sordid when the parties refuse to admit their true relationship. The other inadmissible arrangement is for nonmedical personnel to use the medical model; in order to do so, they would have to attempt to acquire Aesculapian authority, which would make them impostors.

Of the two admissible arrangements, let us consider first one in which nonmedical personnel operate a center based on some nonmedical model or models appropriate to their training and credentials. We have seen a mental health center run without a physician because none was available, and although its services were thereby limited, the people who came to it were fully aware that they could not get advice or help with medical problems at the center but would have to go elsewhere. The center confined itself to dealing with interpersonal and community problems and to improving mental health; it did not treat diseases. Insofar as anything can be described accurately as being a "mental health center," that was it. However, it may by now have secured the services of a physician, thus becoming another of those small psychiatric clinics or hospitals masquerading as a "mental health center." It is unclear whether the public would be willing to pay for nonmedical mental health centers such as the one described, however admirable they might be. It seems that at present the public is only willing to pay for medical facilities which treat actual psychiatric diseases, for the new centers are supposed to replace the old mental hospitals. No one believes that calling municipal hospitals "physical health centers" would increase public support and understanding, let alone have any effect on the incidence of disease.

The first possibility, which is the one we favor, is the use of the medical model by doctors exercising Aesculapian authority and conferring the sick role. The present plan for community mental health centers derives from the so-called Saskatchewan Plan, which was a blueprint for decentralizing *medical* facilities. The Yorkton Psychiatric Centre [8] is an example of that plan in operation. There is no difficulty about including under one roof all kinds of therapies designed to aid recovering patients in the many areas of their lives which may have been affected by their illnesses; however, there is no doubt that the purpose of such a center or small hospital is to treat diseases. Those who do not believe that such diseases exist will see no need for facilities of this kind.

The Cummings did not realize how impractical their model appeared to the Blackfooters, nor how attractive the medical model can be to a community. In the end they concluded that they ought to get rid of the remaining vestiges of the medical model which they still used. Oddly enough, some years later in similar rural Canadian town about fifty miles away, a community heard that an explicit medical model for a psychiatric hospital might be provided by the Health Service. After some brisk and effective lobbying which included several thousand letters from Canadian Mental Health Association members, a not very enthusiastic government was persuaded to build the Yorkton Psychiatric Centre.[9] We do not know whether Gardner and Gardner [10] ever read Cumming and Cumming, but if they did, they learned little from it. They compounded the latter's errors by overextending themselves even further into nonmedical areas where they had no authority and no competence, and by undermining still more the relations between ill people and their doctors. The social model which they claimed to be using was a mere fig leaf barely concealing a covert and hence distorted version of the clinical medical model.

Another segment of the community whose views were not explored by those advocating community mental health centers were the other community agencies. In spite of lip service given to the importance of "systems analysis," little thought has been given to the effect of "dumping" large numbers of mental patients from the hospitals onto other parts of the social service network. One county official in New York State assailed the Department of Mental Health for discharging one thousand patients, at a cost to the Welfare Department of $700,000 per year.[11] In addition to mentioning the financial hardship, the county executive said: "We find former mental institutional patients, because of lack of follow-up aftercare, finding their way in and out of the Suffolk County jail and shuttling between the jail and admission and discharge to state hospitals."

It was no doubt the intention of community psychiatrists to remove the mentally ill from the impaired model of the old state hospitals, but the unintended consequence of this action is that these same patients are in the community, not as participating citizens, but as social victims and jailbirds. They have yet to be given their rights as medical patients under the medical model.

"The community" is a mythical beast, but the people who live in various geographical areas are real enough, as are the diseases from which some of them suffer, and their views have yet to be taken into account.

Although the Cummings Blackfoot study suggested that community concern for mental health (however defined) is not necessarily easy to direct or to tap, professional zeal for this solution to the mental hospital and perhaps even to the problem of mental illness has not abated. Indeed, it has become so much a part of the conventional wisdom that there is a community ever willing and anxious to assist in resocializing the mentally ill that it is almost heretical to question the assumption. It may be that this creature—the community—like other mythical beasts reveals itself only to the pure in heart. Dr. Henry R. Rollin [12] has observed that "community care to me is one of the most seductive and yet one of the most treacherous catch-phrases ever devised for the very simple reason that in my experience of a catchment area largely concerned with Metropolitan London there is very little evidence that the community cares a tuppeny damn." He added: "The doss-house is, of course, an alternative to the mental hospital and the prison or the park bench." Recent studies in Canada by

H. B. M. Murphy and his associates [13] support Rollins's view and suggest that, at least in Canada, community care is often an illusion based upon slogans. This is not surprising; the Cummings pioneer work showed that the reason people are extruded from their community is that they have exhausted the patience and resources of a system whose tolerance is far higher than that of most professionals.

Yet the sobering implications of the Cummings own work, Rollins's predictions and observations, Enid Mills's splendid book, [14] Murphy's recent investigations in the field, and the catastrophes which beset the Gardners during their foray into community mental health and preventive psychiatry, have in no way diminished the taste for this beguiling activity. A recent *Roche Report* [15] shows that the siren's song, sung here by Dr. Maxwell Jones, is as entrancing as ever. Dr. Jones is widely known for his development of "therapeutic communities" originally intended for psychopaths, which specifically excluded schizophrenia and other psychotic conditions, but he has apparently extended his range over the years. Addressing the South Beach Psychiatric Center, he said, "I hope you will retain your enthusiasm for preventive psychiatry." He emphasized that "It needs imaginative leaders to fire people to new ideas. One doesn't change results simply through sanctions from above—charismatic leadership is also needed. I have never seen any exciting change in a system without charismatic leadership." Dr. Jones is not too explicit as to what exactly these preventive measures should be. However, he states:

My present feeling about preventive measures is that if all the money spent on psychiatry were focused on getting into the school system to try to help children to learn about learning, about problem solving and about behavior as it occurs in the classroom, I think the world might have some hope, despite what Toffler says in *Future Shock*. I've seen enough of this sort of program to know that if you take any group of children at any level in school and ask them to focus on their inner selves, they don't know how to approach the subject. These are the people who are going to end up in your consulting rooms. These are the people who are going to try to kill themselves because they don't know how to cope with a problem. This has been said before, but it's ridiculous to wait like spiders in our webs until someone really gets caught up in some failure in life, and then go rushing to his help. This is another aspect of psychiatry's role in social interaction, and in this respect I think we would agree that our profession is a bit out of focus. Most modern therapy in the public sector is done by social workers and paraprofessionals.

With Dr. Jones, as with the Cummings, it is not wholly clear as to just what communities are expected to do in order to prevent people from becoming mentally ill. What is quite clear is that an urge to exhort them to do something or other remains as strong as ever—despite the fact that we seem to have no more idea now than in years gone by as to *what* they should do.

We suspect that preventive psychiatry is an example of an unfortunate false analogy based upon misunderstandings sustained by the model-muddle which was so clearly present in the Blackfoot project. In such confused situations, imaginative people like Dr. Jones undoubtedly do "fire up" people's enthusiasm for some supposedly good end. It is debatable whether a combination of admirable aspirations and vague but grandiose notions should be dignified with the title of "new ideas," for most of them have altered not one whit since the days of Adolf Meyer. Charismatic leaders are notorious for lack of discrimination, and throughout history they have often used their capacity to "fire people up" with excitement and lead them on a Gaderene stampede into the depths of the lake below, but just as often, over the hills and far away to nowhere in particular.

7

The Models
of Madness Compared

MOST ATTEMPTS TO RESOLVE conflicts in psychiatry focus on a single dimension, usually etiology or treatment. The medical model is at its weakest in regard to these two most discussed dimensions. The proponents of nonmedical models are often puzzled that the supposedly moribund medical model, whose demise they report so frequently, nevertheless obstinately survives its poor prognosis. A psychologist friend [1] told us recently that a senior colleague of his discussing an early paper of ours at a teaching seminar said, "There is no doubt that many schizophrenics see themselves in terms of the medical model and that they derive great benefit from this—I find this very disturbing and we must do something about it." He did not, however, say what must be done. If indeed the survival of the medical model depended upon its disputed and often muddled theories, there would be cause for puzzlement; but if we compare the models dimension by dimension, a different picture emerges. At almost every point—even, unexpectedly, with regard to etiology and treatment—the medical model is at least equal to, and usually has an edge over, all its competitors.

Take, for example, the dimension of diagnosis. It is only the medical model which seriously admits of the possibility that the person applying for help may have made a mistake; only medicine offers a "clean bill of health" for someone who thinks he might have an illness but does not. None of the other models allows for errors of this type, so it might be said that medicine is the most discriminating of the models. Medical errors in this dimension tend to be those of failing to recognize obscure illnesses or atypical cases, and while such errors are often serious and even fatal, the opposite error is even worse: assuming that every person who applies for help is a suitable candidate. This latter error is seen in its purest and most harmful form among some proponents of psychoanalysis who consider that everyone would be the better for psychoanalysis, in order to alleviate the universal neurosis which their theory requires. This can and has been extended to people who, one might suppose, were unequivocal candidates for medical treatment; at one time general paresis was considered by adventurous psychoanalysts as suitable for their science, but this beachhead into medicine disappeared with the work of Moore and Noguchi, who demonstrated the presence of the *Treponema pallidum*, the causal agent of syphilis, in the brains of paretics.

A more recent error has been described by Dr. I. S. Cooper,[2] a surgeon who treats dystonia musculorum deformans, an extremely painful, progressive, crippling and eventually fatal inherited disease of children. Dr. Cooper reports that some of his young patients, whom he treated successfully with surgery, had spent months and years in the hands of psychiatrists and psychologists. Psychoanalytic, family interaction, and similar methods were used upon these unlucky children and their families with ruthless zeal, but with no judgment or compassion. In consequence of this a grave and agonizing illness became compounded with anguish, guilt, shame, and the disintegration of family life. Eventually, in spite of these inquisitorial rigors, the steady progress of this formidable illness made it clear to the parents that their ill children needed a surgeon. In at least one case the diagnosis had been made several years earlier by an observant doctor whose views were discounted since they did not accord with the model within which this child and her family were then being treated.

Another aspect of this discriminatory bias of medicine is its unique concern with differential diagnosis. As a result of this, some applicants may be given a clean bill of health; but for those who are given the sick role, their diagnosis must be weighed against all the other diagnoses which fit the same clinical picture. While the moral and impaired models at least imply that one must measure the extent of the damage, the other five models are concerned with a single condition which afflicts every applicant in principle, in practice, or both.

This willingness to consider a number of alternative explanations gives the medical model a greater scientific potential than the others, which is not surprising, for during its long history medicine has spawned dozens of sciences from systematic botany to biometrics. An active search for error is an essential feature of the scientific process, and its absence in many of the other models has allowed the same hackneyed ideas to be resurrected decade after decade and century after century without correction or development. Mark Altschule [3] has shown with wit and aplomb that the notions that civilization favors the development of madness and that social change inevitably increases the numbers of mentally ill people have been advanced for millennia. Although these ideas have changed little, each time they reappear newly minted they carry the same quality of inescapable doom which they had hundreds or even thousands of years ago.

There is in the medical model, however, a source of internal conflict in this dimension which must be recognized and understood if it is to be avoided, namely: the sapiential aspect of Aesculapian authority requires differential diagnosis and the possibility of error, while the charismatic element favors the appearance of omniscience. When we are ill, we need both sapience and charisma, and lucky is the patient whose doctor has found a way to balance these two requirements of his role. Indeed, since very few doctors receive any instruction about the nature, quality, and appropriate use of their ancient authority, which has only recently been clearly defined, it is encouraging that many of them use it so well. Once knowledge about their authority and the rights and duties which accompany it becomes available and receives formal recognition by medical schools, we predict that even more doctors will become competent in this very important aspect of the clinical art. In our opinion many of the current dissatisfactions expressed by patients regarding their doctors derive from the clumsy, careless, or even downright inept use of Aesculapian authority. The abuse of a great and respected authority inevitably causes the greatest offense and dismay.

In the dimension of etiology, the historical record of the medical model shows that one by one, mysterious illnesses have yielded their secrets to medical investigation. We may never be able to secure any ultimate proof as to why a particular person becomes ill at a particular time, or to prove why a particular disease comes into existence and flourishes, but etiological knowledge which enables us to prevent or control diseases to some extent is usually forthcoming, and there is every reason to believe this to be so for psychiatric diseases as well. In other models, etiological knowledge is either held to be unimportant (e.g., the moral model) or is held to be important and known (e.g., the psychoanalytic and social models), but this knowledge does not seem to contribute in any practical way to the prevention or control of madness.

It is sometimes argued that schizophrenia cannot be an illness because the etiology is still unknown, or is at least hotly disputed. But within the medical model, a disputed etiology is no bar to considering the condition an illness. If there is any correlation, it is the other way around: illnesses with known etiologies, such as pellagra psychosis or general paresis, tend to be treated successfully and are thus removed from clinical into public health medicine. At any given time, clinical medicine consists mainly of just those illnesses which are most poorly understood. The medical model, then, has an impressive record for discovering the etiology of illnesses, and also can claim to offer social support where that knowledge is not yet available.

It might be added that those using nonmedical models have rejected etiological evidence for schizophrenia which would be considered quite good when seen from within the framework of the medical model. If we had as many etiological clues for cancer, multiple sclerosis, or cystic fibrosis as we have for schizophrenia, we would hold ourselves to be very fortunate. The standard for acceptable evidence must be appropriate to the model in use.

Regarding interpretation of the behavior of the mad person, the five continuous models imply that someone is to blame, either the family, society, or some combination of these. The moral and impaired models are concerned with normalizing behavior, and the medical model with physiological normalcy; neither of these goals requires that anyone be blamed, nor would they in any way be facilitated by blaming someone for the condition of madness. The advantage of a blame-free interpretation of behavior is that energy is not wasted in vendettas but can be spent on returning the mad person to normal.

The medical model has the additional advantage that the patient's behavior sometimes offers valuable clues for diagnosis. For example, a pamphlet intended for thyroid patients shows a cartoon of a shivering person, wrapped in layers of winter clothing, sitting between a blazing fire and a heating lamp. The caption indicates that this behavior, a reaction to cold intolerance, tells the doctor that something might be wrong with the body's thermostat, the thyroid gland. In schizophrenia, behavioral clues can help establish a diagnosis. The American Schizophrenia Association, like all such national organizations, gives a list of "danger signs" which should alert people to the possibility of schizophrenia. Among them are: unaccountable changes in personality, confusion, memory loss, fatigue, insomnia, and disturbances in seeing, hearing, smelling, touching, and tasting. The behavioral consequences of these symptoms are observable from the outside, although the inner experience which generates them is not directly observable.

After people recover from suffering many years of schizophrenia, they often find that they have acquired patterns of behavior which, however unavoidable or even essential for survival they may have been during the illness, become increasingly dysfunctional with recovery. Here the impaired and moral models are frequently the appropriate tools for retraining the the recovered patient to enable him to acquire behavior which will allow him to work, to sustain relationships, and to do those many other things which normal people take for granted. Recovery Incorporated [4] is an example of a program using the moral model which was designed by a psychiatrist to help his patients acquire new and useful ways and to divest themselves of unsuitable and even destructive behavior patterns acquired when ill.

By contrast, the psychoanalytic model, especially in some of the exotic or vulgarized derivatives which are now prevalent, sometimes teaches and often encourages (at great expense) dysfunctional social behavior. For the standard of behavior appropriate to the psychoanalytic couch, or whatever may be used as a substitute when this has been rendered obsolete, is seldom acceptable anywhere else. Those who add bad manners learned on the couch to the initial misfortune of growing up with, or developing, schizophrenia may find themselves living in a community of one. Those who have been led to believe that their mental health, well-being, and personal integrity oblige them to express their feelings, however extreme these may be, no matter what the cost in personal relationships, will find it difficult to rally much social support when they most need it. We do not suggest that well-trained psychoanalysts encourage their analysands to act out in an anti-social manner, but there are few well-trained psychoanalysts, compared with the very large numbers of psychotherapists using the psychoanalytic model. The public conception of the psychoanalytic model and its social consequences derives at least as much from the enthusiastic many as from the austere, orthodox few.

The medical model offers the same advantages in the dimension of treatment as it does in etiology. Its historical record for discovering useful treatments is encouraging, and in their absence the social support of the sick role can sustain the ill person until such time as better treatments are available. There is almost always something that can be done to ameliorate the sick person's condition, to prevent it from getting worse, or, failing that, to slow down the progress of the disease. In view of the ultimate threats of disease—pain, impairment, death—even a very modest improvement may be of great comfort to a particular patient. As in the case of etiology, the standards of acceptability must be suitable to the model in use. A treatment which resulted in improvement of 5 percent of cancer patients would be considered valuable in the absence of anything better, for those 5 percent may represent hundreds or even thousands of suffering human beings. No one using a medical model would reject a treatment because it did not instantly cure a disease for 100 percent of the afflicted population. Those who reject new treatments for schizophrenia because they are not 100 percent effective ought to be asked whether they believe these new treatments to be 100 percent ineffective, for if they help any schizophrenics, no matter how few, they ought to be used with that lucky fraction of the total schizophrenic population. Further, it would be worthwhile to investigate what those who are helped have in common, in the hope that some underlying principle may be revealed, thus pointing the way to other treatments for the less fortunate.

In order to be acceptable, a new treatment must meet certain requirements: it must be more effective and at least as safe as the existing treatments, and it must be technically and economically feasible. Also, it must be intellectually respectable—it must make sense in terms of what we know about the illness and about treatments in general. We would probably not accept, today, a treatment compounded of eye of newt and skin of toad unless it could be shown that these substances contained active ingredients of an appropriate kind, such as some new hormone or enzyme. Further, a treatment must be moral; it must not require the participants to engage in morally repugnant activities. Just what treatments will be considered moral or immoral depends upon the time and the place. When King William the Third of England was Duke of Orange he developed smallpox and was thought to be dying. His doctors considered that, in accordance with the theories of the day, his only hope lay in "an access of animal spirits." This sovereign remedy was to be found in young people and was respired in their breath. They therefore recommended that one of his young pages should sleep with him. William was said to sleep with his pages when well, but for sexual and recreational rather than for medical reasons. The lad returned to his master's bed, contracted smallpox and very nearly died, but both William and his page eventually recovered. William felt deeply indebted to his page, who continued to be a favorite for the rest of the king's life, and was later made Duke of Portland. Yet today, in an age of Gay Liberation, neither the doctors nor the public would countenance this very successful life-saving treatment, which would be considered morally distasteful. Nevertheless, if we transposed from the seventeenth to the twentieth century and young Bentinck, the page, offered a pint of blood or his kidney to his monarch, something which would have been quite unacceptable in his own time, who would doubt that his courage would be applauded and the royal doctors praised for their acumen!

A contemporary example of an immoral treatment would be to require an alcoholic to denounce all drinkers, including his former drinking companions. This would not be acceptable today and has seldom worked in the past. Far more acceptable are treatments which view the alcoholic as the unfortunate victim of a metabolic error, from which his companions have luckily escaped. None of the continuous models have yet offered or are likely to offer a treatment for alcoholism or schizophrenia which is morally acceptable, as well as feasible, intellectually respectable, and better than the existing treatments.

It is important to understand that the mere presence of a medical treatment, for example, a prescription "drug," is no guarantee that the medical model is in use. The original methadone maintenance program of Dole and Nyswander [5] was unequivocally within the medical model, and while it was recognized that methadone had serious drawbacks as a medical treatment, it was offered as being better than any existing treatment. In recent years, programs have developed in which methadone is still being prescribed by physicians, but the sick role does not seem to be conferred and the necessary rehabilitative measures are not being taken. The evidence for this is that the word "crutch" is being used to criticize these programs. A daily dose of medicine, say, insulin for diabetes or thyroid for hypothyroidism, is not referred to as a "crutch" within the medical model. Methadone is seen as a "crutch" by people using a moral model who perceive the methadone programs as using an impaired model improperly.*

The same problem presents itself with tranquilizers as with methadone. Tranquilizers may be used by a physician exercising Aesculapian authority as a medical treatment for patients installed

---

* When we constructed our models of drug addiction, we were not aware of the possibility of an impaired model; it was only the repeated use of the word "crutch" in critical articles which called our attention to this additional model.

in the sick role. Exactly the same substances may also be used as chemical restraints in a hospital ward run by those using the moral model; or as a "drug" in the pejorative sense of the word to maintain a population of impaired schizophrenics in the community. It is notable that many nonhospitalized schizophrenics who take tranquilizers appear to have given up any hope of ever getting better and show little interest either in other treatment possibilities or in rehabilitating themselves. They appear to be resigned to living as second-class citizens, in the community but not of it. By contrast, schizophrenics who do occupy the sick role are constantly on the alert for newer and better treatments, which is a right enjoyed by all *patients*, but *not* by the impaired.

In the dimension of prognosis, the five continuous models offer pie in the sky. If society substantially reforms, there will be no more mental illness; if family therapy is successful, the index patient will give up his symptoms; if psychoanalysis works, the underlying trauma will be revealed and overcome; if sufficiently enlightened gurus can be found, the mad will be conducted on guided "trips" from which they will emerge better than the rest of us; if civil libertarians are vigilant enough, the mental hospitals will be emptied. Should these miracles fail to occur, there is silence about the alternative moves to be made. The medical model, built for disaster, cannot promise a cure but can almost always hold out some hope of betterment, even if temporary. But should an illness grow steadily worse, the social support offered by the medical model grows correspondingly stronger. The fatal illness of young Johnny Gunther brought his divorced parents together at his bedside, called for special exertions on the part of his doctors, brought encouragement from friends and well-wishers. Yet the prognosis, stated directly by the famous brain surgeon Wilder Penfield, was: "Your child has a malignant glioma, and it will kill him." [6]

The proponents of the various models are generally silent on the subject of suicide, but this neglected issue has an important effect on another dimension, that of personnel. Lay therapists, of whatever persuasion, often come to realize that schizophrenics may kill themselves, and that if this occurs, only a doctor with

Aesculapian authority can reduce its impact on families, friends, the community, and upon the therapist, too. This may lead to an unacknowledged preference for patients with less serious disorders. The fact is that schizophrenia is a killer, and that only the medical profession is equipped to handle death. Osmond and Hoffer [7] estimated that schizophrenics commit suicide twenty times more often than the normal rate for their country. While there has been a gratifying reduction in the loss of life from other causes, there has been no corresponding reduction in suicide, the relative importance of which has greatly increased. The picture is even worse when one realizes that schizophrenic suicides are almost always those of young adults, who have thereby lost much of their expected life-span, whereas the suicides of the elderly may shorten their lives by only a few years. While there is little official recognition of the importance of suicide in schizophrenia, there is enough accumulated experience to give pause to anyone planning to set up a totally nonmedical program for schizophrenics.

The medical model, when working properly, is not only the best equipped to handle the stress of suicide on the family and community should it occur; it is also the most likely to be able to prevent it. Watching out for signs that an illness is getting worse and may end fatally is a familiar medical maneuver. Once aware that suicide is a special risk in this illness, a doctor can use his clinical experience, as well as suitable psychological tests,[8] to monitor the illness. The continuous models have no such built-in equipment, as the Wechslers [9] learned to their sorrow when their son committed suicide after being treated by a series of eight psychoanalytically oriented therapists.

Whatever model is in use, the person seeking help and the practitioner offering it usually meet in some building. In the medical model, this building is called a "hospital" and its function is so well known that television writers, pulp novelists, and writers of children's books are able to use it as a setting with little effort of the imagination. This is not the case with the other models. The most extreme case is that of the conspiratorial model, which is in principle anti-institutional. In practice, however, there has been little concern for the fate of mental patients who have been "liberated" from mental hospitals only to find themselves living in flophouses or jails. The rub is that the buildings called "mental hospitals" are not hospitals within the sense implied by the medical model; it is this discrepancy which has called forth the conspiratorial model, for there is no comparable agitation to liberate people from general hospitals. There have been very few instances to date of attempts to house the psychedelic model, but in those that we know of, there has been a marked antagonism on the part of the surrounding community, which is understandable, since this model views society as a repressive force that both creates madness and prevents its resolution. Presumably the inmates of such psychedelic establishments perceive themselves as a beleaguered garrison of the elect surrounded by implacable enemies. In such circumstances their behavior, while wholly appropriate for their model, would be unlikely to evoke a favorable community attitude. Thus we have another destructive self-fulfilling prophecy.

In the psychoanalytic and family interaction models, there is a great deal of confusion in this dimension: both are noninstitutional in principle, but in fact seriously ill schizophrenics have to live somewhere while being treated, and so we find that there are doctors, nurses, wards, attendants, tours of duty, nursing stations, and all the other paraphernalia of hospital life in buildings where the sick role is denied. This discrepancy is covered over by using Aesculapian authority: doctor knows best.

Behavior therapy can be conducted anywhere, although one can imagine that some forms of it might best be conducted in a correctional institution to which the clients could voluntarily commit themselves for a period of time. Some weight-reduction and physical-fitness camps appear to run along these lines. Where the moral model is used within a so-called mental hospital, the greatest architectural confusion occurs, for patients in real hospitals are moved around according to the severity of their illnesses (e.g., to intensive care units if worse), but within the moral model, the worst behaved inmates are moved to progressively worse quarters. Instead of intensive care, they get isolation in punishment cells, as Clifford Beers [10] and Frances Farmer [11] have so vividly described.

The impaired and social models both imply protective institutions or asylums for those unable to manage in the outside world. When these two models are mixed in with a deteriorated version of the medical model, one gets an inhospitable, nonprotective human warehouse, run under medical auspices. It was this hydra-headed monster that Goffman observed and described in his famous paper, "On the Characteristics of Total Institutions." [12] Since Goffman did not concern himself with the nature of the illnesses (chiefly schizophrenia) that had generated all these models, he was forced to construct a conspiratorial model [13] in which people designated as mental patients were living miserable lives in total institutions for no apparent reason. Only a grasp of the actual nature of schizophrenia as a solvent which destroys the social glue of human relationships can make sense of the plight of its helpless victims and the peculiar architectural arrangements which have grown up around them.

It is not difficult to construct a building which is suitable for the treatment of schizophrenic patients and which evokes the best behavior both in them and in the staff who treat them: the architectural features of such buildings have been known for at least 170 years.[14] In schizophrenia there are frequent disturbances of space and time perception which cause patients to be frightened and distressed by complicated and ambiguous architectural features. What is required is a straightforward and simple building in which patients are not forced unnecessarily into each other's company. Since schizophrenic patients ofen suffer from overstimulation, they are best off in a building in which they can retreat gracefully to their own quarters should they feel overwhelmed by the presence of other people. Since the goal of the medical model is to get patients out of the hospital once their illness has subsided, the hospital does not need to have bowling alleys, swimming pools, theaters, and other features which would be appropriate for a permanent population of impaired people. Among the new psychiatric hospitals, Kyo Izumi's Yorkton Psychiatric Centre,[15] Haverford State Hospital,[16] and the Sibley Memorial Hospital [17] incorporate these desirable features. In addition to being suitable for both patients and staff, these buildings provide concrete evidence to the community that the object of the enterprise is to benefit those who are ill. Local people take pride in these buildings and consider them a community asset, just as they do with attractive and modern general hospitals.

In the dimension of personnel, the medical model offers the best-known and most clearcut role for the practitioner: the doctor, invested with Aesculapian authority. The comparable roles in the other models are lightweight by comparison; none has anything like the massive authority of the doctor. When proponents of the various models are gathered together under one psychiatric roof, several kinds of difficulties arise. Those psychologists and social workers who use nonmedical models will see no reason why they should be underpaid, undervalued, and exploited by the psychiatrists, especially if they believe themselves more skilled in psychotherapy than their medical colleagues. This is especially true in establishments whose rhetoric is that of the psychoanalytic model: if psychotherapy is the most important skill, then why are the staff not graded according to their psychotherapeutic talents? The hidden agenda, of course, is the ever-present but inexplicit medical model. Another difficulty arises when the psychiatrists invite sociologists and anthropologists to come and help them with their work, only to subordinate these scientists to psychiatry. As Professor Paul Roman, a sociologist, says:

In these settings one can observe sociologists often placed in auxiliary or even "minion" roles in research, with their primary contribution being methodological advice (Tucker; Larsen). Their counsel seems frequently to exclude *critical evaluation* of psychiatric models and practices, with the result that the sociologist's role is almost exclusively that of a research technician (e.g., Pasamanick *et al.*). When direct sociological incursions are attempted, rejection is the reported experience (Tucker).[18]

Since clinical doctors have no special problem in relating themselves appropriately to pharmacologists, pathologists, radiologists, physiologists, physiotherapists, or medical social workers, it is clear that the difficulty in psychiatry is the lack of a complete, consistent, and explicit medical model. As soon as the patients in psychiatric hospitals are perceived as having illnesses rather than problems, the psychiatrists' Aesculapian authority will seem not only tolerable but welcome, as few lay people wish to shoulder the responsibility of treating the ill. On the other hand, if psychiatric patients have problems in living rather than illnesses, there is no reason to put up with the high-handed ways of psychiatrists; indeed, there is no reason to have medically qualified staff at all.

Within the medical model, another kind of personnel problem arises, that of the relation of doctors to nurses. At the Saskatchewan Hospital, Weyburn, where T. T. Paterson undertook his original studies, doctors were rather loosely put in charge of wards. It was never clear what "being in charge of a ward" meant, and a good deal of wrangling used to occur with the nursing staff over this. Paterson advised that the physicians should have no structural authority, the structural authority being carried by the nurses, as it has long been done in general hospitals. This system proved to be very successful and was much appreciated by the doctors, who, it turned out, were delighted to be rid of an authority which they had never particularly wanted, did not understand, and did not use very adroitly.

The dimension of personnel defines not only who the practitioners shall be, and their relation to other professionals, but also their rights and duties toward the person seeking help, the other half of the subject's role. In the cases of the sick role, these are the rights and duties of the doctor vis-à-vis the patient. One of the questions that has been raised recently about the doctor-patient relationship is whether or not it might include sexual intercourse.[19] In the Hippocratic oath it was clearly recognized that the sexual seduction of patients by means of Aesculapian authority was considered a grave and serious abuse. As long as psychiatry stays within the medical model it is unlikely that its members or the public would countenance its great authority being used to allow physicians to take sexual advantage of patients. Paradoxically, the more liberal society's sexual mores become, the more necessary it may be for physicians to desist from what would be a growing temptation, since the forces of conscience acting against such license would clearly be less in a promiscuous society than in a straight-laced one. The question at issue is not a general one regarding the advantages or disadvantages of sexual laxity or puritanism, but that of the effect of sexual mores upon the sick role, the doctor-patient relationship, and Aesculapian authority.

Psychiatrists who use a medical model and wish to persuade their fellow psychiatrists to do likewise may not be able to persuade them on the basis of etiological theories or experimental evidence for new treatments, because the standards in these two dimensions vary so much with the model in use. What they can do, if we may paraphrase Thomas Kuhn,* is to provide a clear exhibit of what psychiatric practice will be like for those who adopt the new view. Those psychiatrists who have never used the medical model consistently and explicitly may not be able to imagine what it would look like if they did. Here their fellow psychiatrists who have either learned how to do this or have never forgotten it can be of service in offering a clear example of the medical model in operation.

Of the eight possible subject roles in our schema, the two chief contenders are the sick role and the "psych" role. The impaired role, while widespread among hospitalized schizophrenics and those living untreated in the community, is usually conferred by default. There comes a fateful moment in the lives of those suffering from schizophrenia when they first present themselves for help, either to a private physician or psychiatrist in his office, or in a hospital admitting office. Upon giving an account of his symptoms and his current state, the person seeking help learns from the practitioner either that he has a disease, or that he has problems in living. (He probably has problems in living in any case, but the doctor conferring the sick role will elect to postpone any discussion of these problems until his disease is brought under control.) The course of action in the two cases is almost entirely different. If the sick role is conferred, some kind of diagnosis will be offered,

* Kuhn says: "The man who premises a paradigm when arguing in its defense can nonetheless provide a clear exhibit of what scientific practice will be like for those who adopt the new view of nature. That exhibit can be immensely persuasive, often compellingly so. Yet, whatever its force, the status of the circular argument is only that of persuasion. It can not be made logically or even probabilistically compelling for those who refuse to step into the circle." (Thomas S. Kuhn, *The Structure of Scientific Revolutions* [Chicago: University of Chicago Press, 1962].)

laboratory tests will be ordered, a temporary treatment regimen will be started, some supportive and hopeful remarks will be made, and a second appointment will be scheduled. If the "psych" role is conferred, the need for diagnosis will be disclaimed, hopeful and supportive remarks will be made, a series of appointments for psychotherapeutic sessions will be made, and perhaps there will be some discussion of the person's family or life situation. In both cases there may be discussions of fees, but in the case of the "psych" role this is likely to be more urgent, since psycho-therapy sessions are often not covered by insurance, and it is known in advance that there will be a large weekly expenditure. The subjective experience of accepting the sick role or the "psych" role is entirely different, as anyone who has experienced both knows. Although we have extolled the virtues of the sick role, we do not wish to imply that learning that one has a major illness which is difficult to treat and will probably be lifelong is any reason for rejoicing. It is just that the alternative—having such an illness, not learning about it, and not getting the sick role—is much worse. In the case of the "psych" role, there are two often reported responses. The person may feel: "It's not so bad after all —at least I'm not really sick—this man seems kind and helpful— he seems to think I can work out my problems." However, a hope-ful prognosis at this point may lead to bitter disappointment later if the expected relief of symptoms does not occur. The other reported response is: "This is really frightening—he doesn't seem to believe I am really sick—I don't see how talking to him will make any difference—maybe my personality is hopeless." In the case of the sick role, there is the rational fear upon learning that one has a serious illness; in the case of the "psych" role there is the equally rational fear that the proposed solution does not sound adequate to the anguish experienced.

It is a vital matter for the family of the schizophrenic, as well as the schizophrenic himself, to discover whether he has been installed in the sick role or the "psych" role. How can one tell? The word "sick" is unfortunately no clue at all, any more than the use of a prescription drug guarantees the presence of the medical model. In today's usage, to say that someone is "very sick" may just as well mean that he has an extremely warped and unpleasant personality, or that he is "too sick" to undertake any responsibilities, i.e., impaired. This is so much the case that we have advised both psychiatrists and families to stay away from the word "sick" altogether and use the less-corrupted word "ill" instead. One of the greatest disservices of the psychoanalytic model is that because of it the word "sick" has been lost to our vocabulary as a way of describing the state of being ill or suffering from a disease. The litmus-test for the sick role is whether the afflicted person is receiving what Benjamin Rush [20] called the "immediate and universal compassion" for which disease is the signal. If the practitioner, the family, or others who know the supposedly sick person are treating him with condescension or contempt, or are moralizing with him about his erring ways, he is not in the sick role, whether or not the word "sick" is used to describe him.

Suppose that it is not clear whether the person seeking help is suffering primarily from a disease or from a problem in living. What then should be done? We have already indicated that this may be difficult to determine on the basis of generally acceptable scientific evidence. The rule is: a disputed condition is best considered an illness when the conferral of the sick role is the least harmful course of action. In A. J. Cronin's novel *The Citadel*, Dr. Manson accepts as patients a number of people whom he knows are not really sick in order to build his practice. In a moment of truth, he decides to throw them all out, knowing full well that in depriving them of the sick role he is not harming them but, if anything, doing them a favor. In the case of schizophrenia, the conferral of the "psych" role instead of the sick role may doom the person seeking help to months or years of irrelevant or useless psychotherapy when he needs medical help. In addition, the "psych" role may have the effect of worsening the family relations, especially if the person does not improve or gets worse. Each year that medical treatment is delayed will find the illness more firmly entrenched, and in young people valuable years of socialization and education may be lost. Worst of all, the schizophrenic may lose hope and commit suicide, leaving behind a family either implicitly or explicitly accused of his death. These are the risks which must be weighed if the practitioner elects, and the family accepts, the conferral of the "psych" role rather than the sick role.

We believe that the sick role/"psych" role dichotomy is more useful than the corresponding body-mind dichotomy. There does not seem to be any reliable way of choosing between body and mind in a disputed ailment, but the choice of roles carries with it a set of knowable consequences, some of which are likely to be more harmful than others. By weighing these consequences one can attempt to make the least harmful choice. "Body" and "mind" are simply two words we have invented in order to describe two kinds of experiences that we have of ourselves that are sufficiently different most of the time to make it awkward and impracticable to use the same word for both. The problem is that we forget to include the brain as part of the body. We all know that inside the skull is the brain, not the "mind," but since the brain does not have palpitations or cramps, since it does not hurt, itch, or sting, we have no direct experience of it and we do not know when it is "sick." Our model for a disease of the brain is a brain tumor, but in fact most illnesses affect our brains. Illnesses make us groggy, or irritable, or depressed, or forgetful—even the common cold has a profound effect upon our mental abilities and our mood. Yet a doctor may examine a patient system by system—the digestive system, the respiratory system, the skeletal system, the nervous system, etc.—and finding nothing wrong, may ask: "Do you think it might be psychological?" How seldom doctors ask: "Do you think this illness is affecting your brain?" Very often the answer would be "Yes."

Three of the models, the psychoanalytic, the psychedelic, and the conspiratorial, offer no rights to the family at all: the family stands accused of creating schizophrenia, thereby forfeiting its natural rights. The family interaction model offers the family the right to be treated as "sick" along with the index patient, but this right exists in theory only, for in practice this is the most virulent of all the models toward the family, often compounding blame with ridicule and even accusations of crime. In the social model, poor families are told that it is their right to live in a more just and equitable world, at which time they will no longer be plagued with mental illness. This news must be cold comfort to a poor family trying to find help for a schizophrenic child.

One of the rights of the family in the impaired model is to be spared unreasonable hope. When such families approach psychiatrists with questions about new treatment possibilities, the response is often: "Who has dared to offer you hope?" The right to be spared unreasonable hope is indeed valuable in a true, permanent impairment, but these families are raising the question of whether schizophrenia is such an impairment or whether it is not an illness for which hope is appropriate.

In the moral model, families have the right to expect that there are behavioral experts who can induce in their errant member better behavior than they are able to promote. This is sometimes expressed by angry and frustrated families as: "They'll teach you how to behave at that hospital!" The behavioral arrangements in the hospital ward may very well induce a person to give up the behavior which his family found so offensive, but if this is done under coercion and without real consent, it is not likely to last when he is at home again. The changes which come about in voluntary behavior therapy sessions or self-help groups such as Recovery Incorporated, are more likely to be lasting.

Compared with the medical model, the other models have little to offer families. Only the medical model can bring real sympathy and comfort, realistic hope, and a well-known set of rights and duties which will relate them constructively to their ill member, to the practitioner, and to the community. The families of schizophrenics are badly treated because they do not know their rights. Perhaps it is their duty to know their rights, and then, knowing them, to demand the sick role for their ill child or relative. Aesculapian authority is legitimate only when it is used in conjunction with the sick role, and if the sick role is withheld, the family has no obligation to respond to the doctor's authority. If there is anything that families ought to be guilty about, it is their uncritical medical piety. If they withhold their deference to Aesculapian authority until their child is safely within the sick role, they will call forth better behavior from the doctor. Doctors do not wish to mistreat families, but they do not know any better. Since the burden of the ignorance of the doctor-patient relationship falls upon the families, it is they who have the strongest motive for making it explicit, and therefore it is their responsibility to learn as much as they can about it.

Families should not underestimate their own capacity to change their doctors' behavior once they themselves understand the nature of the sick role and that of Aesculapian authority. The sick role is a morally acceptable social invention of great antiquity. It was not made by doctors; indeed, its roots lie in our prehuman evolution. We share the sick role with many other mammals, and most of us acquired the rudiments of the role at about the same time we took our first steps—before we could speak. Doctors are no less susceptible to the morality, the rightness, and the goodness of the sick role than anyone else; hence they are unlikely to undermine it purposely, although they might do so by inadvertence. An appeal to a doctor, urging him to confer the sick role properly and effectively in accordance with medical custom, cannot fall on deaf ears once the issue has been clearly understood by all those involved.

Many people are afraid to confront doctors, for there are circumstances when to challenge Aesculapian authority endangers life. However, the very fact that this authority is so massive gives patients, families, and the public the right to insist that something so mighty is always used in the best possible way. No authority is more susceptible to such an appeal than Aesculapian authority which is based, above all else, upon its use of wisdom, goodness, and intuition acting for the benefit of suffering humanity.

In their hearts most good doctors know that their high prestige derives from the value the public places on their services. Because so much has been given to doctors, the public has a right to a sympathetic hearing from the profession. In the last analysis Aesculapian authority derives neither from universities, nor from medical societies, nor from examination boards, nor from governments, but from the public who, as patients, confers it by placing their lives in the hands of doctors. The doctor is a servant of the public, his patients; sometimes haughty, self-willed, overbearing, even arrogant, but still a servant. It is his privilege and pleasure to serve in so serious a matter, just as Mr. Winston Churchill proudly referred to himself as a servant of the House of Commons. Good service of this kind is not unrewarding.

By some quirk of their history and education, possibly due to the exacting nature of their occupation, doctors are little concerned with these matters, which play a negligible part in their training and seldom appear in their academic examinations. Since neglect of such vital matters can lead to serious misunderstandings about the very nature of medicine, it may now be necessary for doctors to be reminded that they have a duty to sustain, nourish, and if possible expand that relationship between doctor and patient which has done so much good for humanity. When such an appeal is made firmly but without malice, it will be difficult for exemplary doctors to resist it, although on reflection they may regret the negligence which has made it necessary.

Those psychiatrists who have deprived their patients of the sick role, who have ignored, ridiculed, and even abused hard-pressed families, have acted from ignorance, not from unkindness or viciousness. This ignorance derives from an intellectual laziness that has often plagued medicine in the past, for the art, craft, and science of medicine is exacting enough to distract its practitioners from large, apparently philosophical issues. Psychiatrists have accepted, often uncritically, the fashionable notions of their specialty, combined with some gleaned from psychologist and sociologist colleagues, just as their blood-letting forebears were swept away by Broussais's theory of bowel inflammation, which led to the pandemic of bleeding during the early nineteenth century. That particular enthusiasm cost tens of thousands of lives. Doctors are craftsmen, little given to social and historical analyses of their own activities; they are usually far too busy to concern themselves with what often seem to them to be abstract and impractical matters, far removed from the needs of patients. Nevertheless, doctors are social creatures, not fanatics forever bound to strange new principles, and once they discover that the patients and their families, and the public at large, do not relish their employing nonmedical models, they will probably take heed. It would not surprise us if they returned to their customary behavior with little rancor and even with relish. Recent reports suggest that the endless model-muddles are causing psychiatrists such distress that they consider themselves to be under siege.[21] It may come as a relief if patients and their families encourage psychiatry to return again to medicine, from which it sprang.

What are the rights of society or the community when one of its members who is thought to be mad commits some heinous and destructive crime of the order of murder, treason, or blasphemy? What should the response be to that kind of crime which assails the values of the particular culture head-on and presents an inescapable and unavoidable challenge to its morality?

Schizophrenics seldom resort to violence—considering the fears, suspicions, and uncertainties resulting from their illness and the fact that their world often seems to be populated by enemies or, worse still, the simulations of relatives and friends plotting their downfall and destruction. Most schizophrenics feel far too wretched and insecure to attack anyone; indeed, they usually have much difficulty in coping with aggression by other people. Their social ineptitude tends to erode the patience of all but the most kindly and forbearing. Nevertheless, schizophrenics do commit murders, and these are sometimes so unpredictable, bizarre, spectacular, and excessive as to color our attitude toward the mentally ill.

In two of our models, the moral and the conspiratorial, the schizophrenic murderer, like any other wrongdoer, is subject to the law just the same as the rest of us. In these two models the issue is one of guilt or innocence: did he or did he not commit the murder (or other crime)? Once guilt has been established, the outcome depends upon which of the five subdivisions of the moral model happens to be used by that particular community. In the retributive submodel, the guiding principle is that of an eye for an eye and a tooth for a tooth: the murderer must pay for his crime in a manner which will uphold and strengthen the morality of society. Since the effect of retribution is greatly strengthened by an admission of guilt, which much reduces the possibility of error, the accused person is always strongly encouraged to confess. For should it be discovered that an innocent person has been convicted by mistake and retribution exacted, morality will be endangered and belief in justice undermined. For this reason, if no other, those employing retribution are very unwilling to admit even the possibility of error. In the deterrent submodel, punishment must be harsh enough to deter others who might be tempted to wrongdoing. The main purpose of the rehabilitative submodel is to restore the erring person to proper moral functioning. Although our society shows very little interest in the restitutive submodel, in which the murderer must reimburse the bereaved family, some other societies have used it successfully. Among the Eskimo, the killer is sometimes obliged to marry his victim's wife and support her children; perhaps there were circumstances in which this carried an element of deterrence. Once murder has been committed, the preventive model is no longer applicable, for it is then too late. The advantage of the moral submodels and the conspiratorial model is that they resolve the problem of the mad murderer by denying that such a category exists. Provided there is an agreement as to which of the moral submodels is to be used, the appropriate course of action regarding the murderer can be determined easily enough. However, neither the various moral nor conspiratorial models provide much scope for human compassion or even for common observation: throughout recorded history, it has been recognized that people commit grievous crimes because they are not themselves, but are afflicted by madness.

Those models derived from psychoanalysis lie at the other extreme, for with them society is held responsible for creating madness either directly through the agency of the family. Such models show little concern for the rights of society, but instead focus attention upon the duty of the body social to become more tolerant, more understanding, more accepting, and more open-minded toward different lifestyles. At their most sanguine, those who use these models believe that if this were to happen, mental illnesses such as schizophrenia and crimes such as murder would completely disappear. These models have the advantage of encouraging a compassionate attitude to the schizophrenic murderer who is seen as being a victim of forces beyond his control. However, they do not meet our need to uphold the morality of society; neither do they provide for safety from murderers. Consequently, by denying the moral basis which is a requisite for any society, they generate fear and insecurity in members of the community which erode rather than increase their tolerance and understanding. People who are frightened are rarely kind, forbearing, and detached. Indeed, there are many examples of legal defenses based on the psychoanalytic model which appear to have provoked a punitive rather than a compassionate attitude on the part of judges and juries. So far, only the medical model has shown a capacity for resolving these complicated problems: the often criticized but seldom improved M'Naghten Rules were an attempt to do just this about 130 years ago. These rules, propounded by the judges in the House of Lords in England, provide for a class of people who, although they have committed a criminal act, are nevertheless at the same time entitled to the sick role. In the original Judges' Rules, the sick role has to be conferred retrospectively to the time of committing the act, a legal device which engendered many difficulties. What was gained by this approach, clumsy though it may appear today, was that the morality of society was maintained because it is admitted that the action of the accused was both immoral and illegal. At the same time, the Rules, whose flexibility in practice has been much greater than might appear at first reading, enabled people to act compassionately toward an ill person. This reinforces the moral worth of medicine, and in so doing, indicates that a society using the Rules is as much concerned with goodness as with rightness. In other words, such a society does not consider it good enough to give ill people the same rights they would have if well. In addition, the needs of public safety are met because the mad murderer can be seen in the same light as someone suffering from a dangerous and contagious disease, such as the plague, who must be isolated from the rest of us until such time as his illness has been brought under control and has ceased to be a danger to others.

While the crimes committed by the mentally ill provide a dramatic illustration of the rights and duties of society as related to our models, they represent a minuscular part of the greater issues involved. Each of the models specifies some kind of service required by a person seeking help and, in the final analysis, it is the society to which the individual belongs that must provide those services. In all the models time, manpower, energy, and money must be provided in such a manner as not to lead to inequities which would be intolerable to that particular society. Psychoanalysis and family therapy require highly trained therapists, and since they often continue for months and years, they are very expensive. There seems to be a shortage of gurus for the psychedelic model, for they, too, are few and hard to find. Those behavior modification experts so necessary for some of the moral models are also few in comparison with the massive task confronting them. There do not seem to be many of those champions of the persecuted required for the conspiratorial model, and their case load seems rather small. Merely dumping people from mental hospitals by fiat or preventing them from getting there by refusing to admit them without extraordinary legal exertions may provide employment for lawyers, a profession which does not seem to be in any great need at this time, but hardly meets the human requirements of those suffering from mythical mental illnesses. Social psychiatrists and well-trained rehabilitation experts are also in short supply. Neither are there enough doctors for first-rate medical treatment, but it does not take long or cost much to confer the sick role; indeed, any doctor can do this. Providing basic medical care for schizophrenics takes less time and money than the services required to make most of the other models work effectively. Furthermore, in any particular disease, treatment tends to become more effective as time goes on. Penicillin, for instance, was once almost priceless, but today it costs very little; yet it is more effective than it was thirty years ago. Those with extremely costly illnesses such as kidney disease or hemophilia can reasonably expect a diminution in costs and an increase in efficiency as time passes. Psychoanalysis, on the other hand, seems to have gained prestige as it has become increasingly lengthy and expensive over the last three-quarters of a century.

One purpose of the various health-care delivery systems now beginning to be developed is to ensure that rich and poor alike have an equal opportunity to obtain the best medical treatment for their illnesses. If this is so, it may be pertinent to ask just what model poor people prefer when confronted with serious psychiatric illnesses such as schizophrenia or grave depression. The poor, like anyone else, have a right to have their preferences examined with that respectful attention which all citizens in a democracy should demand of its politicians, planners, and bureaucrats. The record is clear enough: poor people much prefer the familiar and easily understood medical model.[22] They have never shown much enthusiasm for the class-biased psychoanalytic model and its derivatives. It is true that they seldom had much access to it, but they do not seem to believe themselves deprived for lack of it; what they want is what they consider to be the best medical treatment available. Psychiatrists, with that all too frequent medical obtuseness about such matters, do not seem to have noticed that they are in the process of being given an enormous constituency of poor people whose medical piety is legendary. All they have to do to acquire this basis of political support which they so far lack is to pit themselves with zeal and resolution against those illnesses from which poor psychiatric patients suffer. If they are to succeed in gaining the confidence of their patients, they must learn to use the medical model which their patients prefer and understand in a far more adroit and skillful manner than has been done for much of the last century or so. To do this, we believe that psychiatrists will have to pay far greater attention to acquiring a clear and humane understanding of the medical model which they have heretofore treated with benign neglect, to the harm of all. In our opinion it is not only the poor who will benefit from such an innovation; for, where grievous illnesses are concerned, most human beings are remarkably conservative in preferring the medical model. One can only hope that, after some reappraisal which, we predict, will not be especially agonizing, psychiatry will have the good sense to seize this convenient opportunity to return to the medical model.

Our five continuous models all share goals for changing the individual, the family, and society in ways which, if possible, appear admirable. Each one of us hopes for a world in which mutual understanding and forbearance is greater than it is today, where family life is better, where social reforms result in less repression, freer communication, and a better time for all. This is the stuff from which Utopias have been formed, and can be found through all the millenarian literature.[23] Only the basest could deny the desirability of such changes for the better and only the most cynical would consider that such aspirations are not admirable and may indeed encourage improvements in the human condition—although a study of Utopianism and millenarianism might lead one to doubt whether they have been a royal road to human betterment.

However that may be, the question remains whether or not the lot of actual schizophrenics has been, is being, and will be improved in the future by vague aspirations and great expectations. Who can doubt that schizophrenics and all other afflicted people would be better off if they lived in a world that was tolerant, gentle, and compassionate; but in this they are no different from the rest of us who yearn for the world to be a better place. Where they do differ is that they are sufferers from a particular disease or group of diseases which, curiously enough, seems to be unusually resistant to the beneficial consequences of social and economic improvement. Raised standards of living, massive changes in governmental forms, and wholly different lifestyles seem to have done little or nothing to change the incidence of schizophrenia in particular cultures; indeed, it is remarkable for its cross-cultural similarities rather than differences. Child-rearing practices, sexual patterns, the nature of religious practices, the fluidity or rigidity of social customs, and linguistic patterns seem to make very little difference regarding the general form of this most human of illnesses, although they do change its content somewhat. It seems that we are faced with a serious disease which afflicts 1 to 2 percent of humankind and which has so far been unusually resistant to those social and public health measures which have proved so beneficial with many other illnesses.

As with other puzzling illnesses, there have been all kinds of suggestions for helping the afflicted. At one time it was held both humane and medically sound to congregate schizophrenics in those buildings, initially rather small and intimate, called asylums and later, as they became larger, called mental hospitals. The object of this was twofold: first, to avoid having patients wandering around the countryside, being imprisoned in private lockups, or confined with criminals in jails or with paupers in workhouses; second, so they they could receive medical treatment and care sometimes of a very humane and skillful kind. At the present time, there has been a change in fashion owing to a combination of advances in psychopharmacology and improved psychiatric management which caught the attention of social reformers and administrators. Consequently, the residents of mental hospitals are being returned to the "community" again, rather than living in these total institutions. There is now evidence that many thousands of these patients are drifting into jails, flophouses, rundown hotels, utter seclusion in single rooms, and perhaps most questionable, private madhouses run in their off-time by the staff of those mental hospitals from which the patients have been extruded. It does not seem that those who, over the years, have arranged for these migrations of thousands of ill people first into and now out of institutions have concerned themselves greatly with the nature of the illnesses with which they have been dealing. The institutions themselves, the design of their buildings, the quality of their furnishings, and the nature of their organization bear melancholy witness to this lack of imaginative understanding. Furthermore, devoted and often energetic people have seldom asked those who have suffered from schizophrenia what they believe is needed, for these experts prefer to argue among themselves. Since this kind of debate is frequently conducted in terms of different models which have never been made explicit, the acrimony and ill-will generated rarely result in great benefits to those suffering from schizophrenia. As one recovering schizophrenic put it: "Schizophrenia is like the blind men and the elephant—everyone who touches it says it's something different. But why don't they ever ask the elephant?" [24] The elephant has been stating its point of view with dignity and sobriety for at least 150 years,[25] but it still receives very little sustained attention, for the experts are usually devoted to explaining and interpreting its behavior rather than attending to its account of its experiences.

It has always been the business of clinical medicine to "ask the elephant," to discover what a particular patient is experiencing and to relate that experience to the existing body of medical knowledge. If a patient says something to the doctor that he has never heard before, a doctor who is "good" and not merely "all right" will use this new information to enlarge the body of medical knowledge. What T. T. Paterson calls the "art of doctoring" and the "techne of medicine" are the warp and woof of the medical fabric.[26] Both are part of medicine's double goal, to treat "that article there," the irreducible, individual patient who is never an abstraction, and yet at the same time to accumulate medical knowledge for the benefit of all patients both now and in the future, who clearly are and cannot be other than an abstract conception. This is a modest goal compared with that of changing society in accordance with one's plans or theories, to the uttermost limits of vision and so bringing in the millennium of the kingdom of heaven on earth; but in spite of its limitations, the treatment and understanding of disease has been in the past and continues to be a source of one of the greatest of human aspirations. To conquer disease and enlarge health is still one of the most exciting and exacting activities; and, curiously enough, it has proved to be an unrivaled generator of social and political change. As a part of medicine, psychiatry has access to the mountain ranges of unconquered and little-understood diseases, and the massif of schizophrenia is the Everest of psychiatry.

8

The Future
of Psychiatry

IN EVERY SOCIAL SITUATION, there is a level of behavior which
people will accept as being "all right" or as "doing the right thing."
If behavior sinks below this socially acceptable level, people will
say that it is "not right." This level is arrived at by social consensus; its violation is identified as immorality and, at times, as
illegality. Psychiatry has at present sunk below this bare minimum
standard of behavior; as a result, cries of moral indignation can be
heard from its constituents. Above this minimum standard of behavior are actions which are aimed at the betterment of an enterprise, not merely to make it "all right" but to make it "good." *
This implies a different standard or, rather, an aspiration, an open-
ended thrust toward the future of an infinitely improvable enterprise. How can these two standards be applied to psychiatry and
its many models?

We would suggest as a bare minimum standard for psychiatric
models that they be complete, that they be used consistently, and
that they be used with the consensus of all the participating members. This will not be sufficient to make psychiatry "good," but it
will at least prevent it from sinking into the immorality and even

---

* For our understanding of this distinction, we are indebted to our colleague,
T. T. Paterson; he in turn acknowledges his debt to G. E. Moore.

illegality * which have often characterized its efforts both in the past and today.

In order to be considered complete, a model of a disputed ailment such as schizophrenia, alcoholism, or drug addiction must be able to answer to some degree all the questions that arise in connection with that ailment, and it must be able to provide a course of action for every situation which the participants will have to face, whether they are professional people, patients, their families, or the general public. Once the dimensions are determined, one must be able to fill in every dimension; there can be no gaps or holes in the model. This is the same demand that one makes of a set of rules for a game, such as checkers, chess, go, Monopoly, etc. Whoever made the game, or purveys sets of that game, should have anticipated all the difficulties that might arise in playing the game, so that a rule exists for each of them.

Dr. Szasz's rule-book, for instance, contains no clear and explicit instructions about a situation such as this. Suppose an old friend, a successful, usually happy and likable person, develops a severe endogenous depression. This is a well-known and fairly frequent illness which occurs in otherwise stable people, usually in their middle years. It is self-limiting and, today, is highly treatable. Apart from this condition, the patient enjoys excellent health and has prospects of a long and productive life with a devoted family which includes young dependents. Unfortunately, as sometimes happens in this appalling illness, the patient is absolutely convinced that life is now devoid of hope, his past achievements have become Dead Sea fruit, while the future holds nothing for him. He believes that he is a sinner of unimaginable depravity whose fate is present disgrace, impending doom, and eternal damnation. The only way to prevent his family from sharing in this catastrophe and being sucked into the maelstrom of his ruin lies in suicide. This he is determined to do and his intention is not idle or histrionic, for he is well known for courage and resolve; however, due to that lethargy, indecision, and slowness which are other features of his illness, he has so far been unable to execute his in-

---

* To our knowledge, there has not yet been a test case, but it is only a matter of time before some psychiatric patient sues a psychiatrist for failing to confer the sick role.

tention. Unluckily, this slowness or retardation, as it is called technically, may lift before recovery from depression and despair is complete, thus allowing him to carry out his fatal resolve and so to lose life just when hope is being rekindled. He refuses treatment of every kind because all is hopeless and he himself worthless: assurance to the contrary, however frequently and impressively given, is of no avail whatever.

What ought the doctor and the family to do? Should they leave the matter to chance or should they intervene whether the patient agrees or not, recognizing that provided the patient does not kill himself he may have thirty more productive and happy years ahead without ever having a recurrence of depression? According to Szasz's general principles, all mental illnesses are equally nonexistent, and in a free society anyone who wishes to kill himself has the right to do so; but a general principle is not a set of instructions and procedures. One cannot look up endogenous depression in Szasz's works and find out just what to do and what not to do in these distressing circumstances. How exactly does the doctor break the news to the family that nothing whatever can or should be done against the patient's wishes for self-destruction because that would be violating his civil rights? How does he explain that they must await the possibility of the patient's self-destruction or grave self-injury, for even the most determined suicides are not always successful, with such philosophy as they can muster? It is a serious fault and a gaping discontinuity in Szasz's model.

Second, this minimum standard requires a person using a particular model to stick to the rules of that model, and not shift to the rules of some other model, whether from lack of awareness that he is doing so or from a desire to better his position by so doing. The same standard applies to games: if one is playing chess, one must play by the rules of chess, and not shift to the rules of checkers or go in order to defeat one's opponent. After a certain age children know the rules of a game, but are not quite socialized enough to resist shifting to some other rules when it is to their advantage. So it is with mental health professionals. One patient, a man named Davidson,[1] was told repeatedly that he would have no trouble if he obeyed the rules; he asked a doctor if that were true.

The doctor replied that it was indeed true. Davidson then asked for a copy of the rules, to which the doctor angrily replied that there were no rules! Davidson says: "I was surprised and taken aback, for I had no idea that there was not such a copy as I wanted; and I remarked that in any place or club where there are rules to be obeyed, they were printed and hung up, or copies were obtainable by all the members. . . ."

The doctor in this instance used a model, probably a moral model, in which there were rules. But since these rules had not been made explicit, he could not produce them upon demand and therefore shifted to some other model in which there were no rules.

It is possible to make a model which is complete and internally consistent, but yet is unlikely to enable one to achieve consensus with anyone else on the basis of it. Delusional systems are models of this kind. As an intellectual exercise, we once constructed a "pixie" model of schizophrenia, in which pixies were held to be the cause of the illness and the treatments were all aimed at stamping out pixies. All the dimensions were filled out and all were consistent with each other, but the likelihood of getting much agreement about this model was small. In psychiatry it is difficult to get consensus about any model other than the medical model. Even when the staff agree on some nonmedical model, which is rare enough, the patients won't go along with it. Mary Cecil found herself in an awkward spot when, after she had admitted herself voluntarily to a mental hospital because she was feeling ill, she was thrown out again by a psychiatrist who believed that she was bad rather than ill:

> The psychiatrist was the cold kind. He said bitingly:
> "You've made a pretty good fool of yourself, haven't you?"
> "Very," I agreed. . . .
> "Your parents will fetch you tomorrow and you'd better behave yourself in the future. Try to think a little of their feelings. Next case."
> . . . They were throwing me out. They didn't think I was ill. What was I to do? [2]

If one knows how to achieve consensus with the others in a situation or in a game, one can shift models by mutual agreement. If two chess players decide in the middle of a game to abandon the game and play checkers instead, there will be no problem, provided only that both agree to make the necessary shift in rules. One can even imagine a master gamesman setting up a series of different board games, making a move in one game, moving to the next board and making a move in that game, etc. This would be workable provided that all the games were complete, that the gamesman played each consistently, and that he had consensus with the person facing him as to which game they were playing. In the absence of consensus, either in games or in psychiatry, one feels that "something has gone wrong here," "something is not right." This is precisely the feeling reported to us by many psychiatric patients and their families when they are confronted with a serious gap in consensus between themselves and the psychiatric professionals to whom they turn for help.

If psychiatrists and other mental health professionals used models that were complete, used them consistently, and were careful to achieve consensus among themselves as well as with those they serve, psychiatry would be "all right," but it would not be much good. In order for psychiatry to achieve positive goodness, we believe it would be necessary to have real commitment to a particular model. What would this entail?

The philosopher George Burch,[3] discussing similar problems in religion, distinguishes liberalism and orthodoxy from commitment. Liberalism, he says, follows the formula *this and that*. You don't have to give up anything, because we are really all going in the same direction anyway. He says: "It is possible to be both a Christian and a Buddhist simultaneously, but you have to sacrifice two things—the essence of Christianity and the essense of Buddhism." The problem with liberalism, or what we have called model-muddle, is that it is impoverished, for if one fails to commit oneself to a particular model, or religion as the case may be, one cannot reap the full benefits which it has to offer.

The next possibility is orthodoxy, or dogmatism. The formula here is *this, not that*. Here one considers mutually incompatible doctrines, one of which is true and the other or others of which are false. Professor Burch states that orthodoxy is not inconsistent with tolerance, since one may consider that other people are entitled to their views as a matter of civil liberties. What orthodoxy fails to provide for is the possibility that the other person may be right, or that there may be more than one right. At its worst, however, orthodoxy leads to intolerance and even fanaticism.

Commitment, says Professor Burch, follows the formula *this or that*. There is a real choice between two or more possibilities which have value. When we make a commitment, we actualize one choice as against the others. If we come to a fork in the road, we choose to go left or right, not because one is necessarily better than the other, but because in order to go anywhere, one must commit oneself to a direction.

How does this affect one's attitudes toward those who make other choices? Professor Burch says: "The disjunctive attitude when applied leads to a policy of coexistence . . . . Commitment reflects a true and robust humility which, while maintaining its own way without compromise or qualification, still recognizes the equal validity of others' ways not as errors to be tolerated but as alternatives also freely chosen."

One of the difficulties which has to be faced when making a commitment is that none of the models is entirely satisfactory. Although any model can be made complete in the sense that it offers a *general* solution to the problems it raises, as one asks of it more and more refined questions, there will inevitably be fewer and fewer easy answers. For example, in the medical model, the instruction for the dimension of "treatment" is that it is to be as specific as possible to the disease determined under "diagnosis." This differentiates the medical model from all our other models, where the action to be taken has some other basis. And if the treatment does not work, there are further instructions: the dosage may be too small or too large, the patient may have an idiosyncratic response, some other treatment might work better, the patient may have been misdiagnosed, etc. What if no known treatments work for any of the patients manifesting a particular disease? Then one can at least prevent it from getting worse, some medicines alleviate it a little, medical science is searching for the answer, etc. But even the all-but-infinitely elastic medical model can finally run out of answers, and then doubt starts as to whether this disease can really be conquered (as with cancer) or whether it is really a disease at all (as with tuberculosis in the past and schizophrenia now). So it is with all the other models. Only lack of refinement and incompleteness have prevented them from reaching their various dead ends sooner. Clearly, if one model worked perfectly and had all the answers, the others would soon disappear. They all exist because none of them works well enough to sweep the field.

Commitment to a model, therefore, must always be made in the face of the knowledge that there are many questions it cannot answer and, in fact, the better one knows one's model, the more unanswerable questions there are. Commitment, then, has to be made on the basis of faith, the faith that one's model has more promise of answering these questions in the future than the alternative models. We are all aware that people commit themselves to religions on the basis of faith, but it now appears that even in areas which seem at first to be more amenable to reason and demonstration, the same problem arises.

Thomas Kuhn has been most eloquent on this point in relation to the commitments that scientists make toward a particular paradigm:

A scientist's willingness to use a conceptual scheme in explanation is an index of his commitment to the scheme, a token of his belief that his model is the only valid one. Such commitment or belief is always rash, because economy and cosmological satisfaction cannot guarantee truth, whatever "truth" may mean. The history of science is cluttered with the relics of conceptual schemes that were once fervently believed and that have since been replaced by incompatible theories. There is no way of proving that a conceptual scheme is final. But, rash or not, this commitment to a conceptual scheme is a common phenomenon in the sciences, and it seems an indispensable one, because it endows conceptual schemes with one new and all-important function. Conceptual schemes are comprehensive; their consequences are not limited to what is already known. Therefore, an astronomer committed to, say, the two-sphere universe will expect nature to show the additional, but as yet unobserved properties that the conceptual scheme predicts. For him the theory will transcend the known, becoming first and foremost a powerful tool for predicting and exploring the unknown. It will affect the future of science as well as its past.[4]

Commitment to a model which is complete in a general way enables one to direct one's energies toward more and more specific questions and problems. If this process goes on long enough, and if the particular model has sufficient creative potential, it is almost inevitable that one will eventually come across a question or questions which the model cannot answer, even provisionally, and then the model itself may be in trouble. In a group of scientists, or in a particular scientific field, a crisis may arise when such anomalous findings are made. It is not known why some unanswered questions are simply seen as matters which the future will resolve, while others are seen as a threat to the validity of the model itself. But, Kuhn says, the one thing that scientists never do is give up the paradigm that led them into crisis, unless there is another and more promising paradigm at hand. This is certainly our experience with the models of madness: no one using a medical model ever gives it up because there is insufficient evidence for a particular etiological theory, or because none of the medical treatments is entirely satisfactory; no one using a psychoanalytic model ever renounces it because he cannot prove that certain events actually happened in a patient's family, or because the treatment doesn't seem to get very far. All the models contain the implicit promise that if only one used them long enough and patiently enough, they would yield up the desired evidence. Yet models, like empires, rise and fall, and people do shift from one to another. How does this come about?

Since no old paradigm has ever fully exhausted its potential for solving the questions put to it and any new paradigm consists, by definition, of promises rather than achievements, there is no rational or scientific way of making the choice between them. However, a person committed to a new paradigm can, as Kuhn says, "provide a clear exhibit of what scientific practice will be like for those who adopt the new view of nature." Yet however persuasive that exhibit may be, it cannot be made scientifically compelling for those who refuse to abandon the paradigm which has guided their work in the past. According to Kuhn, it is young men or men new to a particular field who are most likely to come up with new paradigms. As with political or religious ideologies, some people prefer to live out their lives under the old paradigm, even though they recognize that it is in grave difficulty and that there are other choices. This was the choice made by Erasmus when confronted with the new paradigm, Lutheranism, which was to solve the unsolved problems of the Catholic Church. He wrote to Luther:

Neither death nor life shall draw me from the communion of the Catholic Church. I have never been an apostate from the Catholic Church. I know that in this Church, which you call the Papist Church, there are many who displease me, but such I also see in your Church. One bears more easily the evils to which one is accustomed. Therefore I bear with this Church, until I see a better, and it cannot help bearing with me, until I shall myself be better. And he does not sail badly who steers a middle course between two several evils.[5]

Commitment and coexistence go hand in hand. One must commit oneself to a model in order to act responsibly, and one must make a choice to some extent on the basis of faith, since one cannot know whether one's chosen model will hold up under future explorations. And the deeper we go into our own model, the more we realize how elusive the truth is and how unlikely that anyone has a monopoly of it. As Galileo put it: "For anyone who had experienced just once the perfect understanding of one single thing, and had truly tasted how knowledge is accomplished, would recognize that of the infinity of other truths he understands nothing."[6] Following Galileo's example, we must be committed and yet relativistic.

The models we have been discussing are conceptual or ideological models, but in physics and other "hard" sciences, the term "model" is often used to mean experimental model, which implies a set of testable hypotheses. Sometimes the same distinction is made when contrasting models with theories. As the physicist David Park says of the use of models in science:

Models provide the definitions of the terms we use and are the basis of our theories. Some models are better than others. The criteria are that the best model leads to the theory having the widest range of agreement with experiment, and that it is the one most fruitful of new models and theories.[7]

Our conceptual models cannot be "proved" true or false, although like consumer models they can be shown to be preferred or not by various populations.* However, each of our conceptual models can generate experimental models or theories, and most of them have. The medical model has generated a great deal of biochemical and pharmacological work, aimed at demonstrating the presence of unusual substances in the bodies of those suffering from schizophrenia, depression, and other psychiatric diseases, or else attempting to show that certain medical treatments have some effect on the biochemistry and/or symptoms of the ill person. There have also been genetic, epidemiological, and psychological studies designed to test various hypotheses.

The social model has generated epidemiological studies as well, but there have not yet been a great many of these, and, according to Elliot Mishler and Norman Scotch, very few are done in such a way as to permit comparison.[8] Both the psychoanalytic and the family interaction models hypothesize certain disturbed patterns of child-rearing and family interaction, and some experiments have been done showing that the families of schizophrenics interact differently from the families of normal people. However, the chicken-and-egg problem has not been solved, nor have these studies as yet taken into account the recent genetic findings [9] which suggest that there is often more than one schizophrenic in the same family. Another problem posed by these two models, but never, it seems, tackled by their users, is that of prediction: if so much is known about schizophrenic families, why cannot such families be identified early and appropriate steps taken to prevent the illness from getting started?

---

* Soskis did such a study of our models (David Soskis, "Aetiological Models of Schizophrenia: Relationships to Diagnosis and Treatment," *The British Journal of Psychiatry*, Vol. 120, No. 557, April 1972). Questionnaires tapping ideological views were mailed to 132 psychiatrists in a New York county. Soskis found that most psychiatrists in his sample used mixed models, but that there was a dichotomy between those using organic and those using psycho-social models. Having available only our earliest models, he did not inquire into role or authority, the dimensions we now believe to be most crucial.

The conspiratorial model needs a great deal more statistical data: what proportion of the total number of people said to have schizophrenia have been railroaded into hospitals by scheming relatives and corrupt, illiberal doctors? No one denies that this is possible and there is evidence that it has sometimes happened, but that is a long way from explaining the phenomena of schizophrenia or mental hospitals in conspiratorial terms.

The behavior modification version of the moral model has drawn on a large body of knowledge from the field of animal psychology, notably the work of B. F. Skinner, so that it is in fairly good shape experimentally: its problem, as we have noted, lies in the tiny scope of these experiments relative to the whole phenomena of schizophrenia. The psychedelic model, so far as we know, has restricted itself to case studies, and has not undertaken experiments or epidemiological studies, but there is no theoretical reason why enlightenment could not be demonstrated, provided of course that it could be defined. The impaired model is in the odd position that it exists by default rather than intention; no one at the present time is actually advocating it as the model of choice. Nevertheless, the measurement of many different kinds of impairments in schizophrenia could lead to greater understanding, more rational rehabilitation programs, and better living arrangements.

Our models can and have generated experiments. Indeed they must, for although these models have a heavy ideological component, they must ultimately lead to an answer to a scientific question: what is madness? Faith in a model generates experiments— and experiments, if successful, generate faith. Who can say when, in this interplay, the balance may tip in favor of one model rather than the others? At this time, faith in the medical model is more widespread and runs deeper than faith in any other model, and there are many more relevant experiments being done. Here our commitment lies. But as Kuhn has shown, there is no way of proving that a conceptual scheme is final.

Suppose that psychiatry, instead of being "all wrong" or even "all right" was positively "good"? How would an enlightened psychiatrist behave? Our version of an enlightened psychiatrist is one who knows that he is a physician, knows that he has

Aesculapian authority and how to use it well, and confers the sick role on patients whom he diagnoses as having some psychiatric illness, referring elsewhere those who come to his office with either nonmedical problems or medical problems that are the province of some other specialist. He would take a medical history, conduct a physical examination, and order appropriate laboratory and psychological tests. If he determined that the patient had some illness, he would explain to the patient what illness he had in a language that the patient could understand. He would make it clear that neither the patient nor his family were to blame for the illness. He would explain the treatment that he was prescribing and indicate that of the treatments available this was the one most likely to do good and least likely to harm. He would explain the probable cost of the treatment. He would compare this patient's illness with that of other patients whom he had treated for the same illness, so that the patient would know if he had a mild or severe case of the illness. He would explain how likely it was that the patient would recover, how soon he might hope for this, and how fully he might hope to recover. He would tell the patient how to avoid making himself sicker and how to avoid relapses. He would inquire into how much the illness had damaged the patient, psychologically, vocationally, socially, etc., and recommend various kinds of rehabilitative measures to correct this. He would show himself to be knowledgeable about the state of research in his field and, above all, he would make it clear that he *hoped* that medical science would be able to shed further light on psychiatric illnesses and provide better treatments.

In many illnesses, particularly major and/or chronic illnesses, the doctor must take into account the family and community matrix of the patient, as well as his intellectual level, his spiritual strength, his willingness to pit himself against the illness, and a host of other factors. Every patient is a unique human being and his ability to occupy the sick role will depend to a very great extent on what kind of human being he is. In a doctor who is really good, and not just all right, these factors are computed automatically and are difficult to separate out and enumerate.

Dr. Behrens of the Sanitorium Berghof was such a doctor; he knew from his vast experience what kind of patient Joachim was, and he was not fooled by appearances. This physicianly behavior has been alternately derogated as "bedside manner" by some, and elevated to "psychotherapy" by others. Following the fashions of the day, we will call it psychotherapy also, but we will designate it as Psychotherapy I—medical psychotherapy, in order to distinguish it from two other kinds of psychotherapy that have nothing in particular to do with medicine.[10]

The goal of medical psychotherapy is to restore health or functioning to someone who has been ill and to reduce pain and suffering. The doctor exercises Aesculapian authority; the patient occupies the sick role. This kind of psychotherapy also includes the treatment of distress from known psychological causes, such as grief, fear, shame, and other traumas. In some cases, the doctor might delegate this therapy to some other professional who would work under his supervision, just as an orthopedist might send a patient to a physiotherapist.

Psychotherapy II, or educational psychotherapy, is aimed at promoting social and psychological skills in people who are not ill and do not occupy the sick role. Its goal is to help a person to develop his assets and reduce his liabilities. This kind of therapy includes some forms of psychoanalysis, various kinds of counseling, guidance, behavior therapy, teaching of unacquired social skills, and so forth. To these activities might be added Dale Carnegie courses, Arthur Murray dance classes, public speaking courses, Berlitz language courses, and other twentieth-century versions of the schools of deportment which Dickens described, such as Mr. Turveydrop's School in *Bleak House*. In order to qualify to do these kinds of therapy, it seems logical that the therapist ought to be able to demonstrate his mastery of the particular subject matter. There is no reason to believe that a medical education prepares people to undertake this vast assortment of ways for promoting health, wealth, and happiness.

Psychotherapy III, or enlightenment psychotherapy, can be practiced only by the enlightened. As to who is enlightened, those that say they know don't, and those that know don't say. The goal of enlightenment is to transcend natural limitations, and so the candidates, as a general rule, are not thought to be in need of Psychotherapy I or II. The number of people seeking enlightenment is probably smaller than those seeking the other two kinds of therapy, but this may change in the future. One becomes enlightened by finding a suitable master or guru, becoming his disciple, and abiding by his rule until it "takes," when one is recognized in some still obscure way as being a member of the elect.

The enlightened psychiatrist, then, restricts himself normally to Psychotherapy I, which he carries on in conjunction with his pharmacological and other medical treatments. If he decides to practice Psychotherapy II or III, he understands that since he cannot make his Aesculapian authority go away, the burden is on him to explain to his analysands, disciples, students, or whatever that he has taken off his medical hat and put on some other hat instead. But in his role as psychiatrist, the enlightened psychiatrist knows that he is not a guru; that is his enlightenment.

Schizophrenia is a many splendored thing. No one imagines for a moment that this great illness can be totally conquered by taking a pill. That is magic, not medicine. Great illnesses require great exertions by doctor, patient, family, and sometimes the community as well. They have psychological, social, moral, spiritual, financial, vocational, and other aspects—and they cause major catastrophes. But fortunately medicine is not merely an all-right institution, like the post office (at its best); it is a good institution, an institution aimed at human betterment, and psychiatrists have only to tap this source of moral strength in order to start back up on the path to enlightenment.

Final Remarks

We have traveled a long way since those puzzling hours spent in a particular mental health center nearly a decade ago. What seemed puzzling, perhaps incomprehensible, then seems understandable now and, far from feeling that communications in such places are bad, what now surprises us is that they are not a great deal worse. As we now see it, that particular mental health center and probably most others which use a goulash of models maintain themselves largely because their patients (who have to be very patient), the relatives of the ill, and the community are bent on humoring their doctors. Doctors are well known for their eccentricities and peculiarities, and if these should include the idea that they are not doctors at all, which might be inferred from Dr. Maxwell Jones's insistence that his patients call him Max, then with their customary loyalty and forbearance patients will call him Max. There are, however, limits to loyalty.

We suspect, indeed we are prepared to bet, that the same patients who call Dr. Maxwell Jones "Max" think of him as Dr. Jones and are far more concerned with their doctor than they are with their friend Max. That he and probably other psychiatrists like to believe that their patients see them more as friends than as doctors is a fancy which their patients will not disturb so long as they show evidence of concern in a medical way. Dr. Maxwell Jones, for instance, ran two rather successful hospitals. In our opinion the results of these hospitals derived not at all from the fact that he was called Max and a great deal from the air of confidence and zeal which he exuded and transmitted to his staff, for such qualities have always been essential ingredients of good medicine. However, as we have noted, Dr. Jones's methods are not the only ones which generate zeal and confidence. The medical model, as used by Drs. Woodward and Conolly and many others, does much the same and is far better known than most other models.

Our inquiry into the mental health center also resulted in a prolonged encounter with not only the practice of model-making, but into the theory of model-making as well. As Dr. David Park pointed out, when we have only one model, we often behave as if we are dealing with "the facts," but the presence of even one additional model alters the level of discourse and opens up a whole new set of possibilities.[11] As long as there was only the Ptolemaic earth-centered model of the universe, only those questions were raised which that model suggested, but the emergence of the Copernican sun-centered model resulted in an extraordinary stimulus to the astronomy of that time. When a new model is constructed, it may do nothing more, at first, than give an alternative explanation for the same set of observed phenomena, but once one looks through the lens of the new model, entirely new and unanticipated data may be observed and new questions may be raised which go far beyond the problems for which the new model was originally constructed. While we do not expect the consequences of our model-making efforts to be so momentous as those of the Copernican revolution, our models have served much the same purpose. They have allowed an ordering of well-known facts and inquiry into other facts which were less known or hardly known at all, which would not have otherwise been undertaken simply because there would have been no particular reason to do so.

We shall not labor the point that within psychiatry the need for these model-making techniques and careful comparisons between models is not only essential for the well-being of patients, the protection of the public, and the guidance of professionals, but provides a variety of clues for resolving the many muddles and puzzles which have afflicted this branch of medicine. Some of psychiatry's official journals allow scarcely a month to go by without articles regarding the future of this specialty and the critical, indeed one would sometimes suppose catastrophic, nature of its affairs. Although one does not have to take these public breast-beatings too seriously, we must suppose that they mean something and reflect some kind of concern and distress within this branch of medicine and among its patients and the public as well; it seems unlikely that the responsible doctors concerned are merely engaged in exhibitionism. Accumulating evidence now suggests that the benefits obtained from boarding out chronically ill mental patients in the community have not been as great as those theorists who believed in the panacea of community involvement supposed. While even a small knowledge of history would have made this much less surprising, it appears to us that the use of our models of madness *before* engaging in these inflated hopes might have suggested a different approach likely to do more good in the long run. What is more, it would have avoided the considerable disappointment and dismay now spreading among psychiatrists which must surely affect their patients and which, according to some of them, is spreading demoralization through this important branch of medicine.[12]

Since medical confidence is such a vital ingredient in the success of any treatment, it is hardly surprising that worried and apprehensive psychiatrists produce even more worried patients. This occurs in spite of the fact that we can probably do more about these illnesses today than we have ever been able to do. One would never guess this from many of the public statements made by responsible and even exemplary members of our profession.

These findings alone would have been a rich harvest for a morning's work ten years ago, but we have been even more fortunate because our inquiries into the models of madness forced us to attend to the whole nature of medical authority and here, thanks to the prior work of T. T. Paterson and his concept of Aesculapian authority, we have been able to advance our understanding beyond that which Wilfred Trotter developed over forty years ago. In this complicated age of medical bureaucracies in which physicians play greater or lesser parts, it becomes necessary that they should have some understanding of that extraordinary authority with which they are invested as clinical doctors. This was probably of less importance forty or fifty years ago when public health doctors and science doctors, however eminent they may have appeared in their own subspecialty, had little or no bearing upon the treatment of patients, the running of hospitals, or the provision of health services. This, however, is no longer true. Public health and its closely related administrative medicine, combined with the enormous ferment deriving from scientific medicine, impinge ever more heavily upon clinical medicine. Since those who practice these specialties do not possess Aesculapian authority, their proper goals should be to help and support those who do. Our models of medicine suggest that many careful inquiries are needed into the relationship between the three kinds of medicine, the consequences of that relationship for medicine as a whole, and so for the public who are our patients.

We believe that a great variety of different publics will be able to gain a greater understanding regarding the nature of medicine by means of these models, and since all medical activities depend in the last analysis upon public sanction and support, it seems essential to us that these many publics should be provided with a means by which they can understand the nature and the complexity of the problem.

It appears to us from casual observation that there is a great confusion, even among experienced politicians, regarding the three kinds of medicine and the way in which they relate to each other. This confusion has not been in the least bit reduced by the pronunciamentos of medical associations and the critics within medicine itself. Indeed, their immoderate statements tend, if anything, to make things a good deal worse. To exercise good judgment and so further good legislation for bettering medicine, the nature of this ancient craft and its relationship to the modern world must be understood. We believe that our models provide as good a method of enlarging that understanding as any that exists. While we do not doubt that they will be bettered in the future, we hope that their very existence will stimulate others to improve and even transform them.

APPENDIX

PAPERS ON CONCEPTUAL MODELS IN PSYCHIATRY

The authors' indexed notes, accumulated over a period of some twenty years, which are essentially the raw research materials for *Models of Madness, Models of Medicine* and future writings, are available in microfiche. Approximately 3,600 pages on 40 microfiche, the notes explore and develop in a multitude of ways the themes and inquiries of this book. They are available from Princeton Datafilm, Inc., Princeton Service Center, Box 231, Princeton Junction, New Jersey, 08550.

1. Miriam Siegler and Humphry Osmond, "Models of Madness," *British Journal of Psychiatry*, 112 (1966), 1193-1203.
2. Miriam Siegler and Humphry Osmond, "Models of Drug Addiction," *The International Journal of the Addictions*, 3 (1968), 3-24.
3. Miriam Siegler, Humphry Osmond, and Stephens Newell, "Models of Alcoholism," *Quarterly Journal of Studies on Alcohol*, 29 (1968), 571-591.
4. Miriam Siegler, Humphry Osmond, and Frances Cheek, "Attitudes Toward Naming the Illness," *Mental Hygiene*, 52 (1968), 226-238.
5. Miriam Siegler and Humphry Osmond, "The Impaired Model of Schizophrenia," *Schizophrenia*, 1 (1969), 192-202.
6. Miriam Siegler, Humphry Osmond, and Harriet Mann, "Laing's Models of Madness," *British Journal of Psychiatry*, 115 (1969), 947-958.
7. Humphry Osmond, "The Medical Model in Psychiatry," *Hospital and Community Psychiatry*, 21 (1970), 275-281.
8. Humphry Osmond, "Acceptable Risks in Medicine," *Medical Counterpoint*, Feb., 1970, pp. 27-30.
9. Miriam Siegler and Humphry Osmond, "Goffman's Model of Mental Illness," *British Journal of Psychiatry*, 119 (1971), 419-424.
10. Humphry Osmond, "The Medical Model in Psychiatry: Love It or Leave It." *Medical Annals of the District of Columbia*, 41 (1972), 171-175.
11. Miriam Siegler and Humphry Osmond, "Some Differences Between the Sick Role and the 'Psych' Role," presented at the American Society for Psychosomatic Dentistry and Medicine, Oct. 6, 1972, Mt. Pocono, Pa.
12. Miriam Siegler and Humphry Osmond, "Aesculapian Authority," *Hastings Center Studies*, 1, No. 2 (1973), 41-52.
13. Miriam Siegler and Humphry Osmond, "The 'Sick Role' Re-visited," *Hastings Center Studies*, 1, No. 3 (1973), 41-58.
14. Miriam Siegler and Humphry Osmond, "Schizophrenia and the Sick Role," *Journal of Orthomolecular Psychiatry*, 2 (1973), 25-38.
15. Miriam Siegler and Humphry Osmond, "'Closed Ranks' Twenty Years Later," *Journal of Orthomolecular Psychiatry*, 2 (1973), 150-163.
16. Humphry Osmond, "Psychiatry under Siege: The Crisis Within," *Psychiatric Annals*, 3 (1973), 59-82.
17. Humphry Osmond and Miriam Siegler, "Notes on Orthomolecular Psychiatry and Psychotherapy," *Journal of Orthomolecular Psychiatry*, 2 (1973), 118-126.

18. Miriam Siegler and Humhpry Osmond, "The Three Medical Models," *Journal of Orthomolecular Psychiatry,* 3 (1974).

NOTES

I. Introduction

1. Thomas S. Kuhn, *The Structure of Scientific Revolutions* (Chicago: University of Chicago Press, 1962).

2. Mirîam Siegler, Frances E. Cheek, and Humphry Osmond, "Attitudes Toward Naming the Illness," *Mental Hygiene,* 52 (1968), 226-238.

3. Robert Sommer and Humphry Osmond, "Autobiographies of Former Mental Patients," *Journal of Mental Science,* 106 (1960), 443.

4. Humphry Osmond and Robert Sommer, "The Schizophrenic No-Society," *Psychiatry,* 25 (1962), 244-255.

5. Roland Fischer, "Selbstbeobachtungen im Mezkalin-Rausch," *Schweizerische Zeitschrift für Psychologie,* 5 (1946), 308. R. Fischer, F. Georgi, and R. Weber, "Modellversuche zum Schizophrenieproblem Lysergsaurediathylamid und Mezcalin," *Schweizerische Medizinische Wochenschrift,* 81 (1951), 817.

6. Humphry Osmond, "A Review of the Clinical Effects of Psychotomimetic Agents," *Annals of the New York Academy of Science,* 66 (1957), 418-434.

7. Abram Hoffer and Humphry Osmond, *The Hallucinogens* (New York: Academic Press, 1967), pp. 267-442.

8. Harold Kelm, Humphry Osmond, and Abram Hoffer, *Hoffer-Osmond Diagnostic Test Manual* (Saskatoon, Saskatchewan, Canada: Modern Press, 1967).

9. S. Fogel and Abram Hoffer, "Perceptual Changes Induced by Hypnotic Suggestion for the Post-Hypnotic State: I. General Account of the Effect on Personality," *Journal of Clinical and Experimental Psychopathology,* 23 (1962), 24-35.

10. Bernard S. Aaronson, "Hypnosis, Depth Perception, and Schizophrenia," presented at the Eastern Psychological Association meetings, Philadelphia, Pa., 1964. Bernard S. Aaronson, "Behavior and the Place Names of Time," *American Journal of Clinical Hypnosis,* 9 (1966), 1-17. Bernard S. Aaronson, "Distance, Depth and Schizophrenia," *American Journal of Clinical Hypnosis,* 9 (1967), 203-207. Bernard S. Aaronson, "Mystic and Schizophreniform Perception as a Function of Depth Perception," *Journal of the Scientific Study of Religion,* 6 (1967), 246-252. Bernard S. Aaronson, "Hypnosis, Time Rate Perception and Personality," *Journal of Schizophrenia,* 2 (1968), 11-41. Bernard S. Aaronson, "Hypnotic Alterations of Space and Time," *International Journal of Parapsychology,* 10 (1968), 5-36.

11. Humphry Osmond, "Models of Madness," *New Scientist,* 12 (1961), 777-780.

12. René Dubos, *Mirage of Health* (Garden City: Doubleday Anchor Books, 1959). Celsus, *On Medicine,* trans. W. G. Spencer, *The Loeb Classical Library* (Cambridge: Harvard University Press, 1935).

13. Sinclair Lewis, *Arrowsmith* (New York: Harcourt, Brace and World, 1925).

14. A. J. Cronin, *The Citadel* (Boston: Little, Brown and Co., 1937).

15. Wilfred Trotter, *The Instincts of the Herd in War and Peace* (New York: The Macmillan Co., 1915).

16. Wilfred Trotter, *The Collected Papers of Wilfred Trotter* (London: Oxford University Press, 1946), p. 94.

17. *Ibid.*, p. 157.

18. *Ibid.*, p. 163.

19. *Ibid.*, p. 159.

20. Harvey Cushing, *The Life of Sir William Osler, Volume I* (Oxford: Clarendon Press, 1926), pp. 504-505.

21. Miriam Siegler and Humphry Osmond, "Models of Madness," *British Journal of Psychiatry*, 112 (1966), 1193-1203.

22. Gerald Gordon, *Role Theory and Illness: A Sociological Perspective* (New Haven: College and University Press, 1966).

23. T. Kraft, "Social Anxiety Model of Alcoholism," *Perceptual and Motor Skills*, 33 (1971), 797-798.

24. Ederyn Williams, "Models of Madness," *New Society*, Sept. 30, 1971.

25. Humphry Osmond and Miriam Siegler, unpublished letter to *New Society*, Nov. 22, 1971.

26. Arnold J. Mandell, "Exploring Psychiatry's Own Identity Crisis," *Roche Report*, 1 (1971).

27. Silas Weir Mitchell, "Address before the Fiftieth Annual Meeting of the American Medico-Psychological Association," *American Medico-Psychological Association Proceedings* (1894), 101-121.

28. "Statement of Principles," *Psychiatric News*, Feb. 3, 1971.

29. Edward W. Hughes, Jr., Correspondence, *Psychiatric News*, Dec. 1, 1971.

30. Mitchell, Address to American Medico-Psychological Association, 1894.

31. Dennis Kussin, *Medical Post*, Feb. 9, 1971.

32. Thomas S. Szasz, *Law, Liberty and Psychiatry* (New York: The Macmillan Co., 1963).

33. Siegler and Osmond, "Models of Madness," *op. cit.*

34. Gerald Gordon, *Role Theory and Illness: A Sociological Perspective, op. cit.*

35. R. D. Laing, *The Politics of Experience* (New York: Pantheon Books, 1967).

II. The Discontinuous Models of Madness

1. Henry B. Adams, " 'Mental Illness' or Interpersonal Behavior?" *American Psychologist*, 19 (1964), 191-197. George W. Albee, "The Dark at the Top of the Agenda," *The Clinical Psychologist*, Fall issue (1966), 7-9. George W. Albee, "Conceptual Models and Manpower Requirements in Psychology," *American Psychologist*, 23 (1968), 317-320. W. D. G. Balance, Paul P. Hirschfield, and Wolfgang G. Bringmann, "Mental Illness: Myth, Metaphor, or Model," *Professional Psychology*, 1 (1970), 133-137. D. A. Begelman, "Misnaming, Metaphors, The Medical Model and Some Muddles," *Psychiatry*, 34 (1971), 38-58. Norman W. Bell and Roger Bibace, "Policy by Prescription?" *Canada's Mental Health*, 12 (1964), 11-14. Bernard L. Bloom, "The 'Medical Model,' Miasma Theory and Community Mental Health," *Community Mental Health Journal*, 1 (1965), 333-338. Marc H. Hollender and Thomas S. Szasz, "Normality, Neurosis and Psychosis," *Journal of Nervous and Mental Diseases*, 125 (1957), 599-607. Ronald Leifer, "The Medical Model as Ideology," *International Journal of Psychiatry*, 9 (1970–1971), 13-21. Irwin G. Sarason and Victor J. Ganzer, "Concerning the

Medical Model," *American Psychologist,* 23 (1968), 507-510. Theodore R. Sarbin, "On the Futility of the Proposition that Some People Be Labelled 'Mentally Ill,'" *Journal of Consulting Psychology,* 31 (1967), 447-453. Sohan Lal Sharma, "A Historical Background of the Development of Nosology in Psychiatry and Psychology," *American Psychologist,* 25 (1970), 248-253. Thomas S. Szasz, "The Problem of Psychiatric Nosology," *American Journal of Psychiatry,* 114 (1957), 405-413.

2. Michael Crichton, *Five Patients* (New York: Alfred A. Knopf, 1970), pp. 18, 154-155.

3. David R. Hawkins, "Treatment of Schizophrenia Based on the Medical Model," *Journal of Schizophrenia,* 2 (1969), pp. 3-10.

4. T. T. Paterson, "Notes on Aesculapian Authority," unpublished manuscript, 1957.

5. Talcott Parsons, *The Social System* (Glencoe, Ill.: The Free Press, 1951).

6. T. Ayllon, personal communication.

7. Samuel Butler, *Erewhon* (New York: The New American Library, 1960). Originally published in 1872.

8. *Ibid.,* p. 79.

9. W. Glasser, *Reality Therapy* (New York: Harper & Row, 1965), p. 46.

10. Thomas Szasz, *Law, Liberty and Psychiatry* (New York: The Macmillan Co., 1963).

11. Henry Davidson, "The New War on Psychiatry," *American Journal of Psychiatry,* 121 (1964), 528-534.

12. Ivan Belknap, *Human Problems of a State Mental Hospital* (New York: McGraw-Hill, 1956).

13. James A. Wechsler, *In a Darkness* (New York: W. W. Norton and Co., 1972).

14. Alex Comfort, *The Anxiety Makers* (New York: Dell Publishing Co., 1967).

15. O. H. Mowrer, *The Crisis in Psychiatry and Religion* (New York: Van Nostrand Co., 1961).

16. David Rothman, *The Discovery of the Asylum* (Boston: Little, Brown and Co., 1971).

17. Begelman, "Misnaming, Metaphors," *op. cit.*

18. Harold Kelm, Humphry Osmond, and Abram Hoffer, *Hoffer-Osmond Diagnostic Test Manual* (Saskatoon, Saskatchewan, Canada: Modern Press, 1967). A. Moneim El-Meligi and Humphry Osmond, *Manual for the Clinical Use of the Experiential World Inventory* (New York: Mens Sana Publishing Co., 1970).

19. Samuel Butler, *Erewhon, op. cit.,* pp. 100-101.

20. A somewhat different version of this section appeared in our paper, "The Impaired Model of Schizophrenia," *Schizophrenia,* 1 (1969), 192-202.

21. Gerald Grob, *The State and the Mentally Ill: A History of Worcester State Hospital in Massachusetts: 1830–1920* (Chapel Hill: University of North Carolina Press, 1966), p. 118.

22. *Ibid.,* p. 130.

23. Gerald Gordon, *Role Theory and Illness: A Sociological Perspective* (New Haven: College and University Press, 1966), p. 75.

24. *Roche Report: Frontiers of Hospital Psychiatry,* Vol. 4, March 1, 1967.

25. Gerald Grob, *op. cit.,* p. 89.

III. The Continuous Models of Madness

1. Aubrey Lewis, "Sigmund Freud: 1856–1939," in Aubrey Lewis, *The State of Psychiatry* (New York: Science House, 1967), p. 52.
2. Sigmund Freud, "Heredity and the Aetiology of the Neuroses," in Philip Rieff, ed., *Early Psychoanalytic Writings: The Collected Papers of Sigmund Freud* (New York: Collier Books, 1963). Sigmund Freud, "Further Remarks on the Defence Neuro-Psychoses," in Philip Rieff, ed., *Early Psychoanalytic Writlngs: The Collected Papers of Sigmund Freud* (New York: Collier Books, 1963). Sigmund Freud, "The Aetiology of Hysteria," in Philip Rieff, ed., *Early Psychoanalytic Writings: The Collected Works of Sigmund Freud* (New York: Collier Books, 1963).
3. Sigmund Freud, *The Origins of Psychoanalysis* (New York: Basic Books, 1954), p. 215.
4. Sigmund Freud, *The Interpretation of Dreams* (New York: Avon Books, 1965). Originally published 1900.
5. Sigmund Freud, 'My Views on the Part Played by Sexuality in the Aetiology of the Neuroses," in Philip Rieff, ed., *Sexuality and the Psychology of Love: The Collected Papers of Sigmund Freud* (New York: Collier Books, 1963). Sigmund Freud, *On the History of the Psychoanalytic Movement* (New York: W. W. Norton and Co., 1966). Sigmund Freud, *An Autobiographical Study* (New York: W. W. Norton and Co., 1952).
6. Karl Popper, *The Logic of Scientific Discovery* (New York: Harper & Row, 1965).
7. Sigmund Freud, *On the History of the Psychoanalytic Movement, op. cit.*
8. Ernest Jones, *The Life and Work of Sigmund Freud,* edited and abridged by Lionel Trilling and Steven Marcus (Garden City: Doubleday Anchor Books, 1963).
9. Paul Roazen, *Brother Animal: The Story of Freud and Tausk* (New York: Vintage Books, 1971).
10. Franz Alexander and Sheldon T. Selesnick, *The History of Psychiatry* (New York: Harper & Row, 1966).
11. Paul Roazen, *Brother Animal, op. cit.*
12. Miriam Siegler and Humphry Osmond, "Some Differences Between the Sick Role and the 'Psych' Role," presented at the 23rd Annual Meeting of the American Society of Psychosomatic Dentistry and Medicine, October 1972, Mt. Pocono, Pa.
13. Francis Schrag, "Psychoanalysis as an Educational Process," in *Philosophy of Education 1972: Proceedings of the Philosophy of Education Society,* ed. MaryAnne Raywid (Edwardsville, Ill.: Studies in Philosophy and Education, 1972).
14. Sigmund Freud, *The Question of Lay Analysis, with Freud's 1927 Postscript,* trans. and Ed. James Strachey (Garden City: Doubleday Anchor Books, 1964).
15. Ernst Federn, "How Freudian are the Freudians?" (Merck, Sharp and Dohme: *Reflections,* 1968). Reprinted from *The Journal of the History of the Behavioral Sciences,* July 1967.
16. *Ibid.*
17. Sigmund Freud, *The Question of Lay Analysis, op. cit.,* p. 103.
18. Ernst Federn, "How Freudian are the Freudians?" *op. cit.*

19. Paul Federn, *Ego Psychology and the Psychoses* (New York: Basic Books, 1955), pp. 241-260.
20. Heinrich Kramer and James Sprenger, *Malleus malificarum*, trans Rev. Montague Summers (London: Pushkin Press, 1948). Originally published 1486.
21. Louise Wilson, *This Stranger My Son* (New York: Signet Books, 1968).
22. Nancy Mitford, *The Sun King* (London: Hamish Hamilton, 1966).
23. Edward Jarvis, *Insanity and Idiocy in Massachusetts: Report of the Commission on Lunacy, 1855,* introduction by Gerald Grob (Cambridge: Harvard University Press, 1971).
24. E. E. Southard, "Alienists and Psychiatrists," *Mental Hygiene,* 1 (1917), 567-571. Norman Bell and John Spiegel, "Social Psychiatry: Vagaries of a Term," *Archives of General Psychiatry,* 14 (1966).
25. Stephen J. Kunitz, "Equilibrium Theory in Social Psychiatry: The Work of the Leightons," *Psychiatry,* 33, No. 3, August (1970), pp. 312-328.
26. Alexander H. Leighton, *An Introduction to Social Psychiatry* (Springfield: Charles C. Thomas, 1960), p. 38.
27. Leo Srole, Thomas S. Langner, Stanley T. Michael, Marvin Opler, and Thomas A. C. Rennie. *Mental Health in the Metropolis: The Midtown Manhattan Study,* Vol. I (New York: McGraw-Hill, 1962).
28. Paul M. Roman and Harrison M. Trice, "Schizophrenia and the Poor," *ILR Research,* published by the New York State School of Industrial and Labor Relations (Cornell University, Ithaca, N.Y.), Vol. XI, No. 3 (February 1966), pp. 3-9.
29. Norman Bell and John P. Spiegel, "Social Psychiatry," *op. cit.*
30. Elmer Gardner and Mary Gardner, "A Community Mental Health Center Case Study: Innovations and Issues," *Seminars in Psychiatry,* Vol. 3, No. 2, May 1971, pp. 172-198.
31. Frank Riessman, Jerome Cohen, and Arthur Pearl, eds., *Mental Health of the Poor* (London: Collier-Macmillan Ltd.; Glencoe, Ill.: The Free Press, 1964).
32. Abram Hoffer, personal communication.
33. Desmond Curran, "Psychiatry Ltd." The Presidential Address to the Section of Psychiatry, the Royal Society of Medicine, delivered on Oct. 9, 1951, in: *The Journal of Mental Science,* Vol. XCVIII, No. 412, July 1952, pp. 373-381.
34. Frederic V. Grunfeld, " 'Shockingly Mad, Madder than Ever, Quite Mad!' " *Horizon,* Vol. XIV, No. 3 (Summer 1972), p. 77.
35. R. D. Laing, *The Politics of Experience* (New York: Pantheon Books, 1967), p. 90.
36. Miriam Siegler, Humphry Osmond, and Harriet Mann, "Laing's Models of Madness," *British Journal of Psychiatry,* Vol. 115, No. 525 (1969), pp. 947-958.
37. Frederic V. Grunfeld, "Shockingly Mad," *op cit.,* p. 76.
38. René Dubos and Jean Dubos, "Consumption and the Romantic Age," *The White Plague* (Boston: Little, Brown and Co., 1952), pp. 65-66. Also in Berton Roueche, ed., *Curiosities of Medicine* (New York: Berkley Publishing Company, 1958), pp. 44-45.
39. George E. Vaillant, "Tuberculosis: An Historical Analogy to Schizophrenia," *Psychosomatic Medicine,* Vol. XXIV, No. 3 (1962), pp. 225-233.
40. C. C. Pfeiffer, V. Iliev, L. Goldstein, E. G. Jenney, and R. Schultz, "Blood

Histamine, Polyamines and the Schizophrenias. Computer Correlations of the Low and High Blood Histamine Types," *Research Communications in Chemical Pathology and Pharmacology*, 1 (1970), 247-265. A. Sohler, R. Beck, and J. J. Noval, "The Mauve Factor: A Corroboration of Its Identity with 2, 4-dimethyl-3-ethylpyrrole and Sedative Effect of this Compound on the CNS," *Nature*, 728 (1970), 1318.

41. A. Arthur Sugerman, Leonide Goldstein, Henry Murphree, Carl C. Pfeiffer, and Elizabeth Jenney, "EEG and Behavioral Changes in Schizophrenia," *Archives of General Psychiatry*, 10 (April 1964), 340-344. Leonide Goldstein and A. Arthur Sugerman, "EEG Correlates of Psychopathology," *Neurobiological Aspects of Psychopathology*, (1969), pp. 1-19.

42. Harold Kelm, "The Hoffer-Osmond Diagnostic Test (HOD)," in *Orthomolecular Psychiatry: Treatment of Schizophrenia*, David Hawkins and Linus Pauling, eds. (W. H. Freeman and Company, February 1973). A. Moneim El-Meligi and Humphry Osmond, "The Experiential World Inventory in Clinical Psychiatry and Psychopharmacology," in *Orthomolecular Psychiatry: Treatment of Schizophrenia*, David Hawkins and Linus Pauling, eds. (W. H. Freeman and Company, February 1973).

43. Thomas J. Scheff, *Being Mentally Ill: A Sociological Theory* (Chicago: Aldine Publishing Company, 1966).

44. Erving Goffman, "The Moral Career of the Mental Patient," in *Asylums* (Garden City: Doubleday Anchor Books, 1961). See also Miriam Siegler and Humphry Osmond, "Goffman's Model of Mental Illness," *The British Journal of Psychiatry*, Vol. 119, No. 551 (October 1971), pp. 419-424.

45. Walter R. Gove, "Societal Reaction as an Explanation of Mental Illness: An Evaluation," *American Sociological Review*, Vol. 35, No. 5 (October 1970), pp. 873-884.

46. Iona Opie and Peter Opie, *The Lore and Language of Schoolchildren* (London: Oxford University Press, 1959).

47. David Rothman, *The Discovery of the Asylum* (Boston: Little, Brown and Co., 1971).

48. Robert Sommer and Humphry Osmond, "The Schizophrenic No-Society," *Psychiatry*, 25 (1962), 244-255.

49. Robert Hyde, personal communication, *ca.* 1955.

50. Humphry Osmond, personal communication, 1956.

51. William Battie, *A Treatise on Madness,* introduced and annotated by Richard Hunter and Ida Macalpine (London: Dawson of Pall Mall, 1962). Originally published 1758.

52. John Conolly, *The Indications of Insanity*, introduction by Richard Hunter and Ida Macalpine (London: Dawson of Pall Mall, 1964). Originally published 1830.

53. D. A. Begelman, "Misnaming, Metaphors, the Medical Model and Some Muddles," *Psychiatry*, Vol. 34 (February 1971), pp. 38-58.

54. Lawrence S. Linn, "The Mental Hospital from the Patient Perspective," *Psychiatry*, Vol. 31, No. 3 (August 1968), pp. 213-223.

55. Miriam Siegler, Frances E. Cheek, and Humphry Osmond, "Attitudes Toward Naming the Illness," *Mental Hygiene*, Vol. 52, No. 2 (April 1968), pp. 226-238.

56. Clifford W. Beers, *The Mind That Found Itself* (Garden City: Doubleday and Company, 1968). Originally published 1908.

57. Silas Weir Mitchell, "Address before the Fiftieth Annual Meeting of the

American Medico-Psychological Association," American Medico-Psychological Association Proceedings (1894), pp. 101-121.

58. Thomas S. Szasz, "Interview: Thomas S. Szasz, M.D." *The New Physician*, 18 (1969), 453-476.

59. Thomas S. Szasz, " 'R. F. K. Must Die!' " *The New York Times Book Review*, Nov. 15, 1970.

60. Homer Bigart, "Bremer Guilty in Shooting of Wallace, Gets 63 Years," *The New York Times*, Saturday, Aug. 5, 1972.

61. W. W. Meissner, "Thinking about the Family—Psychiatric Aspects," *Family Process*, Vol. 3, No. 1 (March 1964), pp. 1-40.

62. Elliot Mishler and Nancy Waxler, "Family Interaction Processes and Schizophrenia: A Review of Current Theories," *The Merrill-Palmer Quarterly*, Vol. 11, No. 4 (October 1965), pp. 269-315.

63. C. M. Binger, A. R. Ablin, R. C. Feuerstein, J H. Kushner, S. Zoger, and C. Mikkelsen, "Childhood Leukemia: Emotional Impact on Patient and Family," *The New England Journal of Medicine*, 280 (1969), 414-418.

64. A. R. Ablin, C. M. Binger, R. C. Stein, J. H. Kushner, S. Zoger, and C. Mikkelsen. "A Conference with the Family of a Leukemic Child," *American Journal of Diseases of Children*, 122 (October 1971), 362-364.

65. A. Bergman, M. Pomeroy, and J. B. Beckwith, "The Psychiatric Toll of the Sudden Infant Death Syndrome," *G.P.*, Vol. XI, No. 6 (December 1969), pp. 99-105.

66. Judy Klemesrud, "A Tragedy with an Aftermath of Guilt," *The New York Times*, June 19, 1972.

67. Jacques May, *A Physician Looks at Psychiatry* (New York: The John Day Company, 1958), pp. 40-41.

68. Louise Wilson, *This Stranger My Son* (New York: The New American Library, 1968), p 10.

69. Jessie Gray Foy, *Gone Is Shadow's Child* (Plainfield, N.J.: Logos International, 1970), p. 30.

70. Clara Claiborne Park, *The Siege* (Boston: The Atlantic Monthly Press; Little, Brown and Co., 1972). First published 1967, pp. 139-141.

71. Louise Wilson, *op. cit.*, p. 213.

72. Sarah E. Lorenz, *Our Son Ken* (New York: Dell Publishing Co., 1969). Originally published as *And Always Tomorrow*, 1963, pp. 80-81.

73. Frances Eberhardy, "The View from 'The Couch,' " *J. Child. Psychol. Psychiat.*, 8 (1967), 257-263.

74. Clara Park, *The Siege, op. cit.*, p. 196.

75. H. R. Trevor-Roper, *The European Witch-Craze of the Sixteenth and Seventeenth Centuries and Other Essays* (New York: Harper & Row Torchbooks, 1969).

IV. The Medical Model

1. Konrad Lorenz, *On Aggression* (London: Methuen, 1966).

2. Philip Ziegler, *The Black Death* (Harmondsworth, England: Pelican Books, 1970).

3. T. T. Paterson, "Aesculapian Authority," unpublished manuscript, 1957.

4. A somewhat expanded discussion of Aesculapian authority appears in our paper, "Aesculapian Authority," in Miriam Siegler and Humphry Osmond, *The Hastings Center Studies*, Vol. 1, No. 2 (1973), pp. 41-52.

5. A. Mitscherlich and F. Mielke, *The Death Doctors*, trans. from German by James Cleugh (London: Elek Books, 1962), p. 172.

6. T. T. Paterson, "Aesculapian Authority," *op. cit.* T. T. Paterson, *Management Theory* (London: Business Publications, 1966).

7. T. T. Paterson, "Aesculapian Authority," *op. cit.*

8. Carl M. Grossman and Sylvia Grossman, *The Wild Analyst: The Life and Work of Georg Groddeck* (New York: Dell Publishing Company, 1965).

9. A. J. P. Taylor, *Bismarck: The Man and the Statesman* (New York: Random House; Vintage Books, 1967).

10. Geoffrey Jukes, *Stalingrad: The Turning Point* (New York: Ballantine Books, 1968), p 40.

11. Lord Moran, *Winston Churchill: The Struggle for Survival: 1940–1965* (London: Sphere Books, 1968), p. 108.

12. Richard Hunter and Ida Macalpine, *Three Hundred Years of Psychiatry: 1535–1860* (London: Oxford University Press, 1963), p. ix.

13. A somewhat expanded discussion of the sick role appears in our paper, "The Sick Role Re-visited," in Miriam Siegler and Humphry Osmond, *The Hastings Center Studies*, Vol. 1, No. 3 (1973).

14. Talcott Parsons, *The Social System* (Glencoe, Ill.: The Free Press, 1951). Talcott Parsons, "The Mental Hospital as a Type of Organization," in M. Greenblatt, D. J. Levinson, and R. H. Williams, eds., *The Patient and the Mental Hospital* (Glencoe, Ill.: The Free Press, 1957). Talcott Parsons, "Definitions of Health and Illness in the Light of American Values and Social Structure," in E. G. Jaco, ed., *Patients, Physicians and Illness* (Glencoe, Ill.: The Free Press, 1958). Talcott Parsons, "Illness and the Role of the Physician: A Sociological Perspective," in C. Kluckhohn, H. A. Murray, and D. M. Schneider, eds., *Personality in Nature, Society and Culture* (New York: Alfred A. Knopf, 1961). Talcott Parsons and Renee Fox, "Illness, Therapy and the Modern Urban American Family," in E. G. Jaco, ed., *Patients, Physicians and Illness* (Glencoe, Ill.: The Free Press, 1958).

15. John C. Lilly, *Man and Dolphin* (New York: Pyramid Books, 1970).

16. Jean-Pierre Hallet, *Animal Kitabu* (Greenwich, Conn.: Fawcett Publications, 1967), p. 111.

17. Loren Eiseley, *The Firmament of Time* (New York: Atheneum, 1966), p. 144.

18. Anna Freud, "The Role of Bodily Illness in the Mental Life of Children," in *The Psychoanalytic Study of the Child*, Vol. VII (New York: International Universities Press, 1952), pp. 69-81.

19. Laurent De Brunhoff, *Babar Comes to America* (New York: Random House, 1965).

20. Iona Opie and Peter Opie, *The Lore and Language of Schoolchildren* (London: Oxford at the Clarendon Press, 1959).

21. Nigel Temple, *Seen and Not Heard* (London: Hutchinson, 1970).

22. Jane Werner Watson, Robert E. Switzer, and J. Cotter Hirschberg, *My Friend the Doctor* (New York: Golden Press, 1972; created in cooperation with the Menninger Foundation).

23. H. D. Lederer, "How the Sick View Their World," *Journal of Social Issues*, Vol. 8, No. 4 (1952), pp. 4-15.

24. Fred Davis, *Passage through Crisis: Polio Victims and Their Families* (Indianapolis: Bobbs-Merrill, 1963).

25. Cf. Eileen Ward, *John Keats: The Making of a Poet* (New York: The Viking Press, 1963).

26. John Gunther, *Death Be Not Proud* (New York: Harper & Row, 1949), p. 145.
27. *Ibid.*, p. 45.
28. Betty MacDonald, *The Plague and I* (Philadelphia: J. B. Lippincott Company, 1948).
29. J. A. Roth, *Timetables: Structuring the Passage of Time in Hospital Treatment and Other Careers* (Indianapolis: Bobbs-Merrill, 1963), pp. 37-38.
30. Talcott Parsons, *The Social System, op. cit.,* pp. 476-477.
31. Hugh Barber, *The Occasion Fleeting* (London: H. K. Lewis and Company, 1947), p. 15.

V. Medicine and Its Submodels

1. R. Dubos, *Mirage of Health* (Garden City: Doubleday Anchor Books, 1959).
2. T. T. Paterson, *Management Theory* (London: Business Publications, 1966), p. 81.
3. A. Herbert Schwartz, "Children's Concepts of Research Hospitalization," *The New England Journal of Medicine,* Vol. 287, No. 12 (Sept. 21, 1972), pp. 589-592.
4. P. B. Medawar, *Induction and Intuition in Scientific Thought* (London: Methuen and Company, 1969).
5. Celsus, *On Medicine,* trans. W. G. Spencer, *The Loeb Classical Library* (Cambridge: Harvard University Press, 1935), pp. 8-35.
6. W. Beaumont, *Experiments and Observations on the Gastric Juice and the Physiology of Digestion* (New York: Dover Publications, 1959). Originally published 1833.
7. C. J. Wiggers, "Human Experimentation as Exemplified by the Career of Dr. William Beaumont," in I. Ladimer and R. W. Newman, eds., *Clinical Investigation in Medicine: Legal, Ethical and Moral Aspects* (Boston: Boston University Law-Medicine Research Institute, 1963).
8. Renee Fox, *Experiment Perilous* (Glencoe, Ill.: The Free Press, 1959), p. 151.
9. D. C. Martin, J. D. Arnold, Y. F. Zimmerman, and R. H. Richart, "Human Subjects in Clinical Research: A Report of Three Studies," *The New England Journal of Medicine,* 279 (1968), 1426-1431.
10. Benjamin Waterhouse, *A Prospect of Exterminating the Smallpox* (Boston, 1800).
11. Benjamin Waterhouse, "Kine-Pox Inoculation," in *Columbian Centinel* (Boston, 1806).
12. Claude Bernard, *An Introduction to the Study of Experimental Medicine* (New York: Dover Publications, 1957). Originally published in 1865.
13. A. Mitscherlich and F. Mielke, *The Death Doctors,* trans. from German by J. Cleugh (London: Elek Books, 1962), pp. 26-27.
14. G. A. Soper, "The Curious Case of Typhoid Mary," *Bulletin of the New York Academy of Medicine,* 15 (1939), 698-712.
15. Sinclair Lewis, *Arrowsmith* (New York: Harcourt, Brace and World, 1925).
16. R. H. Anderson, "Soviet Physicians Said to Lack Bedside Manner," *The New York Times,* Sept. 8, 1968.
17. W. P. Butler, "Cuba's Revolutionary Medicine," *Ramparts Magazine,* Vol. 7, No. 12 (1969), pp. 6-14.

18. W. MacMichael, *The Gold-Headed Cane,* 1826 facsimile edition (London: The Royal College of Physicians, 1968), p. 134.
19. José M. Ferrer, III, "An Awful Lot of Lawyers Involved," *Time,* July 9, 1973.
20. Patrick Mallam, "Billy 'O,'" in Kenneth Dewhurst, ed., *Oxford Medicine* (Manor House, Sandford-upon-Thames, Oxford: Sandford Publications, 1970), p. 95.
21. James Parker, "Golden Touch," *Today's Health,* June 1968, pp. 48-68.
22. "Carpenter Indicated as Fake Physician with a Hospital Job," *The New York Times,* June 6, 1969.
23. "Lancaster Cab Driver Identified as 'Doctor' on Chesapeake Island," *The Philadelphia Inquirer,* Apr. 26, 1969.
24. "'Heart Specialist' cited as Impostor as Four Patients Die," *The New York Times,* March 3, 1969.
25. Robert Crichton, *The Great Impostor* (New York: Avon Books, 1968).
26. T. Lidz and M. Edelson, eds., *Training Tomorrow's Psychiatrist: The Crisis in Curriculum* (New Haven: Yale University Press, 1970).

VI. Community Mental Health: What Model?

1. Charles Erasmus, "An Anthropologist Looks at Technical Assistance," *The Scientific Monthly,* 78 (1954), 147-158.
2. Clifford W. Beers, *A Mind That Found Itself* (Garden City: Doubleday and Company, 1968). First published 1908.
3. Adolf Meyer, *Psychobiology—A Science of Man* (Springfield, Ill.: Charles C. Thomas, 1957).
4. Karl Popper, *The Poverty of Historicism* (New York: Harper Torchbooks, 1964).
5. Gerald Grob, *The State and the Mentally Ill: A History of Worcester State Hospital in Massachusetts: 1830–1920* (Chapel Hill: University of North Carolina Press, 1966), pp. 356-357.
6. Manfred Bleuler, "Research and Changes in Concepts in the Study of Schizophrenia, 1941–1950," *Bulletin of the Isaac Ray Medical Library,* 3 (1955), 1-132, 25-26.
7. Elaine Cumming and John Cumming, *Closed Ranks* (Cambridge: Harvard University Press for the Commonwealth Fund, 1957). See also Elaine Cumming, "The Social Control of Mental Illness with Specific Reference to the Strategies of Isolation and Denial," doctoral thesis, Harvard University, 1954; John Cumming and Elaine Cumming, "Mental Health Education in a Canadian Community," in Benjamin Paul, ed., *Health, Culture and Community* (New York: Russell Sage Foundation, 1955). We discuss *Closed Ranks* in greater detail in our paper, *"Closed Ranks* Twenty Years Later," *Journal of Orthomolecular Psychiatry,* Vol. 2 (1973).
8. Raymond Glasscote, David Sanders, H. M. Forstenzer, and A. R. Foley, *The Community Mental Health Center: An Analysis of Existing Models* (The Joint Information Service of the American Psychiatric Association and the National Association for Mental Health, Washington, D.C., 1964).
9. Humphry Osmond, personal communication.
10. E. Gardner and M. Gardner, "A Community Mental Health Center Case Study: Innovations and Issues," *Seminars in Psychiatry,* Vol. 3, No. 2 (1971), pp. 172-198.

11. David L. Andelman, "Suffolk Scores State Hospitals," *The New York Times,* Nov. 12, 1972.
12. Henry R. Rollin, "Has the Mental Hospital Got a Future?" *Proceedings of the Royal Society of Medicine,* 65 (October 1972), 898.
13. H. B. M. Murphy, Bernard Pennee, and Daniel Luchins, "Foster Homes: The New Back Wards?" *Canada's Mental Health,* supplement, September-October 1972.
14. Enid Mills, *Living with Mental Illness* (London: Routledge and Kegan Paul, 1962).
15. Maxwell Jones, *Roche Report,* Vol. 3, No. 13 (1973).

VII. The Models of Madness Compared

1. Ian Mackenzie, personal communication, 1973.
2. I. S. Cooper, *The Victim Is Always the Same* (New York: Harper & Row, 1973).
3. Mark D. Altschule, *Roots of Modern Psychiatry* (New York: Grune and Stratton, 1957).
4. Abraham A. Low, *Mental Health through Will-Training* (Boston: Christopher Publishing House, 1950).
5. Vincent P. Dole, personal communication, 1968.
6. John Gunther, *Death Be Not Proud* (New York: Harper & Row, 1949).
7. Humphry Osmond and Abram Hoffer, "Schizophrenia and Suicide," *Journal of Schizophrenia,* 1 (1967), 54-64.
8. Harold Kelm, Humphry Osmond, and Abram Hoffer, *Hoffer-Osmond Diagnostic Test Manual* (Saskatoon, Saskatchewan, Canada: Modern Press, 1967). A. Moneim El-Meligi and Humphry Osmond, *Manual for the Clinical Use of the Experiential World Inventory* (New York: Mens Sana Publishing Co., 1970).
9. James A. Wechsler, *In a Darkness* (New York: W. W. Norton and Co., 1972).
10. Clifford W. Beers, *A Mind That Found Itself* (Garden City: Doubleday and Company, 1968).
11. Frances Farmer, *Will There Really Be a Morning?* (New York: Dell Publishing Company, 1973).
12. Erving Goffman, "On the Characteristics of Total Institutions," in Erving Goffman, *Asylums* (Garden City: Doubleday and Company, 1961).
13. Miriam Siegler and Humphry Osmond, "Goffman's Model of Mental Illness," *British Journal of Psychiatry,* 119 (1971), 419-24.
14. Samuel Tuke, *Description of the Retreat,* introduction by Richard Hunter and Ida Macalpine (London: Dawson of Pall Mall, 1964). First published 1813.
15. Raymond Glasscote, David Sanders, H. M. Forstenzer, and A. R. Foley, *The Community Mental Health Center: An Analysis of Existing Models* (a publication of the Joint Information Service of the American Psychiatric Association and the National Association for Mental Health, 1964).
16. Laurence B. Holland, *Who Designs America?* (Garden City: Doubleday Anchor Books, 1966).
17. Zigmond Lebensohn, personal communication, 1971.
18. Paul M. Roman, "Labeling Theory and Community Psychiatry: The Impact of Psychiatric Sociology on Ideology and Practice in American Psychiatry," *Psychiatry,* 34 (1971), 378-390.

19. Henry Raymont, "Psychiatry Journal Accused of Ban on Ad for Sex-Exposé Book," *The New York Times*, Sept. 7, 1971.
20. Daniel Boorstin, *The Lost World of Thomas Jefferson* (Boston: Beacon Press, 1960), p. 90.
21. Humphry Osmond, "Psychiatry under Siege: The Crisis Within," *Psychiatric Annals*, 3 (1973), 59-82.
22. Frank Riessman, Jerome Cohen, and Arthur Pearl, eds., *Mental Health of the Poor* (Glencoe, Ill., The Free Press, 1964).
23. Norman Cohn, *The Pursuit of the Millennium* (London: Palladin, 1970).
24. Robert E. Horne, personal communication, 1973.
25. Robert Sommer and Humphry Osmond, "Autobiographies of Former Mental Patients," *Journal of Mental Science*, 106 (1960), 648-662. Robert Sommer and Humphry Osmond, "Autobiographies of Former Mental Patients: Addendum," *Journal of Mental Science*, 107 (1961), 1030-1032. Miriam Siegler and Humphry Osmond, "Schizophrenia and the Sick Role," *Journal of Orthomolecular Psychiatry*, 2 (1973), 25-38.
26. T. T. Paterson, personal communication, 1972.

VIII. The Future of Psychiatry

1. Carney Landis, *Varieties of Psychopathological Experience* (New York: Holt, Rinehart and Winston, 1964).
2. Mary Cecil, "Through the Looking Glass," in Bert Kaplan, ed., *The Inner World of Mental Illness* (New York: Harper & Row, 1964), p. 217.
3. George Bosworth Burch, *Alternative Goals in Religion* (Montreal: McGill-Queen's University Press, 1972).
4. Thomas S. Kuhn, *The Copernican Revolution* (Cambridge: Harvard University Press, 1971), p. 39.
5. Johan Huizinga, *Erasmus and the Age of Reformation* (New York: Harper Torchbooks, 1957).
6. Galileo Galilei, *Dialogue Concerning the Two Chief World Systems—Ptolemaic and Copernican*, trans. Stillman Drake (Berkeley and Los Angeles: University of California Press, 1970), p. 101.
7. David Park, "Are Space and Time Necessary?" *Scientia, Revue Internationale de Synthese Scientifique*, September 1970.
8. Elliot G. Mishler and Norman A. Scotch, "Sociocultural Factors in the Epidemiology of Schizophrenia: A Review," *Psychiatry*, 26 (1963), 315-351.
9. Leonard L. Heston, "The Genetics of Schizophrenic and Schizoid Disease," in David Hawkins and Linus Pauling, eds., *Orthomolecular Psychiatry: Treatment of Schizophrenia* (San Francisco: W. H. Freeman and Company, 1973).
10. These ideas are discussed more fully in our paper "Notes on Orthomolecular Psychiatry and Psychotherapy," *The Journal of Orthomolecular Psychiatry* 2 (1973), 118-126.
11. David Park, personal communication, 1972.
12. Humphry Osmond, "Psychiatry under Siege: The Crisis Within," *Psychiatric Annals*, 3 (1973), 59-82.

Index